# Grids, P2P and Services Computing

T0137915

Frédéric Desprez • Vladimir Getov
Thierry Priol • Ramin Yahyapour
Editors

# Grids, P2P and Services Computing

 Springer

*Editors*
Frédéric Desprez
INRIA Grenoble Rhône-Alpes
LIP ENS Lyon
69364 Lyon Cedex 07
France
Frederic.Desprez@inria.fr

Vladimir Getov
University of Westminster
School of Electronics and
Computer Science
HA1 3TP London
United Kingdom
V.S.Getov@westminster.ac.uk

Thierry Priol
INRIA Rennes - Bretagne
Atlantique
Campus universitaire de Beaulieu
35042 Rennes Cedex
France
Thierry.Priol@inria.fr

Ramin Yahyapour
TU Dortmund University
IT & Media Center
44221 Dortmund
Germany
ramin.yahyapour@udo.edu

ISBN 978-1-4899-8628-3      ISBN 978-1-4419-6794-7 (eBook)
DOI 10.1007/978-1-4419-6794-7
Springer New York Dordrecht Heidelberg London

Printed on acid-free paper

Springer is part of Springer Science+Business Media (www.springer.com)

# Preface

The symposium was organised by the ERCIM[1] CoreGRID Working Group (WG) funded by ERCIM and INRIA. This Working Group sponsored by ERCIM has been established with two main objectives: to ensure the sustainability of the CoreGRID Network of Excellence which is requested by both the European Commission and the CoreGRID members who want to continue and extend their successful co operation, and to establish a forum to foster collaboration between research communities that are now involved in the area of Service Computing: namely high performance computing, distributed systems and software engineering.

CoreGRID[2] officially started in September 2004 as an European research Network of Excellence to develop the foundations, software infrastructures and applications for large-scale, distributed Grid and Peer-to-Peer technologies. Since then, the Network has achieved outstanding results in terms of integration, working as a team to address research challenges, and producing high quality research results. Although the main objective was to solve research challenges in the area of Grid and Peer-to-Peer technologies, the Network has adapted its research roadmap to include also the new challenges related to service-oriented infrastructures, which are very relevant to the European industry as illustrated by the NESSI initiative[3] to develop the European Technology Platform on Software and Services. Currently, the CoreGRID WG is conducting research in the area of the emerging Internet of Services, with direct relevance to the Future Internet Assembly[4]. The Grid research community has not only embraced but has also contributed to the development of the service-oriented paradigm to build interoperable Grid middleware and to benefit from the progress made by the services research community.

---

[1] European Research Consortium for Informatics and Mathematics, http://www.ercim.eu/

[2] http://www.coregrid.net/

[3] Networked European Software and Services Initiative, http://www.nessi-europe.com/

[4] http://www.future-internet.eu/

The goal of this one day workshop, organized within the frame of the Euro-Par 2009 conference[5], was to gather together participants of the working group, present the topics chosen for the first year, and to attract new participants.

The program was built upon several interesting papers presenting innovative results for a wide range of topics going from low level optimizations of grid operating systems to high level programming approaches.

Grid operating systems have a bright future, simplifying the access to large scale resources. XtreemOS is one of them and it was presented in an invited paper by Kielmann, Pierre, and Morin.

The seamless access to data at a large scale is offered by Grid file systems such as Blobseer, described in a paper from Tran, Antoniu, Nicolae, Boug, and Tatebe.

Failure and faults is one of the main issues of large scale production grids. A paper from Andrzejak, Zeinalipour-Yazti, and Dikaiakos presents an analysis and prediction of faults in the EGEE grid.

A paper from Cesario, De Caria, Mastroianni, and Talia presents the architecture of a decentralized peer-to-peer system applied to data-mining.

Monitoring distributed grid systems allows researchers to understand the internal behavior of middleware systems and applications. The paper from Funika, Caromel, Koperek, and Kupisz presents a semantic approach chosen for the ProActive software suite.

The resource discovery in large scale systems deserve a distributed approach. The paper from Papadakis, Trunfio, Talia, and Fragopoulou presents an approach mixing dynamic queries on top of a distributed hash table.

A paper from Carlini, Coppola, Laforenza, and Richi aims at proposing scalable approach for resource discovery allowing range queries and minimizing the network traffic.

Skeleton programming is one promising approach for high level programming in distributed environments. The paper from Aldinucci, Danelutto, and Kilpatrick describes a methodology to allow multiple non-functionnal concerns to be managed in an autonomic way.

In their paper, Moca and Silaghi describe several decision models for resource agregation within peer-to-peer architectures allowing different decision aids classes to be taken into account.

Workflows management and scheduling received a large attention of the grid community. The paper from Sakellariou, Zhao, and Deelman describes several mapping strategies for a astronomy workflow called Montage.

Access control is an important issue that needs to be efficiently solved to allow the wide scale adoption of grid technologies. The paper from Colombo, Lazouski, Martinelli, and Mori presents new flexible policy language called U-XACML that improves the XACML language in several directions.

The paper from Fragopoulou, Mastroianni, Montero, Andrjezak, and Kondo describes several research areas investigated within the Self-* and adaptive mechanisms topic from the Working group.

---

[5] http://europar2009.ewi.tudelft.nl/

Several research issues around network monitoring and in particular network virtualization and network monitoring are presented in the paper from Ciuffoletti.

Research challenges for large scale desktop computing platforms are described in the paper from Fedak.

Finally, a paper from Rana and Ziegler presents the research areas addressed within the Service Level Agreement topic of the Working Group.

The Programme Committee who made the selection of papers included:

Alvaro Arenas, STFC Rutherford Appleton Laboratory, UK
Christophe Crin, Universit de Paris Nord, LIPN, France
Augusto Ciuffoletti, University of Pisa, Italy
Frédéric Desprez, INRIA, France
Gilles Fedak, INRIA, France
Paraskevi Fragopoulou, FORTH-ICS, Greece
Vladimir Getov, University of Westminster, UK
Radek Januszewski, Poznan Supercomputing and Networking Center, Poland
Pierre Massonet, CETIC, Belgium
Thierry Priol, INRIA, France
Norbert Meyer, Poznan Supercomputing Center, Poland
Omer Rana, Cardiff University, UK
Ramin Yahyapour, University of Dortmund, Germany
Wolfgang Ziegler, Fraunhofer Institute SCAI, Germany

All papers in this volume were additionally reviewed by the following external reviewers whose help we gratefully acknowledge:

Gabriel Antoniu
Alessandro Basso
Eddy Caron
Haiwu He
Syed Naqvi
Christian Perez
Pierre Riteau
Thomas Rblitz
Bing Tang

Special thanks are due to the authors of all submitted papers, the members of the Programme Committee and the Organising Committee, and to all reviewers, for their contribution to the success of this event.

Deflt, the Netherlands,                                                            *Frédéric Desprez*
August 2009                                                                           *Vladimir Getov*
                                                                                          *Thierry Priol*
                                                                                    *Ramin Yahyapour*

# Contents

# List of Contributors

**Marco Aldinucci**
Dept. Computer Science, University of Torino, Italy e-mail:
aldinuc@di.unito.it

**Artur Andrzejak**
Zuse Institute Berlin (ZIB), Takustraße 7, 14195 Berlin, Germany, e-mail:
andrzejak@zib.de

**Gabriel Antoniu**
INRIA, Centre Rennes - Bretagne Atlantique, IRISA, Rennes, France e-mail:
gabriel.antoniu@inria.fr

**Luc Bougé**
ENS Cachan/Brittany, IRISA, France e-mail: luc.bouge@bretagne.
ens-cachan.fr

**Emanuele Carlini**
Institute of Information Science and Technologies CNR-ISTI "A. Faedo",
Pisa, Italy, and Institutions Markets Technologies IMT, Lucca, Italy e-mail:
emanuele.carlini@isti.cnr.it

**Denis Caromel**
INRIA - CNRS - University of Nice Sophia-Antipolis, 2004, Route
des Lucioles - BP93 - 06902 Sophia Antipolis Cedex, France, e-mail:
Denis.Caromel@sophia.inria.fr

**Eugenio Cesario**
ICAR-CNR, Rende, Italy, e-mail: cesario@icar.cnr.it

**Augusto Ciuffoletti**
Dipartimento di Informatica Università di Pisa e-mail: augusto@di.unipi.it

**Maurizio Colombo**
Istituto di Informatica e Telematica, Consiglio Nazionale delle Ricerche, via G.

Moruzzi 1, Pisa, Italy e-mail: `maurizio.colombo@iit.cnr.it`

**Massimo Coppola**
Institute of Information Science and Technologies CNR-ISTI, Pisa, Italy e-mail:
`massimo.coppola@isti.cnr.it`

**Nicola De Caria**
DEIS - University of Calabria, Rende, Italy e-mail: `decaria@si.deis.`
`unical.it`

**Marco Danelutto**
Dept. Computer Science, University of Pisa, Italy, e-mail: `marcod@di.unipi.`
`it`

**Ewa Deelman**
USC Information Sciences Institute, 4676 Admiralty Way, Marina Del Rey,
CA90292, USA

**Marios D. Dikaiakos**
Department of Computer Science, University of Cyprus, CY-1678, Nicosia, Cyprus
e-mail: `mdd@cs.ucy.ac.cy`

**Gilles Fedak**
LIP/INRIA Rhône-Alpes, e-mail: `Gilles.Fedak@inria.fr`

**Paraskevi Fragopoulou**
FORTH-ICS, N. Plastira 100, Vassilika Vouton, GR 71003 Heraklion-Crete,
Greece, e-mail: `fragopou@ics.forth.gr`

**Wlodzimierz Funika**
Institute of Computer Science AGH-UST, al. Mickiewicza 30, 30-059, Kraków,
Poland, e-mail: `funika@agh.edu.pl`

**Thilo Kielmann**
Vrije Universiteit, Amsterdam, The Netherlands, e-mail: `kielmann@cs.vu.nl`

**Peter Kilpatrick**
Dept. Computer Science, Queen's University Belfast, UK, e-mail:
`p.kilpatrick@qub.ac.uk`

**Derrick Kondo**
Laboratoire LIG, ENSIMAG - antenne de Montbonnot, ZIRST 51, Av. Jean
Kuntzmann, 38330 Monbonnot Saint Martin, France, e-mail: `dkondo@imag.fr`

**Pawel Koperek**
Institute of Computer Science AGH-UST, al. Mickiewicza 30, 30-059, Kraków,
Poland,
e-mail: `koperek@student.agh.edu.pl`

**Mateusz Kupisz**
Institute of Computer Science AGH-UST, al. Mickiewicza 30, 30-059, Kraków,
Poland,

e-mail: kupisz@student.agh.edu.pl

**Domenico Laforenza**
Institute of Information Science and Technologies CNR-ISTI and Institute of Informatics and Telematics CNR-IIT, Pisa, Italy e-mail: domenico.laforenza@isti.cnr.it

**Aliaksandr Lazouski**
Universita di Pisa, via B. Pontecorvo 3, Pisa, Italy e-mail: lazouski@di.unipi.it

**Fabio Martinelli**
Istituto di Informatica e Telematica, Consiglio Nazionale delle Ricerche, via G. Moruzzi 1, Pisa, Italy e-mail: fabio.martinelli@iit.cnr.it

**Carlo Mastroianni**
ICAR-CNR, Via P. Bucci 41C, 87036 Rende (CS), Italy, e-mail: mastroianni@icar.cnr.it

**Mircea Moca**
Babeş-Bolyai University of Cluj-Napoca, Str. Theodor Mihali, nr. 58-60, Cluj-Napoca, Romania, e-mail: mircea.moca@econ.ubbcluj.ro

**Ruben Montero**
Departamento de Arquitectura de Computadores y Automática, Universidad Complutense, 28040 Madrid, Spain, e-mail: rubensm@dacya.ucm.es

**Paolo Mori**
Istituto di Informatica e Telematica, Consiglio Nazionale delle Ricerche, via G. Moruzzi 1, Pisa, Italy e-mail: paolo.mori@iit.cnr.it

**Christine Morin**
INRIA, Centre Rennes - Bretagne Atlantique, Rennes, France, e-mail: Christine.Morin@irisa.fr

**Bogdan Nicolae**
University of Rennes 1, IRISA, Rennes, France e-mail: bogdan.nicolae@irisa.fr

**Harris Papadakis**
Foundation for Research and Technology-Hellas, Institute of Computer Science (FORTH-ICS), Heraklion, Greece, e-mail: adanar@ics.forth.gr

**Guillaume Pierre**
Vrije Universiteit, Amsterdam, The Netherlands,e-mail: gpierre@cs.vu.nl

**Omer Rana**
School of Computer Science/Welsh eScience Centre, Cardiff University, UK, e-mail: o.f.rana@cs.cardiff.ac.uk

**Laura Ricci**
Università di Pisa, Pisa, Italy e-mail: ricci@di.unipi.it

**Rizos Sakellariou**
School of Computer Science, University of Manchester, Manchester M13 9PL,
United Kingdom, e-mail: `rizos@cs.man.ac.uk`

**Gheorghe Cosmin Silaghi**
Babeş-Bolyai University of Cluj-Napoca, Str. Theodor Mihali, nr. 58-60, Cluj-
Napoca, Romania, e-mail: `gheorghe.silaghi@econ.ubbcluj.ro`

**Domenico Talia**
Institute of High Performance Computing and Networking, Italian National
Research Council (ICAR-CNR) and Department of Electronics, Computer
Science and Systems (DEIS), University of Calabria, Rende, Italy, e-mail:
`talia@deis.unical.it`

**Osamu Tatebe**
University of Tsukuba, Tsukuba, Japan e-mail: `tatebe@cs.tsukuba.ac.jp`

**Viet-Trung Tran**
ENS Cachan/Brittany, IRISA, France e-mail: `viet-trung.tran@irisa.fr`

**Paolo Trunfio**
Department of Electronics, Computer Science and Systems (DEIS), University of
Calabria, Rende, Italy, e-mail: `trunfio@deis.unical.it`

**Demetrios Zeinalipour-Yazti**
Department of Computer Science, University of Cyprus, CY-1678, Nicosia, Cyprus
e-mail: `dzeina@cs.ucy.ac.cy`

**Henan Zhao**
School of Computer Science, University of Manchester, Manchester M13 9PL,
United Kingdom

**Wolfgang Ziegler**
Fraunhofer Institute SCAI, Germany, e-mail: `Wolfgang.Ziegler@scai.fraunhofer.de`

# XtreemOS: a Sound Foundation for Cloud Infrastructure and Federations

Thilo Kielmann, Guillaume Pierre, Christine Morin

**Abstract** XtreemOS is a Linux-based operating system with native support for virtual organizations (VO's), for building large-scale resource federations. XtreemOS has been designed as a grid operating system, supporting the model of resource sharing among independent administrative domains. We argue, however, that the VO concept can be used to establish either resource sharing or resource isolation, or even both at the same time. We outline XtreemOS' fundamental properties and how its native VO support can be used to implement cloud infrastructure and cloud federations.

## 1 XtreemOS

Developing and deploying applications for traditional (single computer) operating systems is well understood. Federated resources like in grid environments, however, are generally perceived as highly complex and difficult to use. The difference lies in the underlying system achitecture. Operating systems provide a well-integrated set of services like processes, files, memory, sockets, user accounts and access rights. Grids, in contrast, add a more or less heterogeneous middleware layer on top of the operating systems of the federated resources. This lack of integration has lead to a lot of complexity, for both users and administrators.

To remedy this situation, XtreemOS [7] has been designed as a *grid operating system*. While being based on Linux, it provides a comprehensive set of services as well as a stable interface for wide-area, dynamic, distributed infrastructures com-

Thilo Kielmann and Guillaume Pierre
Vrije Universiteit, Amsterdam, The Netherlands, e-mail: kielmann@cs.vu.nl, gpierre@cs.vu.nl

Christine Morin
INRIA, Centre Rennes - Bretagne Atlantique, Rennes, France, e-mail: Christine.Morin@irisa.fr

posed of heterogeneous resources spanning multiple administrative domains. The
fundamental issues addressed by XtreemOS are scalability and transparency.

**Scalability.**  Wide-area, distributed infrastructures like grids easily consist of
thousands of nodes and users. Along with this scale comes heterogeneity of
(compute and file) resources, networks, administrative policies, as well as churn
of resources and users. XtreemOS addresses these issues by its integrated view
on resources, along with its built-in support for virtual organizations (VO's) that
provide the scoping for resource provisioning and access. For sustained operation, XtreemOS provides an infrastructure for highly-available services, to support both its own critical services and user-defined application services.

**Transparency.**  Vital for managing the complexity of grid-like infrastructures is
providing transparency for the distributed nature of the environment, by maintaining common look–and–feel for the user and by exposing distribution and
federation only as much as necessary. To the user, XtreemOS provides single
sign-on access, Linux look–and–feel via grid-aware shell tools, and API's that
are based on both POSIX and the Simple API for Grid Applications (SAGA).
For the administrators of VO's and site resources, XtreemOS provides easy-to-
use services for all management tasks.

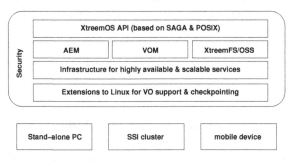

**Fig. 1** The XtreemOS system architecture

Figure 1 summarizes the XtreemOS system architecture. XtreemOS comes in
three flavours; one for stand-alone nodes (PC's), one for clusters providing a single-
system image (SSI), and one for mobile devices. Common to all three flavours are
the Linux extensions for VO support, providing VO-based user accounts via kernel
modules [1]. PC and cluster flavour also share support for grid-wide, kernel-level
job checkpointing.

The infrastructure for highly available and scalable services consists of implementations of distributed servers and of virtual nodes [6]. The *distributed servers*
form a transparent group of machines that provide their services through a shared
(mobile IPv6) address. Within the group, load balancing and fault tolerance are implemented transparent to the clients. The *virtual nodes* provide fault-tolerant service
replication via a Java container, transparent to the service implementation itself.

Central to VO-wide operation are the services AEM, VOM, the XtreemFS file system and the OSS mechanism for sharing volatile application objects. The VO management services (VOM) provide authentication, authorization, and accounting for VO users and resources. VO's can be managed dynamically through their whole life cycle while user access is organized with flexible policies, providing customizable isolation, access control, and auditing. The VO management services, together with the kernel modules enforcing local accounts and policies provide a security infrastructure underlying all XtreemOS functionality.

The Application Execution Management (AEM) relies on the Scalaris [4] peer-to-peer overlay among the compute nodes of a VO that allows to discover, select, and allocate resources to applications. It provides POSIX-style job control to launch, monitor, and control applications.

The XtreemFS grid file system [2] provides users with a global, location independent view of their data. XtreemFS provides a standard POSIX interface, accomodating from multiple VO's, across different administrative domains. It provides autonomous data management with self-organized replication and distribution. The Object Sharing Service (OSS) provides access to volatile, shared objects in main memory segments.

The XtreemOS API's accomodate existing Linux and grid applications, while adding support to XtreemOS' unique features. POSIX interfaces support Linux applications; grid-aware shell tools seemlessly integrate compute nodes within a VO. Grid applications find their support via the OGF-standardized Simple API for Grid Applications (SAGA) [5]. API's for XtreemOS-specific functionality (XtreemOS credentials, AEM's resource reservation, XtreemFS URL's, OSS shared segments, etc.) are provided as SAGA extension packages, commonly referred to as the XOSAGA API.

## 2 Cloud Infrastructure and Federations

Grid infrastructures operate by sharing physical resources among the users of a VO; sharing and isolation are managed by the site-local operating systems and the VO-wide (middleware) services. Although cloud computing as such is still in its infancy, the *Infrastructure as a Service* paradigm (IaaS) has gained importance. Here, virtualized resources are rented to cloud users; sharing and isolation are managed by the Virtual Machine Managers (VMM's). What makes this model attractive is that users get full control over the virtual machines, while the underlying IaaS infrastructure remains in charge of resource sharing and management. An important drawback of this model is that it provides only isolated machines rather than integrated clusters with secure and fast local networks, integrated user management and file systems.

This is where XtreemOS provides added value to IaaS clouds [3]. Figure 2 shows how XtreemOS can integrate resources from one or more IaaS providers to form a clustered resource collection for a given user. Within a single IaaS platform, XtreemOS integrates multiple virtual machines similar to its SSI cluster version,

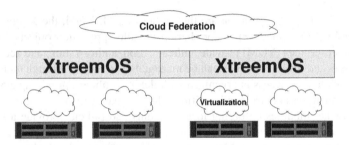

**Fig. 2** XtreemOS integrating IaaS resources

to form a cloud cluster with integrated access control based on its VO-management mechanisms, here applied to a user-defined, dynamic VO. Across multiple IaaS platforms, the same VO management mechanisms allow the federation of multiple cloud clusters to a user's VO. In combination with the XtreemFS file system, such IaaS federations provide flexibly allocated resources that match a user's requirements, while giving full control over the virtualized resources.

XtreemOS extends Linux by its integrated support for VO's. Within grid computing environments, VO's enable sharing of physical resources. Within IaaS clouds, VO's enable proper isolation between clustered resources, thus allowing to form unified environments tailored to their users.

### Acknowledgements

This work has been supported by the EU IST program as part of the XtreemOS project (contract FP6-033576).

## References

1. M. Coppola, Y. Jégou, B. Matthews, Ch. Morin, L.P. Prieto, O.D. Sánchez, E.Y. Yang, H. Yu: Virtual Organization Support within a Grid-Wide Operating System. IEEE Internet Computing, Vol. 12, No. 2, 2008
2. F. Hupfeld, T. Cortes, B. Kolbeck, J. Stender, E. Focht, M. Hess, J. Malo, J. Marti, E. Cesario: The XtreemFS Architecture—a Case for Object-based File Systems in Grids. Concurrency and computation: Practice and experience, Vol. 20, No. 17, 2008.
3. Ch. Morin, Y. Jégou, J. Gallard, P. Riteau: Clouds: a new Playground for the XtreemOS Grid Operating System. Parallel Processing Letters, Vol. 19, No. 3, 2009.
4. T. Schütt, F. Schintke, A. Reinefeld: Scalaris: Reliable Transactional P2P Key/Value Store – Web 2.0 Hosting with Erlang and Java. 7th ACM SIGPLAN Erlang Workshop, Victoria, September 2008.
5. Ch. Smith, T. Kielmann, S. Newhouse, M. Humphrey: The HPC Basic Profile and SAGA: Standardizing Compute Grid Access in the Open Grid Forum. Concurrency and Computation: Practice and Experience, Vol. 21, No. 8, 2009.

6. M. Szymaniak, G. Pierre, M. Simons-Nikolova, M. van Steen: Enabling Service Adaptability with Versatile Anycast. Concurrency and Computation: Practice and Experience, Vol. 19, No. 13, 2007.
7. XtreemOS: `www.xtreemos.eu`

# Towards a Grid File System Based on a Large-Scale BLOB Management Service

Viet-Trung Tran, Gabriel Antoniu, Bogdan Nicolae, Luc Bougé, Osamu Tatebe

**Abstract** This paper addresses the problem of building a grid file system for applications that need to manipulate huge data, distributed and concurrently accessed at a very large scale. In this paper we explore how this goal could be reached through a cooperation between the Gfarm grid file system and BlobSeer, a distributed object management system specifically designed for huge data management under heavy concurrency. The resulting BLOB-based grid file system exhibits scalable file access performance in scenarios where huge files are subject to massive, concurrent, fine-grain accesses. This is demonstrated through preliminary experiments of our prototype, conducted on the Grid'5000 testbed.

## 1 Introduction

The need for transparent grid data management

As more and more applications in many areas (nuclear physics, health, cosmology, etc.) generate larger and larger volumes of data that are geographically distributed, appropriate mechanisms for storing and accessing data at a global scale become increasingly necessary. Grid file systems (such as LegionFS [16], Gfarm [14], etc.)

Viet-Trung Tran and Luc Bougé
ENS Cachan/Brittany, IRISA, France e-mail: viet-trung.tran@irisa.fr, luc.bouge@bretagne.ens-cachan.fr

Gabriel Antoniu
INRIA, Centre Rennes - Bretagne Atlantique, IRISA, Rennes, France e-mail: gabriel.antoniu@inria.fr

Bogdan Nicolae
University of Rennes 1, IRISA, Rennes, France e-mail: bogdan.nicolae@irisa.fr

Osamu Tatebe
University of Tsukuba, Tsukuba, Japan e-mail: tatebe@cs.tsukuba.ac.jp

prove their utility in this context, as they provide a means to federate a very large number of large-scale distributed storage resources and offer a large *storage capacity* and a good *persistence* achieved through file-based storage. Beyond these properties, grid file systems have the important advantage of offering a *transparent access to data* through the abstraction of a shared file namespace, in contrast to explicit data transfer schemes (e.g. GridFTP-based [3], IBP [4]) currently used on some production grids. Transparent access greatly simplifies data management by applications, which no longer need to explicitly locate and transfer data across various sites, as data can be accessed the same way from anywhere, based on globally shared identifiers. Implementing transparent access at a global scale naturally leads however to a number of challenges related to scalability and performance, as the file system is put under pressure by a very large number of concurrent, largely distributed accesses.

From block-based to object-based distributed file systems

Recent research [7] emphasizes a clear move currently in progress from a block-based interface to a object-based interface in storage architectures, with the goal of enabling scalable, self-managed storage networks by moving low-level functionalities such as space management to storage devices or to storage server, accessed through a standard object interface. This move has a direct impact on the design of today's distributed file systems: object-based file system would then store data rather as objects than as unstructured data blocks. According to [7], this move may eliminate nearly 90% of management workload which was the major obstacle limiting file systems' scalability and performance.

Two approaches exploit this idea. In the first approach, the data objects are stored and manipulated directly by a new type of storage device called *object-based storage device* (OSD). This approach requires an evolution of the hardware, in order to allow high-level object operations to be delegated to the storage device. The standard OSD interface was defined in the Storage Networking Industry Association (SNIA) OSD working group. The protocol is embodied over SCSI and defines a new set of SCSI commands. Recently, a second generation of the command set, Object-Based Storage Devices - 2 (OSD-2) has been defined. The distributed file systems taking the OSD approach assume the presence of such an OSD in the near future and currently rely on a software module simulating its behavior. Examples of parallel/distributed file systems following this approach are Lustre [13] and Ceph [15]. Recently, research efforts [6] have explored the feasibility and the possible benefits of integrating OSDs into parallel file systems, such as PVFS [5].

The second approach does not rely on the presence of OSDs, but still tries to benefit from an object-based approach to improve performance and scalability: files are structured as a set of objects that are stored on storage servers. Google File System [8], and HDFS (Hadoop File System) [9]) illustrate this approach.

Large-scale distributed object storage for massive data

Beyond the above developments in the area of parallel and distributed file systems, other efforts rely on objects for large-scale data management, without exposing a file system interface. BlobSeer [11] [10] is such a BLOB (binary large object) management service specifically designed to deal with large-scale distributed applications, which need to store massive data objects and to efficiently access (read, update) them at a fine grain. In this context, the system should be able to support a large number of BLOBs, each of which might reach a size in the order of TB. BlobSeer employs a powerful concurrency management scheme enabling a large number of clients to efficiently read and update the same BLOB simultaneously in a lock-free manner.

A two-layer architecture

Most object-based file systems exhibit a decoupled architecture that generally consists of two layers: a low-level object management service, and a high-level file system metadata management. In this paper we propose to explore how this two-layer approach could be used in order to build an object-based grid file system for applications that need to manipulate huge data, distributed and concurrently accessed at a very large scale. We investigate this approach by experimenting how the Gfarm grid file system could leverage the properties of the BlobSeer distributed object management service, specifically designed for huge data management under heavy concurrency. We thus couple Gfarm's powerful file metadata capabilities and rely on BlobSeer for efficient and transparent low-level distributed object storage. We expect the resulting BLOB-based grid file system to exhibit scalable file access performance in scenarios where huge files are subject to massive, concurrent, fine-grain accesses. We intend to deploy a BlobSeer instance at each Gfarm storage node, to handle object storage. The benefits are mutual: by delegating object management to BlobSeer, Gfarm can expose efficient fine-grain access to huge files and benefit from transparent file striping (TB size). On the other hand, BlobSeer benefits from the file system interface on top of its current API.

The remaining of this paper is structured as follows. Section 2 introduces the two components of our object-based file system: BlobSeer and Gfarm, whose coupling is explained in Section 3. Section 4 presents our preliminary experiments on the Grid'5000 testbed. Finally, Section 5 summarizes the contribution and discusses future directions.

## 2 The building blocks: Gfarm and BlobSeer

Our object-based grid file systems consists of two layers: a high-level file metadata layer, available with the Gfarm file system; a low-level storage layer based on the BlobSeer BLOB management service.

### 2.1 The Gfarm grid file system

The Grid Datafarm (Gfarm) [14] is a distributed file system designed for high-performance data access and reliable file sharing in large scale environments including grids of clusters. To facilitate file sharing, Gfarm manages a global namespace which allows the applications to access files using the same path regardless of file location. It federates available storage spaces of Grid nodes to provide a single file system image. We have used Gfarm v2.1.0 in our experiments.

#### 2.1.1 Overview of Gfarm's architecture

Gfarm consists of a set of communicating components, each of which fulfills a particular role.

Gfarm's metadata server: the *gfmd* daemon.    The metadata server stores and manages the namespace hierarchy together with file metadata, user-related metadata, as well as file location information allowing clients to physically locate the files.

Gfarm file system nodes: the *gfsd* daemons.    They are responsible for physically storing full Gfarm files on their local storage. Gfarm does not implement file stripping and here is where BlobSeer can bring its contribution, through transparent file fragmentation and distribution.

Gfarm clients: Gfarm API and FUSE access interface for Gfarm.    Gfarm provides users with a specific API and several command lines to access the Gfarm file system. To facilitate data access, the Gfarm team developed Gfarm2fs: a POSIX file system interface based on the FUSE library [17]. Basically, Gfarm2fs transparently maps all standard file I/Os to the corresponding routines of the Gfarm API. Thus, existing applications handling files must no longer be modified in order to work with the Gfarm file system.

## 2.2 The BlobSeer BLOB management service

### 2.2.1 BlobSeer at a glance

BlobSeer [11] [10] addresses the problem of storing and efficiently accessing very large, unstructured data objects, in a distributed environment. It focuses on heavy access concurrency where data is huge, mutable and potentially accessed by a very large number of concurrent, distributed processes. To cope with very large data BLOBs, BlobSeer uses striping: each BLOB is cut into fixed-size *pages*, which are distributed among data providers. *BLOB Metadata* facilitates access to a range *(offset, size)* for any existing version of a BLOB snapshot, by associating such a range with the physical nodes where the corresponding pages are located. Metadata are organized as a segment-tree like structure (see [11] for details) and are scattered across the system using a Distributed Hash Table (DHT). Distributing data and metadata is the key choice in our design: it enables high performance through parallel, direct access I/O paths, as demonstrated in [12]. Further, BlobSeer provides concurrent clients with efficient fine-grained access to BLOBs, without locking. To deal with the mutable data, BlobSeer introduces a *versioning* scheme which allows clients not only to roll back data changes when desired, but also enables access to multiple versions of the same BLOB within the same computation.

### 2.2.2 Overview of BlobSeer's architecture

The system consists of distributed processes, that communicate through remote procedure calls (RPCs). A physical node can run one or more processes and, at the same time, may play multiple roles from the ones mentioned below.

Clients.    Clients may issue *CREATE*, *WRITE*, *APPEND* and *READ* requests. There may be multiple concurrent clients. Their number dynamically vary in time without notifying the system.

Data providers.    Data providers physically store and manage the pages generated by *WRITE* and *APPEND* requests. New data providers are free to join and leave the system in a dynamic way.

The provider manager.    The provider manager keeps information about the available data providers and schedules the placement of newly generated pages according to a load balancing strategy.

Metadata providers.    Metadata providers physically store the metadata, allowing clients to find the pages corresponding to the various BLOB versions. Metadata providers are distributed, to allow an efficient concurrent access to metadata.

The version manager.    The version manager is the key actor of the system. It registers update requests (*APPEND* and *WRITE*), assigning BLOB version numbers to each of them. The version manager eventually publishes these updates, guaranteeing total ordering and atomicity.

Accessing data in BlobSeer

To *READ* data, the client contacts the version manager: it needs to provide a BLOB id, a specific version of that BLOB, and a range, specified by an offset and a size. If the specified version is available, the client queries the metadata providers to retrieve the metadata indicating the location of the pages for the requested range. Finally, the client contacts *in parallel* the data providers that store the corresponding pages.

For a *WRITE* request, the client contacts the provider manager to obtain a list of providers, one for each page of the BLOB segment that needs to be written. Then, the client contacts the providers in the list *in parallel* and requests them to store the pages. Each provider executes the request and sends an acknowledgment to the client. When the client has received all the acknowledgments, it contacts the version manager and requests a new version number. This version number is then used by the client to generate the corresponding new metadata. Finally, the client notifies the version manager of success, and returns successfully to the user. At this point, the version manager is responsible for eventually publishing the new version of the BLOB. The *APPEND* operation is a particular case of *WRITE*, where the offset is implicitly the size of the previously published snapshot version. The detailed algorithms for *READ, WRITE* and *APPEND* are given in [11].

## 2.3 Why combine Gfarm and BlobSeer?

Gfarm does not rely on autonomous, self-managing object-based storage, like the file systems mentioned in Section 1. Each Gfarm file is fully stored on a file system node, or totally replicated to multiple file system nodes. If a large number of clients concurrently access small parts of the same copy of a huge file, this can lead to a bottleneck both for reading and for writing. Second, Gfarm's file sizes are limited by the storage capabilities of the machines used as file system nodes in the Gfarm deployment. However, some powerful features, including user management, authentication and single sign-on (based on GSI: Grid Security Infrastructure [1]) are present in Gfarm's current implementation. Moreover, due to the Gfarm's FUSE access interface, data can be accessed in a transparent manner via the POSIX file system API.

BlobSeer brings different benefits: it handles huge data, which is transparently fragmented and distributed at a large scale. Thanks to its distributed metadata scheme, it sustains a high bandwidth is maintained even when the BLOB grows to large sizes, and when the BLOB faces heavy concurrent access [12]. BlobSeer is mostly suitable for massive data processing, fine-grained access, and versioning in a large-scale distributed environment. But BlobSeer lacks a file system interface that may help existing applications to use it directly. As explained above, such an interface is provided by Gfarm, together with the associated file system metadata management. It then clearly appears that making Gfarm cooperate with BlobSeer would enhance their respective functionalities and would lead to an object-based file system with better properties: huge file support (TBs), fine-grain access under heavy concurrency, versioning, user and GSI-compliant security management. In this paper we focus on providing an enhanced concurrency support. Exposing multiversioning to the file system user is currently under study and will not be addressed in this paper.

## 3 Towards an object-based file system based on Gfarm and BlobSeer

### 3.1 How to couple Gfarm and BlobSeer?

Since each *gfsd* daemon running on Gfarm's file system nodes is responsible for physically storing Gfarm's data on its local file system, our first approach aims at integrating BlobSeer calls at the *gfsd* daemon. The main idea is to trap all requests to the local file system, and map them to the corresponding BlobSeer API in order to leave the job of storing Gfarm's data to BlobSeer. A Gfarm file is no longer directly stored as a file on the local system; it is stored as a BLOB in BlobSeer. This way, file fragmentation and striping is introduced transparently for Gfarm at the *gfsd* level.

Nevertheless, this way of integrating BlobSeer into *gfsd* daemon clearly does not fully exploit BlobSeer's capability of efficiently handling concurrency, in which multiple clients simultaneously access the same BLOB. The *gfsd* daemon always acts as an intermediary for data transfer between Gfarm clients and BlobSeer data providers, which may limit the data transfer throughput. For this reason, we propose a second approach. Currently, Gfarm defines two modes for data access, *local access mode* and *remote access mode*. The *local access mode* is the mode in which the client and the *gfsd* daemon involved in a data transaction are on the same physical node, allowing the client to directly access its local disk. In contrast, the *remote access mode* is the mode in which a client accesses data through a remote *gfsd* daemon.

Our second approach consists in introducing into Gfarm a new access mode, called *BlobSeer direct access mode*, allowing Gfarm clients to directly access Blob-Seer. In this mode, as explained in Section 2.2, clients benefit from a better throughput, as they access the distributed BLOB pages in parallel. During data accesses, the risk to create a bottleneck at the *gfsd* level is then reduced, since the *gfsd* daemon no longer acts as an intermediary for accessing data; its task now is simply to establish the mapping between Gfarm logical files and BlobSeer's corresponding BLOB ids. Keeping the management of this mapping at the *gfsd* level is important, as, this way, no change is required on Gfarm's metadata server (*gfmd*), which is not aware of the use of BlobSeer.

## 3.2 The Gfarm/BlobSeer file system design

The Gfarm/BlobSeer cooperation aims at working on a large-scale distributed environment where multiple *sites* in different administrative domains interconnect with each other to form a global network. Therefore, it is vital that our design is scalable to such settings.

A global view

We assume that our object-based file system runs on a multi-site grid, where each site corresponds to a specific cluster. As shown on Figure 1, the whole system consists of a single instance of Gfarm, with one metadata server (*gfmd*), multiple distributed clients and multiple file system nodes (*gfsd*). In addition to this regular Gfarm configuration, we introduce multiple instances of BlobSeer (one per site). Any node of the grid may be a client. On each site, a dedicated node runs a *gfsd* daemon and the other nodes run a BlobSeer instance, with all its entities described in Section 2.2. On each site, the *gfsd* daemon is responsible for mapping Gfarm files to BLOBs and for managing all BLOBs on the site. This approach guarantees the independent administration of the sites. By separating the whole system into different sites, we provide a simple strategy for efficiently using different *access modes* whenever a client access a Gfarm file. Typically, if the client is on the same site with the BlobSeer instance that stores the BLOB corresponding to the desired Gfarm file, it then should use the *BlobSeer direct access mode*, allowing for parallel access of the BLOB pages by the client. Otherwise, the client may not be able to directly access the BlobSeer instance of a remote *site*, due to security policies. In that case, the *remote access mode* is more appropriate: the client may access data through the *gfsd* daemon of the remote *site*, which acts as a proxy.

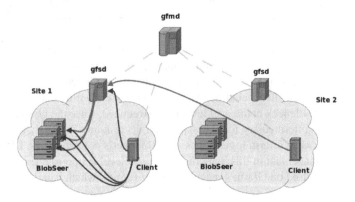

**Fig. 1** A global view of the Gfarm/BlobSeer system.

Description of the interactions between Gfarm and BlobSeer

Figure 2 describes the interactions inside the Gfarm/BlobSeer system, both for *remote access mode* (left) and *BlobSeer direct access mode* (right). When opening a Gfarm file, the *global path name* is sent from the client to the metadata server. If no error occurs, the metadata server returns to the client a *network file descriptor* as an identifier of the requested Gfarm file. The client then initializes the *file handle*. On a *write* or *read* request, the client must first initialize the access node (if not done yet), after having authenticated itself with the *gfsd* daemon. Details are given below.

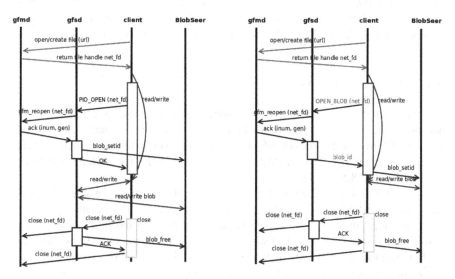

**Fig. 2** The internal interactions inside Gfarm/BlobSeer system: remote access (left) vs BlobSeer direct access mode (right).

Remote access mode.    In this access mode, the internal interactions of Gfarm with BlobSeer only happen through the *gfsd* daemon. After receiving the *network file descriptor* from the client, the *gfsd* daemon inquires the metadata server about the corresponding Gfarm's global ID and maps it to a BLOB id. After opening the BLOB for reading and/or writing, all subsequent read and write requests received by the *gfsd* daemon are mapped to BlobSeer's data access API.

BlobSeer direct access mode.    In order for the client to directly access the BLOB in the *BlobSeer direct access mode*, there must be a way to send the ID of the desired BLOB from the *gfsd* daemon to the client. With this information, the client is further able to directly access BlobSeer without any help from the *gfsd*.

# 4 Experimental evaluation

To evaluate our Gfarm/BlobSeer prototype, we first compared its performance for read/write operations to that of the original Gfarm version. Then, as our main goal was to enhance Gfarm's data access performance under heavy concurrency, we evaluated the read and write throughput for Gfarm/BlobSeer in a setting where multiple clients concurrently access the same Gfarm file. Experiments have been performed on the Grid'5000 [2] testbed, an experimental grid infrastructure distributed on 9 sites around France. In each experiment, we used at most 157 nodes of the Rennes site of Grid'5000. Nodes are outfitted with 8 GB of RAM, Intel Xeon 5148 LV CPUs running at 2.3 GHz and interconnected by a Gigabit Ethernet network. Intra-cluster measured bandwidth is 117.5 MB/s for TCP sockets with MTU set at 1500 B.

Access throughput with no concurrency

First, we mounted our object-based file system on a node and used Gfarm's own benchmarks to measure file I/O bandwidth for sequential reading and writing. Basically, the Gfarm benchmark is configured to access a single file that contains 1 GB of data. The block size for each *READ* (respectively *WRITE*) operation varies from 512 bytes to 1,048,576 bytes.

We used the following setting: for Gfarm, a metadata server and a single file system node. For BlobSeer, we used 10 nodes: a version manager, a metadata provider and a provider manager were deployed on a single node, and the 9 other nodes hosted data providers. We used a *page_size* of 8 MB. We measured the read (respectively write) throughput for both access modes of Gfarm/BlobSeer: *remote access mode* and *BlobSeer direct access mode*. For comparison, we ran the same benchmark on a pure Gfarm file system, using the same setting for Gfarm alone.

As shown on Figure 3, the average read throughput and write throughput for Gfarm alone are 65 MB/s and 20 MB/s respectively in our configuration. The I/O throughput for Gfarm/BlobSeer in *remote access mode* was better than the pure Gfarm's throughput for the write operation, as in Gfarm/BlobSeer data is written in a remote RAM and then, asynchronously, on the corresponding local file system, whereas in the pure Gfarm the *gfsd* synchronously writes data on the local disk. As expected, the read throughput is worse then for the pure Gfarm, as going through the *gfsd* daemon induces an overhead.

On the other hand, when using the *BlobSeer direct access mode*, Gfarm/BlobSeer clearly shows a significantly better performance, due to parallel accesses to the striped file: 75 MB/s for writing (i.e. 3.75 faster than the measured Gfarm throughput) and 80 MB/s for reading.

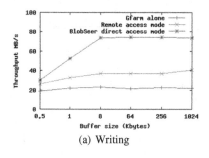
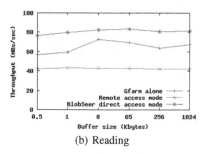

(a) Writing                              (b) Reading

**Fig. 3** Sequential write (left) and read (right).

Access throughput under concurrency

In a second scenario, we progressively increase the number of concurrent clients which access disjoint parts (1 GB for each) of a file totaling 10 GB, from 1 to 8 clients. The same configuration is used for Gfarm/BlobSeer, except for the number of data providers in BlobSeer, set to 24. Figure 4(a) indicates that the performance of the pure Gfarm file system decreases significantly for concurrent accesses: the I/O throughput for each client drops down twice each time the number of concurrent clients is doubled. This is due to a bottleneck created at the level at the *gfsd* daemon, as its local file system basically serializes all accesses. In contrast, a high bandwidth is maintained when Gfarm relies on BlobSeer, even when the number of concurrent clients increases, as Gfarm leverages BlobSeer's design optimized for heavy concurrency.

Finally, as a scalability test, we realized a third experiment. We ran our Gfarm/BlobSeer prototype using a 154 node configuration for BlobSeer, including 64 data providers, 24 metadata servers and up to 64 clients. In the first phase, a single client appends data to the BLOB until the BLOB grows to 64 GB. Then, we increase the number of concurrent clients to 8, 16, 32, and 64. Each client writes 1 GB to that file at a disjoint part. The average throughput obtained (Figure 4(b)) slightly drops (as expected), but is still sustained at an acceptable level. Note that, in this experiment, the write throughput is slightly higher than in the previous experiments, since we directly used Gfarm's library API, avoiding the overhead due to the use of Gfarm's FUSE interface.

## 5 Conclusion

In this paper we address the problem of managing large data volumes at a very large-scale, with a specific focus on applications which manipulate huge data, physically distributed, but logically shared and accessed at a fine-grain under heavy concurrency. Using a grid file system seems the most appropriate solution for this context,

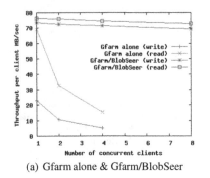

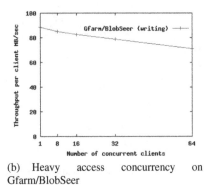

(a) Gfarm alone & Gfarm/BlobSeer        (b)  Heavy   access   concurrency   on
                                        Gfarm/BlobSeer

**Fig. 4** Access concurrency

as it provides transparent access through a globally shared namespace. This greatly simplifies data management by applications, which no longer need to explicitly locate and transfer data across various sites. In this context, we explore how a grid file system could be built in order to address the specific requirements mentioned above: huge data, highly distributed, shared and accessed under heavy concurrency. Our approach relies on establishing a cooperation between the Gfarm grid file system and BlobSeer, a distributed object management system specifically designed for huge data management under heavy concurrency. We define and implement an integrated architecture, and we evaluate it through a series of preliminary experiments conducted on the Grid'5000 testbed. The resulting BLOB-based grid file system exhibits scalable file access performance in scenarios where huge files are subject to massive, concurrent, fine-grain accesses.

We are currently working on introducing versioning support into our integrated, object-based grid file system. Enabling such a feature in a global file system can help applications not only to tolerate failures by providing support for roll-back, but will also allow them to access different versions of the same file, while new versions are being created. To this purpose, we are currently defining an extension of Gfarm's API, in order to allow the users to access a specific file version. We are also defining a set of appropriate *ioctl* commands: accessing a desired file version will then be completely done via the POSIX file system API.

In the near future, we also plan to extend our experiments to more complex, multi-cluster grid configurations. Additional directions will concern data persistence and consistency semantics. Finally, we intend to perform experiments to compare our prototype to other object-based file systems with respect to performance, scalability and sability.

# References

1. The Grid Security Infrastructure Working Group. `http://www.gridforum.org/security/gsi/`.
2. The Grid'5000 Project. `http://www.grid5000.fr/`.
3. Bill Allcock, Joe Bester, John Bresnahan, Ann L. Chervenak, Ian Foster, Carl Kesselman, Sam Meder, Veronika Nefedova, Darcy Quesnel, and Steven Tuecke. Data management and transfer in high-performance computational grid environments. *Parallel Comput.*, 28(5):749–771, 2002.
4. Alessandro Bassi, Micah Beck, Graham Fagg, Terry Moore, James S. Plank, Martin Swany, and Rich Wolski. The Internet Backplane Protocol: A study in resource sharing. In *Proc. 2nd IEEE/ACM Intl. Symp. on Cluster Computing and the Grid (CCGRID '02)*, page 194, Washington, DC, USA, 2002. IEEE Computer Society.
5. Philip H. Carns, Walter B. Ligon, Robert B. Ross, and Rajeev Thakur. PVFS: A parallel file system for linux clusters. In *Proceedings of the 4th Annual Linux Showcase and Conference*, pages 317–327, Atlanta, GA, 2000. USENIX Association.
6. Ananth Devulapalli, Dennis Dalessandro, Pete Wyckoff, Nawab Ali, and P. Sadayappan. Integrating parallel file systems with object-based storage devices. In *SC '07: Proceedings of the 2007 ACM/IEEE conference on Supercomputing*, pages 1–10, New York, NY, USA, 2007. ACM.
7. M. Factor, K. Meth, D. Naor, O. Rodeh, and J. Satran. Object storage: the future building block for storage systems. In *Local to Global Data Interoperability - Challenges and Technologies, 2005*, pages 119–123, 2005.
8. Sanjay Ghemawat, Howard Gobioff, and Shun-Tak Leung. The Google file system. In *SOSP '03: Proceedings of the nineteenth ACM symposium on Operating systems principles*, pages 29–43, New York, NY, USA, 2003. ACM Press.
9. HDFS. The Hadoop Distributed File System. `http://hadoop.apache.org/common/docs/r0.20.1/hdfs_design.html`.
10. Bogdan Nicolae, Gabriel Antoniu, and Luc Bougé. Distributed management of massive data. an efficient fine grain data access scheme. In *International Workshop on High-Performance Data Management in Grid Environment (HPDGrid 2008)*, Toulouse, 2008. Held in conjunction with VECPAR'08. Electronic proceedings.
11. Bogdan Nicolae, Gabriel Antoniu, and Luc Bougé. Blobseer: How to enable efficient versioning for large object storage under heavy access concurrency. In *EDBT '09: 2nd International Workshop on Data Management in P2P Systems (DaMaP '09)*, St Petersburg, Russia, 2009.
12. Bogdan Nicolae, Gabriel Antoniu, and Luc Boug. Enabling high data throughput in desktop grids through decentralized data and metadata management: The BlobSeer approach. In *Proceedings of the 15th Euro-Par Conference on Parallel Processing (Euro-Par 09)*, Lect. Notes in Comp. Science, Delft, The Netherlands, 2009. Springer-Verlag. To appear.
13. P. Schwan. Lustre: Building a file system for 1000-node clusters. In *Proceedings of the Linux Symposium*, 2003.
14. Osamu Tatebe and Satoshi Sekiguchi. Gfarm v2: A grid file system that supports high-perfomance distributed and parallel data computing. In *Proceedings of the 2004 Computing in High Energy and Nuclear Physics*, 2004.
15. Sage A. Weil, Scott A. Brandt, Ethan L. Miller, Darrell D. E. Long, and Carlos Maltzahn. Ceph: a scalable, high-performance distributed file system. In *OSDI '06: Proceedings of the 7th symposium on Operating systems design and implementation*, pages 307–320, Berkeley, CA, USA, 2006. USENIX Association.
16. Brian S. White, Michael Walker, Marty Humphrey, and Andrew S. Grimshaw. LegionFS: a secure and scalable file system supporting cross-domain high-performance applications. In *Proc. 2001 ACM/IEEE Conf. on Supercomputing (SC '01)*, pages 59–59, New York, NY, USA, 2001. ACM Press.
17. FUSE. `http://fuse.sourceforge.net/`.

# Improving the Dependability of Grids via Short-Term Failure Predictions

Artur Andrzejak and Demetrios Zeinalipour-Yazti and Marios D. Dikaiakos

**Abstract** Computational Grids like EGEE offer sufficient capacity for even most challenging large-scale computational experiments, thus becoming an indispensable tool for researchers in various fields. However, the utility of these infrastructures is severely hampered by their notoriously low reliability: a recent nine-month study found that only 48% of jobs submitted in South-Eastern-Europe completed successfully. We attack this problem by means of proactive failure detection. Specifically, we predict site failures on short-term time scale by deploying machine learning algorithms to discover relationships between site performance variables and subsequent failures. Such predictions can be used by Resource Brokers for deciding where to submit new jobs, and help operators to take preventive measures. Our experimental evaluation on a 30-day trace from 197 EGEE queues shows that the accuracy of results is highly dependent on the selected queue, the type of failure, the preprocessing and the choice of input variables.

## 1 Introduction

Detecting and managing failures is an important step towards the goal of a dependable and reliable Grid. Currently, this is an extremely complex task that relies on over-provisioning of resources, ad-hoc monitoring and user intervention. Adapting ideas from other contexts such as cluster computing [11], Internet services [9, 10] and software systems [12] is intrinsically difficult due to the unique characteristics of Grid environments. Firstly, a Grid system is not administered centrally; thus it is hard to access the remote sites in order to monitor failures. More-

Artur Andrzejak
Zuse Institute Berlin (ZIB), Takustraße 7, 14195 Berlin, Germany, e-mail: andrzejak@zib.de

Demetrios Zeinalipour-Yazti and Marios D. Dikaiakos
Department of Computer Science, University of Cyprus, CY-1678, Nicosia, Cyprus e-mail: \{dzeina,mdd\}@cs.ucy.ac.cy

over, failure feedback mechanisms cannot be encapsulated in the application logic of each individual Grid software, as the Grid is an amalgam of pre-existing software libraries, services and components with no centralized control. Secondly, these systems are extremely large; thus, it is difficult to acquire and analyze failure feedback at a fine granularity. Lastly, identifying the overall state of the system and excluding the sites with the highest potential for causing failures from the job scheduling process can be much more efficient than identifying many individual failures.

In this work, we define the concept of *Grid Tomography*[1] in order to discover relationships between Grid site performance variables and subsequent failures. In particular, assuming a set of monitoring sources (system statistics, representative low-level measurements, results of availability tests, etc.) that characterize Grid sites, we predict with high accuracy site failures on short-term time scale by deploying various off-the-shelf machine learning algorithms. Such predictions can be used for deciding where to submit new jobs and help operators to take preventive measures.

Through this study we manage to answer several questions that have to our knowledge not been addressed before. Particularly, we address questions such as: *"How many monitoring sources are necessary to yield a high accuracy?"*; *"Which of them provide the highest predictive information?"*, and *"How accurately can we predict the failure of a given Grid site X minutes ahead of time?"* Our findings support the argument that Grid tomography data is indeed an indispensable resource for failure prediction and management. Our experimental evaluation on a 30-day trace from 197 EGEE queues shows that the accuracy of results is highly dependent on the selected queue, the type of failure, the preprocessing and the choice of input variables.

This paper builds upon on previous work in [20], in which we presented the preliminary design of FailRank architecture. In FailRank, monitoring data is continuously coalesced into a representative array of numeric vectors, the *FailShot Matrix (FSM)*. FSM is then continuously ranked in order to identify the $K$ sites with the highest potential to feature some failure. This allows a Resource Broker to automatically exclude the respective sites from the job scheduling process. FailRank is an architecture for on-line failure ranking using linear models, while this work investigates the problem of predicting failures by deploying more sophisticated, in general non-linear *classification algorithms* from the domain of machine learning.

In summary, this paper makes the following contributions:

- We propose techniques to predict site failures on short-term time scale by deploying machine learning algorithms to discover relationships between site performance variables and subsequent failures;
- We analyze which sources of monitoring data have the highest predictive information and determine the influence of preprocessing and prediction parameters on the accuracy of results;

---

[1] *Grid Tomography* refers in our context to the process of capturing the state of a grid system by sections, i.e., individual state attributes (*tomos* is the Greek word for *section*.)

- We experimentally validate the efficiency of our propositions with an extensive experimental study that utilizes a 30-day trace of Grid tomography data that we acquired from the EGEE infrastructure.

The remainder of the paper is organized as follows: Section 2 formalizes our discussion by introducing the terminology. It also describes the data utilized in this paper, its preprocessing, and the prediction algorithms. Section 3 presents an extensive experimental evaluation of our findings obtained by using machine learning techniques. Finally, Section 4 concludes the paper.

# 2 Analyzing Grid Tomography Data

This section starts out by overviewing the anatomy of the EGEE Grid infrastructure and introducing our notation and terminology. We then discuss the tomography data utilized in our study, and continue with the discussion of pre-processing and modeling steps used in the prediction process.

## 2.1 The Anatomy of a Grid

A Grid interconnects a number of remote clusters, or *sites*. Each site features heterogeneous resources (hardware and software) and the sites are interconnected over an open network such as the Internet. They contribute different capabilities and capacities to the Grid infrastructure. In particular, each site features one or more *Worker Nodes*, which are usually rack-mounted PCs. The *Computing Element* runs various services responsible for authenticating users, accepting jobs, performing resource management and job scheduling. Additionally, each site might feature a *Local Storage* site, on which temporary computation results can reside, and local software libraries, that can be utilized by executing processes. For instance, a computation site supporting mathematical operations might feature locally the Linear Algebra PACKage (LAPACK). The Grid middleware is the component that glues together local resources and services and exposes high-level programming and communication functionalities to application programmers and end-users. EGEE uses the gLite middleware [6], while NSF's TeraGrid is based on the Globus Toolkit [5].

## 2.2 The FailBase repository

Our study uses data from our *FailBase Repository* which characterizes the EGEE Grid in respect to failures between 16/3/2007 and 17/4/2007 [14]. FailBase paves the way for the community to systematically uncover new, previously unknown patterns and rules between the multitudes of parameters that can contribute to failures in a Grid environment. This database maintains information for 2,565 Computing Element (CE) *queues* which are essentially sites accepting computing jobs. For our study we use only a subset of queues for which we had the largest number of available types of monitoring data. For each of them the data can be thought of as a *time-series*, i.e., a sequence of pairs (timestamp,value-vector). Each value-vector consists of 40 values called *attributes*, which correspond to various sensors and functional tests. That comprises the *FailShot Matrix* that encapsulates the Grid failure values for each Grid site for a particular timestamp.

## 2.3 Types of monitoring data

The attributes are subdivided into four groups A, B, C and D depending of their source as follows [13]:

A. *Information Index Queries (BDII)*: These 11 attributes have been derived from LDAP queries on the Information Index hosted on *bdii101.grid.ucy.ac.cy*. This yielded metrics such as the number of free CPUs and the maximum number of running and waiting jobs for each respective CE-queue.
B. *Grid Statistics (GStat)*: The raw basis for this group is data downloaded from the monitoring web site of Academia Sinica [7]. The obtained 13 attributes contain information such as the geographical region of a Resource Center, the available storage space on the Storage Element used by a particular CE, and results from various tests concerning BDII hosts.
C. *Network Statistics (SmokePing)*: The two attributes in this group have been derived from a snapshot of the *gPing* database from ICS-FORTH (Greece). The database contains network monitoring data for all the EGEE sites. From this collection we measured the average round-trip-time (RTT) and the packet loss rate relevant to each South East Europe CE.
D. *Service Availability Monitoring (SAM)*: These 14 attributes contain information such as the version number of the middleware running on the CE, results of various replica manager tests and results from test job submissions. They have been obtained by downloading raw html from the CE sites and processing them with scripts [4].

The above attributes have different significance when indicating a site failure. As group D contains functional and job submission tests, attributes in this group are particularly useful in this respect. Following the results in Section 3.2.1 we regard two of these `sam` attributes, namely `sam-js` and `sam-rgma` as failure indicators. In other words, in this work we regard certain values of these two attributes as queue failures, and focus on predicting their values.

## 2.4 Preprocessing

The preprocessing of the above data involves several initial steps such as masking missing values, (time-based) resampling, discretization, and others (these steps are not a part of this study, see [13, 14]). It is worth mentioning that data in each group has been collected with different frequencies (A, C: once a minute, B: every 10 minutes, D: every 30-60 minutes) and resampled to obtain a homogeneous 1-minute sampling period. For the purpose of this study we have further simplified the data as follows: all missing or outdated values have been set to $-1$, and we did not make difference in severity of errors. Consequently, in our attribute data we use $-1$ for "invalid" values, 0 to indicate normal state, and 1 to indicate a faulty state. We call such a modified vector of (raw and derived) values a *sample*.

In the last step of the preprocessing, a sample corresponding to time $T$ is assigned a *(true) label* indicating a future failure as follows. Having decided which of the sam attributes $S$ represents a failure indicator, we set this label to 1 if any of the values of $S$ in the interval $[T + 1, T + p]$ is 1; otherwise the label of the sample is set to 0. The parameter $p$ is called the *lead time*. In other words, the label indicates a future failure if the sam attribute $S$ takes a fault-indicating value at *any* time during the subsequent $p$ minutes.

## 2.5 Modeling methodology

Our prediction methods are *model-based*. A *model* in this sense is a function mapping a set of raw and/or preprocessed sensor values to an output, in our case a binary value indicating whether the queue is expected to be healthy (0) or not (1) in a specified future time interval. While such models can take a form of a custom formula or an algorithm created by an expert, we use in this work a *measurement-based* model [17]. In this approach, models are extrapolated automatically from historical relationships between sensor values and the simulated model output (computed from offline data). One of the most popular and powerful class of the measurement-based models are based on *classification algorithms* or *classifiers* [19, 3]. They are usually most appropriate if outputs are discrete [17]. Moreover, they allow the incorporation of multiple inputs or even functions of data suitable to expose its information content in a better way than the raw data. Both conditions apply in our setting.

A classifier is a function which maps a $d$-dimensional vector of real or discrete values called *attributes* (or *features)* to a discrete value called *class label*. In the context of this paper each such vector is a sample and a class label corresponds to the true label as defined in Section 2.4. Note that for an error-free classifier the values of class labels and true labels would be identical for each sample. Prior to its usage as a predictive model, a classifier is *trained* on a set of pairs (sample, true label). In our case samples have consecutive timestamps. We call these pairs the *training data* and denote by $D$ the maximum amount of samples used to this purpose.

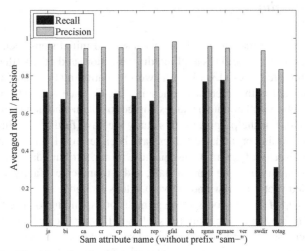

**Fig. 1** Recall and Precision of each `sam` attribute

A trained classifier is used as a predictive model by letting it compute the class label values for a sequence of samples following the training data. We call these samples *test data*. By comparing the values of the computed class labels against the corresponding true labels we can estimate the accuracy of the classifier. We also perform model updates after all samples from the test data have been tested. This number - expressed in minutes or number of samples - is called the *update time*.

In this work we have tested several alternative classifiers such as C4.5, LS, Stumps, AdaBoost and Naive Bayes. The interested reader is referred to [3, 16] for a full description of these algorithms.

## 3 Experimental Results

Each prediction run (also called *experiment*) has a controlled set of preprocessing parameters. If not stated otherwise, the following default values of these parameters are used. The size of the training data $D$ is set to 15 days or 21600 samples, while the model update time is fixed to 10 days (14400 samples). We use a lead time of 15 minutes. The input data groups are A and D, i.e., each sample consists of $11 + 14$ attributes from both groups. On this data we performed attribute selection via the backward branch-and-bound algorithm [16] to find 3 best attributes used as the classifier input. As classification algorithm we deployed the C4.5 decision tree algorithm from [15] with the default parameter values.

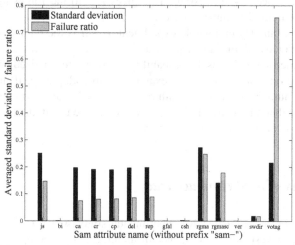

**Fig. 2** Standard deviation and failure ratio for each s am attribute

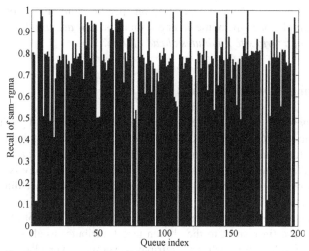

**Fig. 3** Recall of attribute sam-rgma for all 197 queues

## 3.1 Evaluation metrics: recall and precision

During preprocessing, each training or test sample is assigned a *true label*: a value
of 1 indicates a failure at the corresponding sample time, and a value 0 indicates
no failure. During testing, a classifier assigns to each test sample a *predicted label*
with analogous values. Obviously, the more frequently both values agree, the higher
the quality of predictions. For the purpose of failure prediction cases with true label

equal to 1 are especially interesting. This gives rise to the following definitions common in the field of document retrieval.

For all test examples in a single experiment, *recall* is the number of examples with both predicted and true label equal 1 divided by number of cases with true label equal 1. This metrics estimates the probability that a failure is indeed predicted. The *precision* is the ratio of the number of examples with both predicted and true labels equal 1 to the number of examples with predicted label equal 1. It is interpreted as the probability that a predicted failure really occurs. We use in the following these two metrics to evaluate prediction accuracy.

## 3.2 Analysis of prediction accuracy

We shall next present an extensive experimental study, which focuses on two aspects: First, we investigate the influence of monitoring data groups as well as various preprocessing and mining parameters on the accuracy of results. Second, we seek to determine the highest prediction accuracy (measured in terms of recall and precision) that can be achieved depending on specific requirements on the predictions. For example, one type of the latter questions is: *how accurately can we predict the behavior of a Grid site X minutes ahead of time?*

### 3.2.1 Selecting the target attributes

First we study which sam attributes are most interesting in terms of prediction accuracy and variance. We compute recall and precision for each combination of queue / sam attribute. Figure 1 shows these results for each particular sam attribute averaged over all queues. The preliminary conclusion from the figure is that most of the sam attributes (i.e., 12 out of the 14) are good choices for yielding a high recall/precision.

Consequently, we also considered the *failure ratio*: the ratio of all samples indicating a failure (in respect to the chosen target attribute) to all samples. Figure 2 shows these values for each sam attribute, averaged over all queues. The attributes sam-bi, sam-gfal, sam-csh, sam-ver and sam-swdir had a low failure ratio and standard deviation and were consequently excluded from further consideration.

We additionally ranked the remaining attributes according to their importance and their recall values, and consequently decided to only focus on the following two attributes:

- **sam-js**: This is a test that submits a simple job for execution to the Grid and then seeks to retrieve that job's output from the UI. The test succeeds only if the job finishes successfully and the output is retrieved.
- **sam-rgma**: R-GMA [2] is the Relational Grid Monitoring Architecture which makes all Grid monitoring data appear like one large Relational Database that

may be queried in order to find the information required. The `sam-rgma` test tries to insert a tuple and run a query for that tuple. The test returns success if all operations are successful.

Figure 3 shows that the recall of `sam-rgma` varies strongly among the queues. We observed a similar behavior for the failure indicator `sam-js` but omit these results for brevity.

### 3.2.2  Data characteristics and accuracy

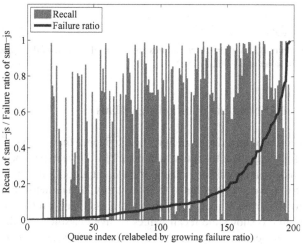

**Fig. 4** Recall vs. sorted failure ratio of `sam-js` for all 197 queues

Next, we investigated the key characteristics of the data and how their variations influence the prediction accuracy. For each of the 197 queues and for the two target attributes (`sam-js` and `sam-rgma`) we computed the failure ratio as defined above. We then sorted all queues by increasing failure ratios and plotted the corresponding recall values for predictions with standard values. As seen in Figure 4 there is obviously no relationship between failure ratio and prediction accuracy. The same conclusions apply for the `sam-rgma` attribute.

We have also inspected visually the failure patterns over time in our data. Typically, an occurrence of a failure or non-failure is followed by a large number of samples of the same kind, i.e., the failure state does not change frequently; see top graph in Figure 5. Also typically the prediction errors occur right after the change in the failure state. This indicates that the value of the last historical sample of the target attribute was a good indicator of its future value.

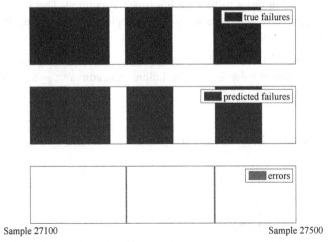

**Fig. 5** Comparison of true and predicted failures for a typical interval of data (queue number 6, attribute `sam-js`, samples 27100 to 27500)

### 3.2.3 Effects of different classification algorithms

Despite the theoretical knowledge and practical evidence that no classification algorithm can perform significantly better than others [8, 1] we experienced substantial deviations in recall and precision values for different algorithms, in the absence of attribute selection. We attribute this to the potentially high dimensionality of the input data (up to 40 attributes if all input groups are used) and a relatively large noise in the data. Figure 6 shows the recall values of five classification algorithms (see [15]) for the attribute sam-js averaged over 10 randomly selected queues (indexes 6, 9, 19, 54, 62, 75, 86, 137, 163, 188) without and with an attribute selection algorithm. Other algorithms such as k-nearest neighbor classifier or Support Vector Machine did not produce representative results due to memory or implementation problems in the used libraries [16, 15]. Figure 6 tells us that the AdaBoost algorithm (combined with Stumps) yielded best recall values. Furthermore, attribute selection improved the accuracy in all cases but for C4.5. Despite of this fact, C4.5 has been used as it had very small running time compared e.g. to AdaBoost.

## 4 Conclusions

In this paper we attack the problem of low reliability in job completion of Grid systems by means of proactive failure detection. Specifically, we predict site failures on short-term time scale by deploying classification algorithms that discover the relationships between site performance variables and subsequent failures. Our

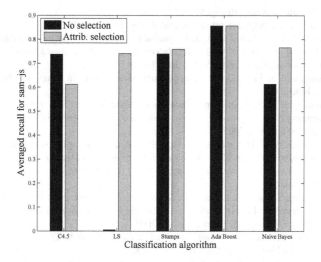

**Fig. 6** Recall (sam-js) for five different classification algorithms without and with attribute selection (averaged over 10 queues)

experimental evaluation on a 30-day trace from 197 EGEE queues shows that the accuracy of results can be significantly high in many cases.

# Acknowledgements

This work was supported in part by the European Union under projects CoreGRID (# IST-2002-004265) and EGEE (#IST-2003-508833). The authors would like to thank Kyriacos Neocleous and Yannis Ioannou from the University of Cyprus for their valuable help in constructing the Failbase repository and Charalampos Gkikas from ICS/FORTH for providing access to the Hellas-FORTH gPing data.

# References

1. A. Andrzejak and L. Silva. Using machine learning for non-intrusive modeling and prediction of software aging. In *IEEE/IFIP Network Operations & Management Symposium (NOMS 2008)*, Salvador de Bahia, Brazil, Apr 7–11 2008.
2. A. Cooke et. al. The Relational Grid Monitoring Architecture: Mediating Information about the Grid. *Journal of Grid Computing*, 2(4):323–339, 2004.
3. R. Duda, P. Hart, and D. Stork. *Pattern Classification*. John Wiley and Sons, 2001. 0-471-05669-3.
4. EGEE. Service availability monitoring (SAM), http://sam-docs.web.cern.ch/sam-docs/.
5. I. Foster. Globus Toolkit Version 4: Software for Service-Oriented Systems. *Journal of Computer Science and Technology*, 21(4):513–520, 2006.

6. Glite. Glite middleware, http://glite.org/.
7. GStat. Grid statistics (gstat), http://goc.grid.sinica.edu.tw/gstat/.
8. E. J. Keogh, S. Lonardi, and C. A. Ratanamahatana. Towards parameter-free data mining. In *Proceedings of the Tenth ACM SIGKDD International Conference on Knowledge Discovery and Data Mining*, pages 206–215, August 2004.
9. E. Kiciman and A. Fox. Detecting application-level failures in component-based internet services, June 2004.
10. E. Kiciman and L. Subramanian. Root cause localization in large scale systems. In *In Proceedings of the 1 st Workshop on Hot Topics in System Dependability (HotDep-05*. IEEE Computer Society, June 2005.
11. S. Krishnamurthy, W. H. Sanders, and M. Cukier. A dynamic replica selection algorithm for tolerating timing faults. In *2001 International Conference on Dependable Systems and Networks (DSN 2001) (formerly: FTCS)*, pages 107–116, Goteborg, Sweden, July 2001. IEEE Computer Society.
12. M. E. Locasto, S. Sidiroglou, and A. D. Keromytis. Application communities: Using monoculture for dependability. In *In Proceedings of the 1 st Workshop on Hot Topics in System Dependability (HotDep-05*, pages 288–292, 2005.
13. K. Neocleous. Failure analysis, prediction and management on the EGEE grid infrastructure. Master's thesis, University of Cyprus, August 2007.
14. K. Neocleous, M. D. Dikaiakos, P. Fragopoulou, and E. Markatos. Failure management in grids: The case of the EGEE infrastructure. *Parallel Processing Letters*, 17(4):391–410, Dec. 2007.
15. D. G. Stork, E. Yom-Tov, and R. O. Duda. *Computer manual in MATLAB to accompany Pattern Classification*. Wiley, second edition, 2004.
16. F. van der Heijden, R. P. W. Duin, D. de Ridder, and D. M. J. Tax. *Classification, Parameter Estimation and State Estimation*. John Wiley & Sons, 2004.
17. R. Vilalta, C. V. Apte, J. L. Hellerstein, S. Ma, and S. M. Weiss. Predictive algorithms in the management of computer systems. *IBM Systems Journal*, 41(3):461–474, 2002.
18. WISDOM. Initiative for grid-enabled drug discovery against neglected and emergent diseases, http://wisdom.eu-egee.fr.
19. I. H. Witten and E. Frank. *Data Mining: Practical machine learning tools and techniques*. Morgan Kaufmann, San Francisco, 2nd edition edition, 2005.
20. D. Zeinalipour-Yazti, H. Papadakis, C. Georgiou, and M. Dikaiakos. Metadata ranking and pruning for failure detection in grids. *Parallel Processing Letters*, 18(3):371–390, Sept. 2008.

# Distributed Data Mining using a Public Resource Computing Framework

Eugenio Cesario, Nicola De Caria, Carlo Mastroianni and Domenico Talia

**Abstract** The public resource computing paradigm is often used as a successful and low cost mechanism for the management of several classes of scientific and commercial applications that require the execution of a large number of independent tasks. Public computing frameworks, also known as "Desktop Grids", exploit the computational power and storage facilities of private computers, or "workers". Despite the inherent decentralized nature of the applications for which they are devoted, these systems often adopt a centralized mechanism for the assignment of jobs and distribution of input data, as is the case for BOINC, the most popular framework in this realm. We present a decentralized framework that aims at increasing the flexibility and robustness of public computing applications, thanks to two basic features: (i) the adoption of a P2P protocol for dynamically matching the job specifications with the worker characteristics, without relying on centralized resources; (ii) the use of distributed cache servers for an efficient dissemination and reutilization of data files. This framework is exploitable for a wide set of applications. In this work, we describe how a Java prototype of the framework was used to tackle the problem of mining frequent itemsets from a transactional dataset, and show some preliminary yet interesting performance results that prove the efficiency improvements that can derive from the presented architecture.

Eugenio Cesario
ICAR-CNR, Rende, Italy, e-mail: cesario@icar.cnr.it

Nicola De Caria
DEIS - University of Calabria, Rende, Italy e-mail: decaria@si.deis.unical.it

Carlo Mastroianni
ICAR-CNR, Rende, Italy e-mail: mastroianni@icar.cnr.it

Domenico Talia
ICAR-CNR and DEIS - University of Calabria, Rende, Italy e-mail: talia@deis.unical.it

# 1 Introduction

In the last few years, volunteer computing has become a success story for many scientific applications. In fact, Desktop Grids, in the form of volunteer computing systems, have become extremely popular as a mean for exploiting huge amount of low cost computational resources with a few manpower getting involved.

Two of the most popular volunteer computing platforms available today are BOINC and XtremWeb. BOINC [2] is by far the most popular volunteer computing platform available today, and to date, over 5 million participants have joined various BOINC projects. The core BOINC infrastructure is composed of a scheduling server and a number of clients installed on users' machines. The client software periodically contacts a centralized scheduling server to receive instructions for downloading and executing a job. After a client completes the given task, it then uploads resulting output files to the scheduling server and requests more work. The BOINC middleware is especially well suited for CPU-intensive applications but is somewhat inappropriate for data-intensive tasks due to its centralized nature that currently requires all data to be served by a group of centrally maintained servers. BOINC was successfully used in projects such as Seti@home, Folding@home, and Einstein@home.

XtremWeb [4][5] is another Desktop Grid project that, like BOINC, works well with "embarrassingly parallel" applications that can be broken into many independent and autonomous tasks. XtremWeb follows a centralized architecture and uses a three-tier design consisting of a worker, a coordinator, and a client. The XtremWeb software allows multiple clients to submit task requests to the system. When these requests are dispensed to workers for execution, the workers will retrieve both the necessarily data and executable to perform the analysis. The role of the third tier, called the coordinator, is to decouple clients from workers and to coordinate tasks execution on workers.

Despite the inherent decentralized nature of the applications for which they are devoted, the current adopted public computing systems generally rely upon centralized algorithms for the assignment of jobs and the distribution of input data. This is a clear limitation for the wide adoption of these systems, due to the lack of flexibility and robustness of centralized architectures. For example, the server in charge of job assignment and data distribution is a clear bottleneck and single point of failure for the system. Moreover, the client/server data distribution scheme does not offer valuable solutions for applications in which input data files can be initially stored in different locations or may be reused by different workers. Finally, the centralized architecture does not allow users to define their own applications and ask the system to execute them: applications are managed centrally, and users can only contribute by running jobs that are useful for applications defined elsewhere.

Recent efforts are investigating the exploitation of distributed infrastructures and protocols to efficiently deliver large data files to Desktop Grid workers. For example, the P2P-ADICS project [7] aims at building a P2P software layer that can be used by scientific applications, specifically those engaged in volunteer computing, to distribute, manage, and maintain their data. BitDew [6] is a programmable environment for automatic and transparent data management on computational Desktop Grids. The Bitdew runtime environment is a distributed service architecture that integrates modular P2P components such as DHT structures for a distributed data catalog and collaborative transport protocols for data distribution.

In the last few years, we have presented a decentralized framework that aims at increasing the flexibility and robustness of public computing applications, thanks to two basic features: (i) the adoption of a P2P protocol for dynamically matching the job specifications with the worker characteristics, without relying on centralized resources; (ii) the use of distributed cache servers for an efficient dissemination and reutilization of data files. Unlike BOINC and XtremWeb, our data distribution scheme does not rely heavily on any centralized mechanisms for job and data distribution.

This framework is exploitable for a wide set of applications. We proposed a framework for the analysis of gravitational waveforms [1]), then it was adapted for the problem of discovering closed frequent itemsets in a transactional dataset (the so called FCIM problem) [3]. So far, the analysis has only been performed through a simulation environment. Now we implemented a Java prototype of the framework, and in this paper we present the first results obtained with the prototype in a real testbed, for the FCIM problem. These results confirm the efficiency improvements that can derive in distributed data mining from the distributed volunteer computing architecture. This paper has also the objective to show that the distributed framework may help the management of a large set of distributed applications, both in the data mining domain and in other application domains. The adopted protocols and algorithms are general and can easily be adapted to different scenarios. In fact, not only this kind of solution can improve the performance of public computing systems, in terms of efficiency, flexibility and robustness, but also it can enlarge the use of the public computing paradigm, in that any user is allowed to define its own application and specify the jobs that will be executed by remote volunteers, which is not permitted by BOINC.

The remainder of the paper is organized as follows. Section 2 describes the distributed framework for the execution of applications according to the public resource paradigm, and illustrates the characteristics of the applications that may benefit from this framework. It is then shown that the FCIM problem is indeed an interesting use case. Section 3 presents the performance results obtained with a prototype of the framework for the FCIM problem. Conclusions and future work are discussed in Section 4.

## 2 A Distributed Framework for Public Computing with Caching Capabilities

In the last few years, we have worked on a decentralized framework for public resource computing having as main goal to overcome the limitations, in terms of flexibility and robustness, of centralized architectures, such as BOINC.

First, we proposed a framework for the analysis of gravitational waveforms [1]), in which the partition of an application into independent jobs is trivial and the input dataset is the same for all the tasks. In [3], the algorithm was adapted for the problem of discovering frequent itemsets in a transactional dataset. When compared to the astronomy application, the input dataset for the data mining problem may be different for different jobs, which requires more attention in the cache management. In [3] performance analysis was obtained through simulation experiments for the data mining case. Recently, we have implemented a Java prototype of the framework, which exploits the presence of a super-peer network for the assignment and execution of jobs, and adopts caching strategies to make the data distribution more efficient. The prototype uses TCP sockets for communication and data exchange, and can be easily adapted for different types of public computing applications. Indeed, both the protocol and the caching algorithm are generic and can be reused for the distributed execution of all those applications that present the following characteristics:

1. the number and complexity of jobs are such that distributed execution can be more efficient than centralized execution. For example, if the duration of jobs is short, the time needed to transfer the input data to the worker nodes over a distributed system may not be compensated by the advantages obtained with the parallel execution of jobs in different machines;
2. it frequently occurs that input data is reused by different jobs, which is the rationale for the presence of distributed cache servers that hold this data and forward it to the workers when needed;
3. the size of input data is sufficiently large, so that its caching can be actually profitable. If the data size is too small, it could be more efficient to let the workers get the data from the original data source instead of exploiting caching strategies.

The problem of mining frequent closed itemsets (FCIM), described in Section 2.1, presents all these characteristics and therefore is a good candidate for the presented distributed framework. However, it is clear that the framework can bring benefits to many other applications, both in the data mining and in completely different domains.

The framework exploits the presence of different types of nodes that are available within a super-peer topology, as detailed in the following:

- the *data source* is the node that stores the entire data set that must be analyzed and mined;
- the *job manager* is the node in charge of decomposing the overall application in a set of independent tasks. This node produces a *job advert* document for every task, which describes its characteristics and specifies the portion of the data needed to complete the task. This node is also responsible for the collection of output results;
- the *workers* are the nodes that are available for job execution. In data mining applications, such as that illustrated in this paper, they are referred to as *miners*.

A miner first issues a *job query* and then a *data query* to retrieve the job advert and the corresponding data;

- *data cachers* are super-peers having the additional ability to cache data and the associated data adverts. Data cachers can retrieve data from the data source or other data cachers, and later provide such data to miners;

- *super-peers* nodes constitute the backbone of the network. Miners connect directly to a super-peer, and super-peers are connected with one another through a high level P2P network. Super-peers play the role of *rendezvous nodes*, i.e. meeting places for job or data providers and consumers. They match miner queries with *job* and *data adverts*.

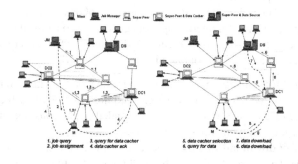

**Fig. 1** Execution of the distributed algorithm for public resource computing in a sample super-peer network.

In order to execute our data mining algorithm, the network works as follows (see Figure 1). A set of *job adverts* are generated by the *job manager* node. A job advert is a job descriptor that collects the characteristics of the job and the minimum processing and storage capabilities required to a node for its execution. An available miner *M* issues a *job query* (step 1), that travels across the super-peer interconnections, to the job manager. A matching *job advert* is sent back to *M* (setp 2). Thanks to the *job advert*, the miner is also informed of the data necessary to complete its job. Thus, it issues a *data query* to discover a data cacher (step 3). Since multiple data cachers may answer (step 4), the miner selects the nearest one [1] and gives it the responsibility to retrieve the required input data. In our example, the selected data cacher $DC_1$ (step 5) does not hold the data needed by $M$, and issues a query to the data source $DS$ or to the other data cachers (step 6). Eventually, $DC_1$ retrieves the data from $DS$ (step 7), stores it and provides it to the miner $M$ (step 8). In the future, $DC_1$ will be able to provide the same data to other miners or to other data cachers. Finally, the miner $M$ executes the job.

Our implementation includes a number of techniques that can speed up the execution, depending on the state of the network and the dissemination of data. For example, in the case that the data cacher $DC_1$ has already downloaded data, steps 6 and 7 are unnecessary. Also, once a miner has discovered the job manager or a data cacher, it could decide to contact them directly without paying the cost of sending a message across the super-peer network.

The presence of data cachers helps the dissemination of data and can improve the performance of the network. An interesting strategic choice concerns the amount of data that is downloaded by a data cacher from the data source. Two different caching strategies have been analyzed and compared:

- **Strategy #1: partial download.** The data cacher downloads from the data source only the portion of the data set that is strictly required by the miner for job execution. If some of this data was already downloaded in previous operations, the data cacher retrieves only the missing data.
- **Strategy #2: full download.** The data cacher downloads the entire data set from the data source. Therefore, the data cacher will not need to turn to the data source in the future, and will be able to provide every portion of data required by the miners for successive job executions.

Of course, the two strategies have pros and cons and can be advantageous in different scenarios. Intuitively, the first strategy is advantageous if the same portion of data is needed several times by miners that are located in the same region of the network. On the other hand, the second strategy performs better if the required portions of data overlap rarely, so that a single download operation can be more efficient that many operations aimed at retrieving the different portions of data in different steps. Moreover, strategy #1 requires that the cacher performs a matching between the data already stored and the data needed for the next job execution, in order to individuate the possible missing data. No such operation is needed with strategy #2.

## 2.1 Parallel Mining of Closed Frequent Itemset

After the general description of the distributed framework given in the previous section, here we show how the proposed architecture can be exploited for distributed

---

[1] The nearest data cacher is individuated by measuring the round trip time, but in general the most convenient data cacher may be chosen according to a different strategy.

data mining algorithms, and in particular for the FCIM problem. In this section, we report a brief description of an FCIM algorithm that has been implemented (and used in our experiments) in order to validate the proposed distributed approach.

Frequent Itemsets Mining (FIM) is a demanding task common to several important data mining applications that look for interesting patterns within databases (e.g., association rules, correlations, sequences, episodes, classifiers). A frequent issue is that the number of frequent itemsets produced from a transactional dataset can be very large. For this reason, it is useful to identify a small representative set of itemsets from which all other frequent itemsets can be derived. Frequent Closed Itemsets provide a minimal representation of itemsets without losing their support information. Formally, an itemset $X$ is closed if none of its immediate supersets has exactly the same support count of $X$ [9].

Historically, the study of parallel algorithms for Frequent Closed Itemsets Mining (FCIM) did not produce good results. However, an interesting parallel algorithm for mining closed itemsets, MT-Closed [8], was recently proposed in literature. Analogously to other FCIM algorithms, MT-Closed executes two scans of the dataset $\mathcal{D}$ in order to initialize an internal data structures. A first scan is needed to discover frequent single items, denoted with $\mathcal{L}^1$. During a second scan, a vertical bitmap representing the dataset is built by considering frequent items only. The resulting bitmap has size $|\mathcal{L}^1| \times |\mathcal{D}|$ bits, where the $i$-th row is a bit-vector representation of the tid-list $g(i)$ of the $i$-th frequent item. The kernel of the algorithm consists in a recursive procedure that exhaustively explores a subtree of the search space given its root. The input of this procedure is a seed closed itemset $X$, and its tid-list $g(X)$. The input should also include the set of items used to calculate closures. Initially, $X = c(\emptyset)$, and $g(X) = \mathcal{D}$. Similarly to other FCIM algorithms, given a closed itemset $X$, new candidates $Y = X \cup i$ are created according to the lexicographic order. If a candidate $Y$ is found to be frequent, then its closure is computed and $c(Y)$ is used to continue the recursive traversal of the search space. for more details, the reader could refer to [8].

An interesting features of MT-Closed is that every single closed itemset $X$ can be thought as the root of a sub-tree of the search space that can be mined independently from any other (non overlapping) portion of the search space. Thus, it is possible to partition the whole mining task into independent regions, i.e. sub-trees of the search space, each of them described by a distinct *job descriptor J*. This perfectly fits with our proposed architecture. In fact, the job manager could assign (by a job descriptor) to each miner the task of searching itemsets in a specific sub-region of the search space. Then the miner sends to the data cacher a request for the input data needed for its mining activity. As soon as the search task has been terminated, the miner returns to the job manager the set of discovered frequent closed itemsets. Then, the miner is ready for a new job assignment.

# 3 Performance Evaluation

To evaluate the performance of the architectural model proposed in the paper, we carried out an analysis by executing different experiments in different scenarios. We have implemented the framework exploiting the super-peer protocol described in Section 2 and deployed it in a real network, composed of 10 nodes of the University of Calabria. The nodes have Intel Pentium 4 processors, CPU frequency 1.36GHz, and 2GB RAM.

The main goal is to carry out a quantitative analysis of performance aimed at evaluating the efficiency of the framework and pointing out how the caching strategies affect the total execution time. The P2P network used in the experiments is composed of 1 data source, 1 job manager, a number of data cachers between 1 and 4, and a number of miners between 1 and 10 [2]. The input dataset used to measure the running times of the various jobs was a subset of the USCensus1990 dataset, composed of 100,000 transactions, for a total size of 560 MB. We run the algorithm by fixing the minimum absolute support threshold to 100.

**Execution Time and SpeedUp.**
A first set of experiments were performed by using the caching strategy #1 (partial download), as described in Section 2. Figure 2 shows the overall time needed to execute all the jobs, i.e. the time elapsed from the submission of the mining task (from the job manager) until its termination. The execution time is reported with respect to the number of miners (from 1 to 10) that are used to execute the data mining jobs. In this figure, we report 4 different curves plotting the execution time obtained when 1, 2, 3 or 4 data cachers are used.

By observing the plot, we can point out two main aspects. The first one is that the total execution time decreases when the number of miners increases. For instance, if we consider the execution with 3 data cachers, it can be seen that the distributed framework execution time decreases from 5368 seconds, when all the jobs are executed on a single miner, to about 840 seconds if 10 miners are active in the network. This is justified by the fact that, in order to complete the whole process, the job manager assigns to each miner the execution of a number of jobs that is less and less as the number of miners increases. For this reason, the whole mining task terminates in a shorter time. From the figure, it is clear that the trend is general and independent from the number of data cachers working in the network.

The second consideration is about the influence that the number of available data cachers has on the execution time. It can be observed that the execution time decreases as the number of data cachers increases from 1 to 4. The reason is that when a higher number of data cachers are available, the miners can concurrently retrieve data from different data cachers, and consequently the length of single download operations decreases. For example, let us consider when 5 miners are used: when a single data cacher is involved the total execution is 1771 seconds, while when 4 data cachers are used it is equal to 1159 seconds.

---

[2] where needed, the same machine was used to host one miner and one data cacher

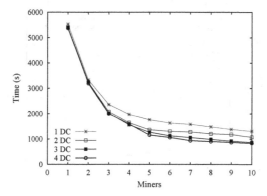

**Fig. 2** Overall execution time vs. the number of miners, for different numbers of available data cachers, and use of caching strategy #1.

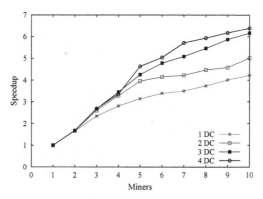

**Fig. 3** Value of speedup vs. the number of miners, for different numbers of available data cachers, and use of caching strategy #1.

In addition to the execution time, another interesting performance index is the relative speedup, that is, the ratio of the execution time when one miner is involved to the execution time with $n$ miners. Figure 3 shows the achieved execution speedup for different number of miners and data cachers. From this figure we can observe that the larger is the number of data cachers, the higher is the speedup value. For example, if one data cacher is used, the speedup ranges from 1.66 (with 2 miners) to 4.21 (with 10 miners); if 4 data cachers are used, the speedup ranges from 1.68 (with 2 miners) to 6.39 (with 10 miners).

**Influence of the caching strategies.**
As mentioned before, another interesting point is the analysis of how the two caching strategies described in Section 2 influence the execution time. Figure 4 shows the overall running time on varying the number of mining peers by using caching strategies #1 and #2, in case of 3 data cachers available in the system. It is worth noticing that the execution time is reduced if the cachers adopt strategy #2.

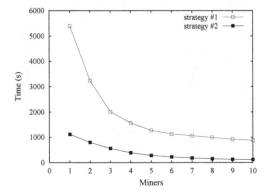

**Fig. 4** Overall execution time vs. the number of miners, with 3 data cachers, and use of caching strategies #1 and #2.

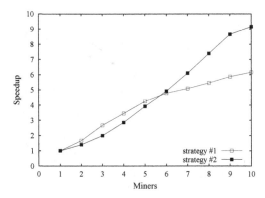

**Fig. 5** Value of speedup vs. the number of miners, with 3 data cachers, and use of caching strategies #1 and #2.

In fact, with strategy #2, each data cacher downloads the entire data set as soon as the first data query is received, and then reuses the data for all the following miner requests. Since the number of miner requests is high (over 4,000 requests) and the requested portions of the input data set are not frequently coincident or overlapping, the strategy #2 is more profitable for this application. As mentioned in Section 2, strategy #1 would be more efficient with a lower number of jobs and/or if the same portion of data is often requested by different jobs. Finally, this trend is confirmed by observing the Figure 5, where the speedup is plotted for the two caching strategies. In particular, strategy #2 obtains better speedup values with respect to the strategy #1 when a larger number of miners are used. For example, the speedup is equal to 9.15 when 10 miners and 3 data cachers exploiting the strategy #2 are used. On the contrary, using the same configuration, with strategy #1, the obtained speedup by using 10 miners is equal to 6.16.

# 4 Conclusions

This paper described the architecture and the performance evaluation of a decentralized software framework for public resource computing. The framework implementation and its use for a P2P data mining algorithm showed how the public resource computing paradigm can be effectively exploited also outside the traditional scientific application areas.

In several scientific and business application domains, it is required to analyze large amounts of data that are distributed over a large number of sites or are originated from many remote data sources (from the sky, sensors, or mobile devices). In those cases, decentralized models and systems can be useful to distribute the mining of data on a large set of computing nodes. The framework presented here can represent a software solution for such scenarios where both data and computation are distributed on a large scale.

Our work will proceed with the adoption of the presented architecture for different data mining applications that may take advantage of distributed execution and caching facilities, such as ensemble learning algorithms and mining of streaming data. Moreover, we are devising efficient strategies to cope with the failure of computing nodes.

**Acknowledgements** This research work continues previous research activities carried out under the FP6 Network of Excellence CoreGRID funded by the European Commission (Contract IST-2002-004265) and activities carried out in the project OpenKnowTech, funded by MIUR (DM 21301). We are very grateful to Claudio Lucchese and Salvatore Orlando for their precious collaboration on early work.

# References

1. Al-Shakarchi, E., Cozza, P., Harrison, A., Mastroianni, C., Shields, M., Talia, D., and Taylor, I. (2007). Distributing workflows over a ubiquitous p2p network. *Scientific Programming*, 15(4):269–281.
2. Anderson, D. P. (2004). Boinc: A system for public-resource computing and storage. In *GRID '04: Proceedings of the Fifth IEEE/ACM International Workshop on Grid Computing (GRID'04)*, pages 4–10.
3. Barbalace, D., Lucchese, C., Mastroianni, C., Orlando, S., and Talia, D. (2008). Mining@home: Public resource computing for distributed data mining. In *CoreGRID Symposium*, Las Palmas de Gran Canaria, Canary Island, Spain.
4. Cappello, F., Djilali, S., Fedak, G., Herault, T., Magniette, F., Neri, V., and Lodygensky, O. (2005). Computing on large-scale distributed systems: Xtrem web architecture, programming models, security, tests and convergence with grid. *Future Generation Computer Systems*, 21(3):417–437.
5. Fedak, G., Germain, C., Neri, V., and Cappello, F. (2001). Xtremweb: A generic global computing system. In *Proceedings of the IEEE Int. Symp. on Cluster Computing and the Grid*, Brisbane, Australia.
6. Fedak, G., He, H., and Cappello, F. (2009). Bitdew: a data management and distribution service with multi-protocol file transfer and metadata abstraction. *Journal of Network and Computer Applications*, 32(5).

7. Kelley, I. and Taylor, I. (2008). Bridging the data management gap between service and desktop grids. In Peter Kacsuk, R. L. and Nemeth, Z., editors, *Distributed and Parallel Systems In Focus: Desktop Grid Computing*. Springer.

8. Lucchese, C., Orlando, S., and Perego, R. (2007). Parallel mining of frequent closed patterns: Harnessing modern computer architectures. In *ICDM '07: Proceedings of the Fourth IEEE International Conference on Data Mining*.

9. Tan, P.-N., Steinbach, M., and Kumar, V. (2006). *Introduction to Data Mining*. Addison-Wesley.

# Integration of the ProActive Suite and the semantic-oriented monitoring tool SemMon

Wlodzimierz Funika, Denis Caromel, Pawel Koperek, and Mateusz Kupisz

**Abstract** In this paper we present our semantic-based approach to the monitoring of distributed applications built with the ProActive Parallel Suite framework. It is based on a semantic description of what is to be monitored, it's measurable capabilities, and related operations. We explore the ability to adapt a semantic-oriented monitoring tool, SemMon to ProActive. The latter provides a stable environment for development of parallel applications, while SemMon is aimed at semantic-oriented performance monitoring support, originally designed for distributed Java applications. We introduce a uniform monitoring environment model which describes the resources provided by ProActive and supports JMX-based notifications. A sample monitoring session is provided as well as plans for further research.

## 1 Introduction

The importance of distributed computing using parallelism techniques continues to grow. Because of the demand for a fast development of robust and reliable applica-

Wlodzimierz Funika
Institute of Computer Science AGH-UST, al. Mickiewicza 30, 30-059, Kraków, Poland,
e-mail: funika@agh.edu.pl

Denis Caromel
INRIA - CNRS - University of Nice Sophia-Antipolis, 2004, Route des Lucioles - BP93 - 06902 Sophia Antipolis Cedex, France,
e-mail: Denis.Caromel@sophia.inria.fr

Pawel Koperek
Institute of Computer Science AGH-UST, al. Mickiewicza 30, 30-059, Kraków, Poland,
e-mail: koperek@student.agh.edu.pl

Mateusz Kupisz
Institute of Computer Science AGH-UST, al. Mickiewicza 30, 30-059, Kraków, Poland,
e-mail: kupisz@student.agh.edu.pl

45

tions, which in many cases are very complex, the use of production-ready development environments is essential. One of such environments is the ProActive Parallel Suite [1]. It enables to develop parallel and concurrent applications in different paradigms, including support for asynchronous communication, load balancing, and migration of computations. ProActive is correlated with the research on grid computing models carried out within the CoreGRID project [2].

The monitoring of distributed applications is essential in the development and production phase. Java runtime provides a standard and production-ready solution for this issue - Java Management Extensions (JMX) [3]. JMX enables observation and management of virtual machine and applications that run in it. Every standard Java Virtual Machine with version number higher than 1.5.0 supports this technology. JMX is used in ProActive as well, by a graphical monitoring system bundled with ProActive (IC2D - Interactive Control and Debugging of Distribution), for control and monitoring of applications.

The benefits of using the existing monitoring applications are unquestionable. These tools are often tailored to specific platform needs - like IC2D from the ProActive Suite. They provide a lot of useful profiling information, but in complex systems there still is a need of more sophisticated and powerful tools that enable *exploring* the monitoring data, like semantic monitoring and analysis of gathered data. Such semi-automatic monitoring facilities provide a controllable solution to the problem of overwhelming amount of information gathered from the observed systems - the information is given a *meaning* and because that semantic description is both human and machine understandable correlations between found meanings can be easily analyzed. This approach is a lot more human - friendly than plain data analysis but still can be easily automated - a standardized semantic description can be extended to fit the needs of more complex and bigger systems. It helps users and administrators to cope with the management and improvement of wide and complex distributed systems, e.g., grids. With such an approach, common problems like network bottlenecks or overloaded machines can be instantly diagnosed and handled. Such analysis can identify, without much effort from the researcher, behavior patterns among the elements of the monitored system and trigger relevant actions. It can also provide *suggestions* on what is worth monitoring next, e.g. when processor usage is too high for a period of time it proposes to start the monitoring of JVM threads since the number of threads running in the JVM is semantically connected with CPU usage.

At the beginning of the paper, following the Related work section, we present the basic concepts of extending the SemMon tool [4] towards the ability to monitor ProActive using the benefits of semantics. Then we discuss elements of integration with the ProActive system: the system architecture after integration and custom changes introduced into SemMon. Next, a sample monitoring session utilizing the new features is presented. At the end we provide our conclusions on the integration work and discuss further research plans.

## 2 Related work

A number of tools can be mentioned when speaking about the monitoring of complex systems.

Autopilot [7] is the very first monitoring tool that used some kind of semantics to help the user with monitoring. Precisely, it used fuzzy logic to interpret gathered data. It was developed in Grid Application Development Software Project (GrADS) [10] as a part responsible for adaptive control of distributed applications. It is mostly used for automatic resource configuration. It provides features like: dynamic performance instrumentation, real-time adaptive control mechanisms and configurable resource management algorithms.

Another monitoring tool employing semantic approach is Aksum [8] - part of the Askalon [9] project. It uses the concept of performance properties to search for performance bottlenecks. It is the first project that uses ontology to represent the performance data, not only to provide data for sharing and reusing between other monitoring tools but also to automatize the performance analysis process.

A different approach is used by PerfOnto [11]. Fundamentally, it is an OWL [13] ontology which describes experiment-related and resource-related concepts. The ontology employed by PerfOnto gives not only detailed information about resources and experiments. Ontological queries can be used in various ways, e.g. to monitor critical sections of a deployed application or submit hints to the scheduler to migrate a task from an overloaded node. Albeit PerfOnto profoundly describes performance data it lacks automation in using them and doesn't contain any adaptation algorithms.

PerfExplorer [12] is aimed at the clustering and reduction of multidimensional performance data, correlation analysis of execution paths. It enables comparative analysis of multiple executions of applications using data mining algorithms available, e.g. in Weka. The tool is very helpful when used on multiprocessor systems, however, its usability in the environments featuring great dynamics, like grids, is constrained.

## 3 Extending SemMon's support for specific platforms

SemMon's modular architecture makes the integration process to any platform easy. The scientist, who wants to extend SemMon, first has to define platform-specific resources and its measurable capabilities. A next step of the process is implementation which consists of:

- Extending the ontology used by SemMon with the resources isolated at the analysis step and their capabilities
- Configuring an existing *Adapter* or making a new one.

In SemMon's architecture, *Adapter* follows the standard adapter design pattern and it's a component which translates requests between SemMon's core component and the monitored system. Since JMX is a standard way of sharing monitorable data, we have provided a widely configurable JMX adapter. In most cases it is not necessary to develop a new adapter, a configuration of the JMX one will be sufficient. JMX Adapter configuration consists of declaring a mapping between the capabilities stored in the ontology and standard JMX queries, which are used to retrieve capabilities values. However, simple JMX queries sometimes are not enough to profoundly use the monitoring capabilities of the platform. That's when a new adapter is needed. Designing an adapter is a platform-specific task and depends on things like: protocol that is used to communicate with the platform, configuration parameters, etc. The design of a sample adapter (for ProActive environment) is covered later on in the paper.

## 4 ProActive integration strategy

Below we show the features of the ProActive system which produce some important implications for the concept of semantic-oriented monitoring architecture and extensions to the SemMon infrastructure.

### 4.1 Features of the systems to be integrated

ProActive is a Java library (Open Source, licensed on GPL2) that is aimed at parallel, distributed, and multi-threaded computing. ProActive simplifies the programming of applications distributed on a variety of platforms. It is used as a base for a reference implementation of Grid Component Model [14] created within Core-GRID project [15]. Using Java both as a programming language and runtime environment, ProActive is a cross-platform solution: it can be run in any environment in which JVM works. ProActive Suite comprises a graphical, real-time monitoring solution - IC2D, an Eclipse-based visualization platform that allows the user to observe the current state of the system and carry out measurements. It enables obtaining extended benchmarking and profiling information concerning computations.

The SemMon project [4, 5] is aimed to create a tool providing semantic analysis of the monitoring data on a distributed system. Knowledge about effective tool usage (the relevance and accuracy of the metrics used during a system examination) may be shared within the research team with a built-in scoring system. All resources and metrics used are elements of a specific ontology which provides a semantic description of gathered data. Based on this approach to monitoring data processing, SemMon has the ability to interpret data and can trigger indispensable actions, e.g. provide some suitable notifications (*alerts*) to users or launch additional, semantically close measurements.

SemMon has been designed with modularity and extendability in mind. It consists of several loosely coupled components: *Ontology subsystem*, *Core subsystem*, and *GUI subsystem*.

Parsing, searching, storing, and sharing of ontology data is handled by *Ontology subsystem*. It features the ability to interpret data coming from monitoring. The knowledge, held in the underlying ontology, is used to point out which metric should be used as next to diagnose the reason of problems. *Core subsystem* provides mechanisms for connecting to "physical" monitoring systems, deployment, initialization, and executing measurements. It is an interface for the *Ontology subsystem* and a public, remote interface for GUI clients (called *Monitoring tool*). The *Core subsystem* comprises three components: *Adapter*, *Resource Registry*, and *Remote interface for GUI*. The first one provides a binding between the underlying monitoring system and SemMon. The *Resource Registry* holds information about all instances of monitored resources and maps them to the identifiers of *Core subsystem*. The *Remote interface for GUI* allows clients to connect to the *Core subsystem* and interact with the SemMon infrastructure.

*GUI subsystem* consists of two components: *the Registrar* and *Monitoring tool*. The first one is a simple graphical interface for web service methods used for registering new machines to *Core subsystem*. *Monitoring tool* is a GUI for the results of the monitoring actions performed by SemMon.

## 4.2 ProActive requirements for monitoring vs. SemMon

The systems created using the ProActive Parallel Suite involve usually a large number of resources. The basic unit in a ProActive-based system is an *Active Object* (AO). Active Objects are grouped in nodes. Nodes are part of ProActive Runtime, which usually corresponds to a single Java Virtual Machine. Active Objects themselves are just Java objects with an assigned thread and own execution queue. Remote access to their methods is provided by the ProActive Suite. The process of communication is transparent for the end user - the application developer. The monitoring of Active Objects requires processing lots of information, which can be burdensome for the user. In case IC2D is used for monitoring, it is the researcher who has to interpret all incoming data. It would often be more helpful, if the system would try to point at the measurements which should be started next or at the actions which should be undertaken automatically or manually. This could help in diagnosing the reason of problems through providing a guidance dependent on the current behavior of system, e.g. in case the value of a system parameter exceeds a threshold.

Such an approach can be illustrated by the following use case:

- ActiveObject (A1) sends a request to another ActiveObject (A2),
- SemMon monitors the responsiveness of A2,
- if the time exceeds a specified threshold an alarm is raised and the system suggests the monitoring of the queue length of A2.

Next, the system might suggest the monitoring of CPU load or network bandwidth. This could reveal the real reasons of problems with the responsiveness of A2. The user could make a decision based on these results, e.g. to migrate the Active Object to another host.

## 4.3 Concept of architecture

The system under discussion (its architecture is shown in Fig. 4.3) consists of:

- a number of Java Virtual Machines (JVM) running ProActive runtimes (may be distributed across the network or reside on a single machine)
- machine running *Core and Ontology* subsystems and *Metrics results database*
- one or several machines running *Monitoring tool*
- machine with *Registration tool*.

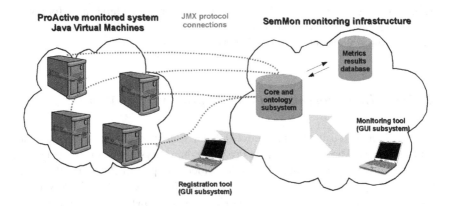

**Fig. 1** Architecture of SemMon and ProActive integration

As mentioned above, the JMX technology is used for the communication of *Core* with the resources under monitoring. ProActive Parallel Suite provides extended JMX connectors. To ensure compatibility with IC2D at the data gathering level, SemMon makes use of these connectors as well (Fig. 2).

Each ProActive runtime instance provides MBeans supplying information about the runtime. A set of these information is extended by JVM statistics gathered by a JIMS MBean (deployed with the application) [6]. All these data is periodically downloaded by the *Core* subsystem, stored in *Metrics results database* and then used to compute the values of metrics. The end user can observe the system state with the graphical *Monitoring tool*.

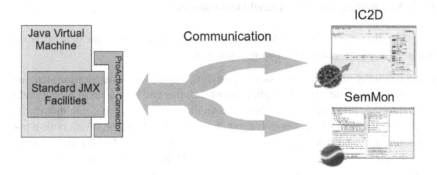

**Fig. 2** Usage of extended ProActive Connector

Connection between *Core* and monitored resources is established with the use of *Registration tool*. Its function is to pass the address of *RMI registry* used by ProActive runtime to a resources registry. The resources registry maps the custom names provided by users to the currently established connections. This provides access to the information held by MBeans as well. Once the address is obtained, a lookup is performed on the newly added *RMI registry* and all the discovered instances of ProActive runtimes are added to the monitored resources list. Parts of SemMon infrastructure may be held on different machines, but it is also possible to run them on the same computer.

## 4.4 Extensions introduced into the integrated system

The integration of both systems required introducing changes to their code. Since modifications to the ProActive Parallel Suite might result in unpredictable errors, so alteration of the source code of the framework has been maximally reduced. The only change in the library's source code is the introduction of JIMS MBean which provides various information about the monitored system (e.g. average load, memory statistics, CPU information). In SemMon, the following enhancements have been introduced:

- a new web service registering ProActive specific resources - it accepts URLs of RMI registries and performs the discovery of the attached ProActive runtimes
- the resource and metric ontologies have been extended by the classes of ProActive specific resources, capabilities and metrics
- the capabilities of the central repository of the monitored JVMs (called "the registry") have been extended to support ProActive resources.

### 4.4.1 New model of the monitored environment

The adaptation of SemMon to ProActive framework revealed that the general model of a monitored system had following limitations:

- the hierarchy of ProActive system's elements was lost at the registration step - the model didn't hold any information about the structure of the environment under monitoring, just information about connections to MBeans, e.g. the monitoring of all Active Objects was possible, but the user didn't know on which node a particular instance of AO operates. Such information is crucial when the dynamics of the environment, e.g. migrations of Active Objects, is taken into account.
- the model was static - once created at runtime, didn't react on later changes of the structure of the observed system.

To match the requirements of integration and to overcome the above constraints, a new data model has been provided. To utilize its full capabilities, the registry has been rewritten from the ground up. The new data model introduces a dedicated, uniform representation of ProActive environment. It consists of "data providers" - objects responsible for single MBean instances. "*Data providers*" create the following structure, which matches the basic structure of ProActive environment (see Fig. 3):

- *ProActiveRuntimeDataProvider* - *root element* containing all ProActive nodes held in a single JVM, an equivalent of ProActive Runtime
- *ProActiveNodeDataProvider* - *container element* for Active Objects, an equivalent of ProActive Node
- *ProActiveActiveObjectDataProvider* - represents a basic unit which can perform computations, an equivalent of ProActive Active Object
- *ProActiveActiveObjectMethodDataProvider* - represents a public method exposed by an Active Object. Such method may be called to obtain specific behavior. Methods are not shown on Fig. 3 due to its clarity.

Another major improvement of the model is support for dynamic changes occurring to the system under monitoring. The information about such events is broadcasted within the ProActive framework with JMX notifications. The new model provides support for these notifications, therefore can be adjusted during runtime.

All notifications defined by ProActive are currently listened to. One of the next problems to be coped with is making the SemMon's GUI to reflect changes introduced by them.

One should remember that the mechanism of JMX notifications, albeit very useful, has a significant drawback: the delivery of a notification is not guaranteed in the JMX Remote API specification [16]. This may lead to the loss of some information and therefore to the inconsistency of the model and the monitored system. Further research should provide methods to minimize the impact of such situations.

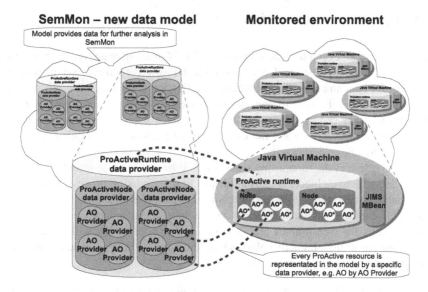

**Fig. 3** Architecture of new data model

### 4.4.2 Registrar tool extensions

Adding new registries led to a new meaning of the data passed with *Registrar* tool, e.g. for ProActive, the address of the system to be monitored is the address of RMI registry and for JMX it is JMX connector's address. In the future SemMon is going to cooperate with other environments e.g. those monitored with the use of J-OCM [18]. It will lead to an increase in the number of registries handled by SemMon. This would require to provide new implementations of *Registrar* tool as well. To reduce the amount of effort in such a case, we have introduced an *Information Service*. This new Web Service provides information about the registries supported by specific instances of SemMon *Core* component. These information includes:

- address of the Web Service used to register specific resources
- label for this address - shown in *Registrar* tool's GUI
- user-friendly help information about this address - shown in *Registrar*'s GUI
- default address value of resources handled by a particular type of registry
- label for default resources address - shown in *Registrar*'s GUI
- help info about default resources address - given in *Registrar*'s GUI.

The address of *Information Service* should be configured before using the *Registrar* tool. During the start procedure, this application will try to connect to the provided location and obtain information about the supported registries. The user don't have to remember different addresses of registering Web Services. This makes the use of SemMon easier and less error-prone.

# 5 Sample monitoring session

Below we give an example of how to use the SemMon monitoring tool to monitor a
ProActive–based application - C3D, bundled with ProActive Suite. It is a distributed
raytracer for benchmarking Java RMI and serialization. The choice is motivated by
the fact it enables the user to measure the performance of the integrated system.
This functionality can be used to evaluate SemMon's impact on the system under
monitoring. However, to make the example more realistic, we modified rendered
image size to 2500x2500 pixels.

The objective of the monitoring session is, on the one hand, to monitor if any of
the rendering active objects is causing delays to the rendering process, and on the
other hand, to examine the impact of monitoring using SemMon on the monitored
host. This example shows how SemMon can support researcher's activities. The
metric results for measurables are shown on a single chart. We will monitor the
*ServeTime* capability of 4 active objects (renderers for the image), which represents
the total time spent on computation.

1. Set up ProActive environment (C3D example application) and start SemMon.
   Both systems need at least a small configuration to allow successful monitoring.
   Gathering the whole information may take a while depending on how many
   threads are started.
2. Monitoring of new resources may be started. In SemMon's GUI win-
   dow, expand the tree in the `Resources` view: `ProActiveRuntime`
   `(Resource->Cluster ->Node ->Software ->ProActiveRuntime`
   `- >ProActiveNode - >ProActiveActiveObject)`. One will see all
   the instances of active objects detected on the monitored machine. For each
   *renderer* Active Object (C3D Dispatcher shows the names of renderers): select
   it, then select *ProActiveActiveObjectServeCapability* in the resources list panel,
   select *Software metric*, and click *Run metric at the background*.
3. Next, proper visualization is performed. Click *Manage run metric* and add all
   metrics to the default visualization. Click *Show visualization* - one can see the
   the *serve* time values in real-time. Sample results of this session are shown in
   Fig. 4.

## 5.1 SemMon's impact on monitored system

Monitoring with SemMon may induce some extra load on the monitored machine.
This is expected behavior, since monitoring in general is a intrusive task. The extra
overhead can have two different reasons:

- listing the resources of the monitored system before an actual system monitoring
- gathering monitoring information during system examination.

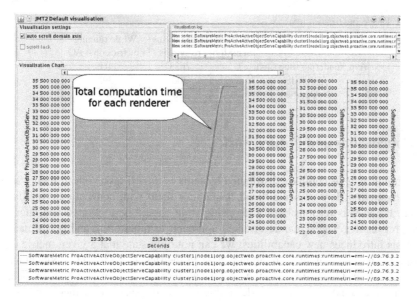

**Fig. 4** Results of a sample monitoring session.

The overhead coming from listing the resources is not significant on the monitored machine. However, since ontology processing is still a resource-expensive task, we can expect high CPU utilization and extensive database usage on the machine running SemMon.

Gathering information during a system examination may induce some extra overhead, which is caused by SemMon polling for capabilities values over JMX.

The sample measurements (presented in Table 1) were taken in the environment consisting of two machines with the following configurations:

- Machine running C3D:
  - Intel Core2 Duo 2,4 GHz
  - 4 GB RAM

- Machine running SemMon's core:
  - AMD Athlon XP 2,2 GHZ
  - 2 GB RAM

The network connection between these machines was a standard 100 Mbit Ethernet connection.

**Table 1** Rendering times

|  | Without SemMon | While listing resources | While running 4 metrics on 4 AOs |
|---|---|---|---|
| Avg. rendering time (ms) | 7754 | 7623 | 8039 |
| Std. dev. (ms) | 357 | 300 | 392 |
| Overhead (%) | — | 3.0 | 8.6 |

# 6 Conclusions and Future work

The monitoring of complex distributed systems is a hard task both in theory and implementation. It is rather difficult to monitor them with conventional facilities where the user is responsible for choosing what should be measured and later to interpret results. The semantic-oriented approach to monitoring and performance analysis introduces new capabilities: we can not only state that a given metric has a value, but also explore correlations between metrics and infer what phenomena influence what. Owing to semantics, tools can provide more meaningful information in the context of systems under monitoring and make use of mechanisms to automate some of the common monitoring activities. The research on integrating SemMon with ProActive or, what would be more correct, porting of SemMon to ProActive proves that the adaptation of a semantic-oriented tool for more complex environments such as ProActive introduces a number of new possibilities for users. The architecture of SemMon, based on components, is prepared for further extensions. Other environments, which e.g. don't expose JMX for monitoring purposes or use a different technology still can be considered for integration.

Our further work will be focused on making SemMon more extensible. All the parts that SemMon is composed of are going to be migrated to the OSGi platform, to enable further extensions to SemMon functionality. Our plan is to redo GUI as a set of Eclipse RCP plugins. This will allow users to run SemMon in the same environment simultaneously with other tools, like IC2D provided by ProActive.

The most important work which has to be done is adding the event support to the the graphical interface. Currently, the monitored resources model exploited by SemMon's GUI is insensitive to changes in the underlying model. It's built upon the connection to a monitored host and remains constant. This means that if, e.g. Active Object has migrated, SemMon's GUI will not be able to display the change. Enabling the graphical interface for dynamic changes is the key to support the monitoring of Active Object migration. Once this is completed, it will be possible to fully integrate JMX notifications sent by ProActive. Furthermore, support for *virtual nodes* is needed. The MBean, which is currently used, is Linux-specific and cannot gather data from non-Linux systems. It has to be extended to support other platforms as well. Also the alarms subsystem has to be remodelled to allow users to set the alarms in a more flexible way. Especially, in terms of Active Object's capabilities - their values are total times, so alarms triggered by exceeding a maximum flat value (that is how alarms are currently triggered) are not so useful. There should be a possibility to trigger alerts based on a sudden change of a value (increase or decrease).

The integration of ProActive and SemMon has proved the concept of the latter's adaptability to new environments. Further implementation work should provide a stable and reliable solution for semantic, semi-automatic monitoring of the distributed applications built with the use of the ProActive Parallel Suite.

**Acknowledgments.** This research is partly supported by the EU IST ViroLab project, the POIG.02.03.00-00-007/08-00 Project PL-GRID and the AGH grant 11.11.120.777.

# References

1. Caromel, D. et al.: ProActive Parallel Suite, http://proactive.inria.fr/
2. CoreGRID project page: http://www.coregrid.net/
3. Sun Microsystems, Inc.: Java Management Extensions (JMX) Technology, http://java.sun.com/javase/technologies/core/mntr-mgmt/javamanagement
4. Funika, W., Godowski, P., Pegiel, P.: A Semantic-Oriented Platform for Performance Monitoring of Distributed Java Applications. In: Proc. ICCS 2008, Part III, pp. 233-242, LNCS 5103, Springer, 2008.
5. Godowski, P., Pegiel, P.: Adaptive monitoring of distributed Java applications, MSc. Thesis, AGH, Krakow, 2007.
6. Zielinski, K., Jarzab, M., Wieczorek, D., Balos, K.: JIMS Extensions for Resource Monitoring and Management of Solaris 10. In Proc. ICCS 2006, Part IV, pp. 1039-1046, LNCS 3994, Springer, 2006.
7. Ribler, R. L., Vetter, J. S., Simitci, H., and Reed, D. A.: Autopilot: Adaptive Control of Distributed Applications. In: Proc. 7th IEEE HPDC, 1998.
8. Fahringer, T. and Seragiotto, C.: Automatic search for performance problems in parallel and distributed programs by using multi-experiment analysis. In Proc. HiPC 2002, Springer, 2002.
9. Fahringer, T., Jugravu, A., Pllana, S., Prodan, R., Seragiotto, C. Jr., and Truong, H.-L.: ASKALON: A Tool Set for Cluster and Grid Computing. In Concurrency and Computation: Practice and Experience, 17:1-27, John Wiley & Sons, 2005.
10. Berman, F., Chien, A., Cooper, K., Dongarra, J., Foster, I., Johnsson, L., Gannon, D., Kennedy, K., Kesselman, C., Reed, D., Torczon, L., and Wolski, R.: The GrAds project: Software support for high-level grid application development. TR Rice COMPTR00-355, Rice University, 2000.
11. Truong, H.-L., Fahringer, T.: Performance Analysis, Data Sharing and Tools Integration in Grids: New Approach based on Ontology . In Proc. ICCS 2004, Part III, pp. 424-431, LNCS 3038, Springer, 2004.
12. K.A.Huck, A.D. Malony, S. Shende, and A. Morris. Knowledge support and automation for performance analysis with PerfExplorer 2.0. In: Scientific Programming, IOS Press, 16(2008), No. 2-3, pp. 123-134, 2008.
13. Sean Bechhofer et al (W3C), OWL Web Ontology Language Reference, http://www.w3.org/TR/owl-ref/
14. OASIS team, GridCOMP partners: Architectural design of the component framework, Deliverable D.CFI.03, June 2007.
15. CoreGRID partners: Basic Features of the Grid Component Model, Deliverable D.PM.04, September 2006

16. Sun Microsystems, Inc.: Java Management Extensions (JMX) - Best Practices, `http://java.sun.com/javase/technologies/core/mntr-mgmt/javama-nagement/best-practices.jsp`

17. Funika, W., Kupisz, M., Koperek, P.: Integration of the SemMon semantic monitoring tool into the ProActive platform, CGW'08, 13-15 October 2008, Krakow, Poland, ACC CYFRONET AGH, Krakow, 2009, pp. 156-163

18. Bubak, M., Funika, W., Wismueller R. Mętel P., Orłowski R., Monitoring of Distributed Java Applications, Future Generation Computer Systems, 2003, no. 19, pp. 651-663.

# An Experimental Evaluation of the DQ-DHT Algorithm in a Grid Information Service

Harris Papadakis, Paolo Trunfio, Domenico Talia and Paraskevi Fragopoulou

**Abstract** DQ-DHT is a resource discovery algorithm that combines the Dynamic Querying (DQ) technique used in unstructured peer-to-peer networks with an algorithm for efficient broadcast over a Distributed Hash Table (DHT). Similarly to DQ, DQ-DHT dynamically controls the query propagation on the basis of the desired number of results and the popularity of the resource to be located. Differently from DQ, DQ-DHT exploits the structural properties of a DHT to avoid message duplications, thus reducing the amount of network traffic generated by each query. The goal of this paper is to evaluate experimentally the amount of traffic generated by DQ-DHT compared to the DQ algorithm in a Grid infrastructure. A prototype of a Grid information service, which can use both DQ and DQ-DHT as resource discovery algorithm, has been implemented and deployed on the Grid'5000 infrastructure for evaluation. The experimental results presented in this paper show that DQ-DHT significantly reduces the amount of network traffic generated during the discovery process compared to the original DQ algorithm.

Harris Papadakis
Foundation for Research and Technology-Hellas, Institute of Computer Science (FORTH-ICS), Heraklion, Greece, e-mail: adanar@ics.forth.gr

Paolo Trunfio
Department of Electronics, Computer Science and Systems (DEIS), University of Calabria, Rende, Italy, e-mail: trunfio@deis.unical.it

Domenico Talia
Institute of High Performance Computing and Networking, Italian National Research Council (ICAR-CNR) and Department of Electronics, Computer Science and Systems (DEIS), University of Calabria, Rende, Italy, e-mail: talia@deis.unical.it

Paraskevi Fragopoulou
Foundation for Research and Technology-Hellas, Institute of Computer Science (FORTH-ICS) and Department of Applied Informatics and Multimedia, Technological Educational Institute of Crete, Heraklion, Greece, e-mail: fragopou@ics.forth.gr

# 1 Introduction

Information services are fundamental components of Grid systems as they allow to locate the resources needed to execute large-scale distributed applications based on application requirements and resource availability. Designing a decentralized but efficient Grid information service is a significant strand of research, with many researches demonstrating the use of peer-to-peer (P2P) models and techniques as an effective alternative to centralized and hierarchical solutions [1]. Such P2P systems are typically classified as *structured* or *unstructured*, based on the way nodes are linked each other and information about resources is placed in the resulting overlay.

Structured systems, like Chord [2], use a Distributed Hash Table (DHT) to assign to each node the responsibility for a specific part of the resources. When a peer wishes to find a resource identified by a given key, the DHT allows to locate the node responsible for that key in $O(\log N)$ hops using only $O(\log N)$ neighbors per node. In unstructured systems, like Gnutella [3], links among nodes can be established arbitrarily and data placement is unrelated from the topology of the resulting overlay. To locate a given resource, the query must be distributed through the network to reach as many nodes as needed, a method known as "flooding." Each node reached by the query processes it on the local resources and, in case of match, replies to the query initiator.

Thanks to the DHT infrastructure, searching in structured systems is more scalable - in terms of traffic generated - than searching in unstructured systems. However, DHT-based lookups do not support arbitrary types of queries (e.g., regular expressions [4]) since it is infeasible to generate and store keys for every query expression. Unstructured systems, on the contrary, can do it effortless since all queries are processed locally on a node-by-node basis [5]. Even though the lookup mechanisms of DHT-based systems do not support arbitrary queries, it is possible to exploit their structure to propagate any kind of information (including arbitrary queries) to all nodes in its overlay. Such queries can then be processed on a node-by-node basis as in unstructured systems. In this way, the DHT can be used for both key-based lookups and arbitrary queries, combining the efficiency of structured networks with the flexibility of unstructured search.

This strategy has been exploited in the design of DQ-DHT [6], a P2P search algorithm that supports arbitrary queries in a Chord DHT by implementing an efficient (i.e., bandwidth-saving) unstructured search technique on top of its overlay. In particular, DQ-DHT combines the Dynamic Querying (DQ) technique [7], which is used to reduce the amount of traffic generated by the search process in unstructured P2P networks, with an algorithm that allows to perform efficient broadcast of arbitrary data over a Chord DHT [8].

In the original DQ algorithm, which is used in unstructured systems like Gnutella, the querying node starts the search by sending the query to a few of its neighbors and with a small Time-to-Live (TTL). The main goal of this first phase (referred to as "probe query") is to estimate the popularity of the resource to be located. If such an attempt does not produce a sufficient number of results, the querying node sends the query towards the next neighbor with a new TTL. Such

TTL is calculated taking into account both the desired number of results, and the resource popularity estimated during the previous phase. This process is repeated until the expected number of results is received or all the neighbors have already been queried.

Similarly to DQ, DQ-DHT dynamically controls the query propagation on the basis of the desired number of results and the popularity of the resource to be located. Differently from DQ, DQ-DHT exploits the structural properties of a DHT to avoid message duplications, thus reducing the amount of network traffic generated by each query. A detailed description of the DQ-DHT algorithm, as well as an evaluation of its performance obtained through simulations, has been presented in a previous work [6].

The goal of this paper is to experimentally evaluate the amount of traffic generated by DQ-DHT compared to the original DQ algorithm in a real Grid infrastructure. To this end, a prototype of a Grid information service, which can use both DQ and DQ-DHT as resource discovery algorithm, has been implemented and deployed on the Grid'5000 infrastructure [9] for evaluation. The experimental results presented in this paper show that DQ-DHT significantly reduces the amount of network traffic generated during the discovery process compared to the original DQ algorithm. These results confirm that combining unstructured search techniques with structured overlays is a simple but effective way to support both DHT-based lookups and arbitrary queries using a single overlay.

The rest of the paper is organized as follows. Sect. 2 provides a background on the DQ-DHT algorithm. Sect. 3 describes the prototype of Grid information service implemented to perform the evaluation and presents the experimental results. Sect. 4 discusses related work. Finally, Sect. 5 concludes the paper.


## 2 Background on DQ-DHT

As mentioned above, DQ-DHT combines the DQ technique with an algorithm that allows to perform a broadcast operation with minimal cost in a Chord network. In order to better explain how DQ-DHT works, Sect. 2.1 introduces the algorithm of broadcast over a Chord DHT, proposed in [8]. Then, Sect. 2.2 briefly describes the DQ-DHT algorithm.


## 2.1 Broadcast over a Chord DHT

Chord assigns to each node an $m$-bit identifier that represents its position in a circular identifier space ranging from 0 and $2^m - 1$. Each node $x$ maintains a *finger table* with $m$ entries. The $j^{th}$ entry in the finger table at node $x$ contains the identity of the first node, $s$, that succeeds $x$ by at least $2^{j-1}$ positions on the identifier circle, where $1 \leq j \leq m$. Node $s$ is called the $j^{th}$ *finger* of node $x$. If the identifier space is not fully populated (i.e., the number of nodes, $N$, is lower than $2^m$), the finger table contains redundant fingers. In a network of $N$ nodes, the number $u$ of unique (i.e., distinct) fingers of a generic node $x$ is likely to be $\log_2 N$ [2]. In the following, we will use the notation $F_i$ to indicate the $i^{th}$ *unique finger* of node $x$, where $1 \le i \le u$.

To broadcast data item $D$, a node $x$ sends a broadcast message to all its unique fingers. This message contains $D$ and a *limit* argument, which is used to restrict the forwarding space of a receiving node. The *limit* sent to $F_i$ is set to $F_{i+1}$, for $1 \le i \le u-1$. The *limit* sent to the last unique finger, $F_u$, is set to the identifier of the sender, $x$. When a node $y$ receives a broadcast message with a data item $D$ and a given *limit*, it is responsible for forwarding $D$ to all its unique fingers in the interval $]y, limit[$. When forwarding the message to $F_i$, for $1 \le i \le u-1$, $y$ supplies it a new *limit*, which is set to $F_{i+1}$ if it does not exceed the old *limit*, or the old *limit* otherwise. As before, the new *limit* sent to $F_u$ is set to $y$. As shown in [8], in a network of $N$ nodes, a broadcast message originating at an arbitrary node reaches all other nodes in $O(\log_2 N)$ steps and with exactly $N-1$ messages.

Fig. 1a shows an example of broadcast in a fully populated Chord ring, where $u = m = 4$. For each node, the corresponding finger table is shown. The broadcast messages are represented by rectangles containing the data item $D$ and the *limit* parameter. The entire broadcast is completed in $u = 4$ steps, represented with solid, dashed, dashed-dotted, and dotted lines, respectively. In this example, the broadcast is initiated by node 2, which broadcasts a message to all nodes in its finger table (nodes 3, 4, 6 and 10) (*step 1*). Nodes 3, 4, 6 and 10 in turn forward the broadcast message to their fingers under the received *limit* value (*step 2*). The same procedure applies iteratively, until all nodes in the network are reached (*steps 3* and *4*).

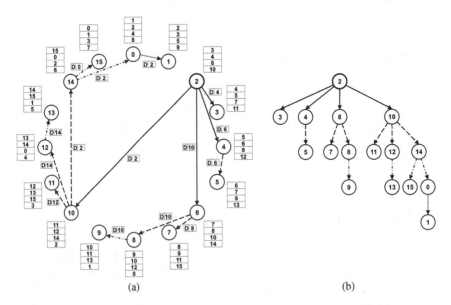

(a)                                        (b)

**Fig. 1** (a) Example of broadcast in a fully populated Chord ring; (b) corresponding spanning tree

The overall broadcast procedure can be viewed as the process of passing the data item through a spanning tree that covers all nodes in the network [8]. Fig. 1b shows the spanning tree corresponding to the example of broadcast shown in Fig. 1a. As discussed in [6], the spanning tree associated to the broadcast over a (fully populated) Chord ring is a binomial tree.

## 2.2 The DQ-DHT algorithm

As mentioned earlier, the goal of DQ-DHT is two-fold: allowing arbitrary queries in a Chord DHT and supporting dynamic adaptation of the search based on the popularity of the resources to be located. To support dynamic search adaptation, DQ-DHT performs the search in an iterative way, similarly to the original DQ algorithm introduced in Sect. 1. In the following, the DQ-DHT algorithm is briefly described.

Let $x$ be the node that initiates the search, $U$ the set of unique fingers of $x$ not yet visited, and $R_d$ the desired number of results. Initially $U$ includes all unique fingers of $x$. Like in DQ, the search starts with a probe query, aimed at evaluating the popularity of the resource to be located. To this end, node $x$ selects a subset $V$ of $U$ and sends the query to all fingers in $V$. These fingers will in turn forward the query to all nodes in the portions of the spanning tree they are responsible for, following the DHT broadcast algorithm described in Sect. 2.1. When a node receives a query, it checks for local resources matching the query criteria and, for each matching resource, sends a query hit directly to $x$. The fingers in $V$ are removed from $U$ to indicate that they have been already visited.

After sending the query to all nodes in $V$, $x$ waits for an amount of time $T_L$, which is the estimated time needed by the query to reach all nodes up to a given level $L$ of the subtrees rooted at the unique fingers in $V$, plus the time needed to receive a query hit from those nodes. The value of $L$ can be chosen to be equal to the depth of the deepest subtree associated to the fingers in $V$. The time needed to pass a message from level to level can be estimated taking into account the network latency measured by the application. After the waiting period, if the current number of received query hits $R_c$ is equal or greater than $R_d$, $x$ concludes the search. Otherwise, the algorithm proceeds iteratively as follows.

At each iteration, node $x$: 1) calculates the resource popularity $P$ as the ratio between $R_c$ and the number of nodes already theoretically queried; 2) calculates the number $H_q$ of hosts in the network that should be queried to hit $R_d$ query hits based on $P$; 3) chooses, among the nodes in $U$, a new subset $V$ of unique fingers whose associated subtrees cumulatively contain the minimum number of nodes that is greater or equal to $H_q$; 4) sends the query to all nodes in $V$; 5) waits for an amount of time needed to propagate the query to all nodes in the subtrees associated to $V$. The iterative procedure above is repeated until the desired number of query hits is reached, or there are no more fingers to contact. If the item popularity is properly

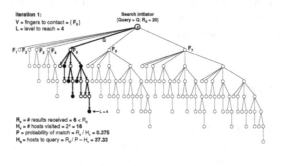

(a)

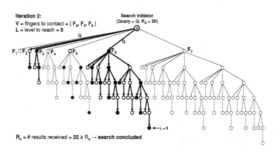

(b)

**Fig. 2** Example of a two-iteration DQ-DHT search in a fully populated Chord network with 128 nodes: (a) first iteration; (b) second iteration. Filled black circles represent nodes that produced a query hit after receiving the query. Empty bold circles represent nodes that received the query but did not produce a query hit. Empty circles are nodes that did not receive the query

estimated after the probe query, only one additional iteration may be sufficient to obtain the desired number of results.

Fig. 2 illustrates an example of a two-iteration DQ-DHT search in a fully populated Chord network with 128 nodes. The root of the binomial tree represents the search initiator, $x$, and its children represent the fingers $F_1...F_7$ of $x$. As discussed in [6], given the structural properties of binomial trees, the subtree rooted at finger $F_i$ has depth $i-1$ and number of nodes equal to $2^{i-1}$. In this example the query to process is indicated as $Q$ and the desired number of results is $R_d = 20$.

Fig. 2a shows the first iteration of search (probe query). Node $x$ chooses to send the query to finger $F_5$ (i.e., $V = \{F_5\}$) in order to probe $2^{5-1} = 16$ nodes at first. Note that in a real scenario (like that described in Sect. 3) the number of nodes to be contacted during the probe query should be larger to obtain a good estimation of the resource popularity, as discussed in [6]. After sending $Q$ to $F_5$, $x$ waits for an amount of time proportional to $L = 4$ (which is the depth of the subtree rooted at $F_5$) before counting the number of results received. The filled black circles represent the nodes, in the subtree rooted at $F_5$, which have sent a query hit to $x$ in response to $Q$. Thus, after the first iteration, the number of results is $R_c = 6$. Since $R_c < R_d$, $x$ proceeds by calculating the resource popularity $P$ and the number $H_q$ of hosts to query to obtain a minimum of $R_d$ results, as shown in the figure.

The second iteration is shown in Fig. 2b. Given $H_q = 37.33$, node $x$ chooses the new set of fingers to contact as $V = \{F_2, F_3, F_6\}$ since the total number of nodes in the subtrees associated to the fingers in $V$ (which is equal to $\sum_{i \in \{2,3,6\}} 2^{i-1} = 38$) is the minimum value, greater or equal to $H_q$, that can be obtained from the fingers not previously contacted. Then, $Q$ is sent to all fingers in $V$ and, after a waiting period proportional to $L = 5$ (depth of the subtree associated to $F_6$), the search is concluded because other 16 nodes (filled black circles in the figure) have sent a query hit to $x$, reaching the goal of obtaining at least $R_d$ results.

# 3 Experimental evaluation

In this section we evaluate the amount of traffic generated by DQ-DHT compared to the original DQ algorithm in a Grid infrastructure. We focus on the traffic generated because it is the performance parameter that mostly affects the overall efficiency of a large-scale P2P system. This is particularly true when a large number of concurrent searches are performed on the same overlay, leading to nodes overload and possible bandwidth saturation even in high-end Grid networks. Sect. 3.1 describes the prototype of Grid information service implemented to perform the experimental evaluation. Sect. 3.2 presents the experimental results obtained by deploying and using the prototype on the Grid'5000 platform.

## 3.1 System prototype

The prototype of Grid information service used to compare DQ-DHT with DQ is an extension of the prototype originally presented in [10]. Such prototype is based on a "superpeer" architecture in which nodes belong either to the category of *peers* or *superpeers* based on the level of service they can offer. Most nodes act as peers, while nodes with higher capacity act as superpeers. Superpeers form the P2P overlay and also act on behalf of peers, which participate in the system indirectly by connecting to superpeers.

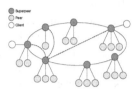

**Fig. 3** The architecture of the original prototype presented in [10], with superpeers organized to form a Chord overlay

Several Grid information services proposed so far are based on superpeer archi-tectures (see [1] for some examples) since they are naturally appropriate to the orga-nizational nature of current Grids. Moreover, the superpeer model allows to improve the scalability of large-scale system by exploiting the heterogeneity of participating nodes. This essentially means that more work can be assigned to those participants that can handle it, while at the same time removing most of the workload from the less capable nodes.

The original prototype organizes superpeers to form a Chord overlay (see Fig. 3). This overlay can be used to perform both key-based lookups using the Chord algo-rithm, and arbitrary queries using the DQ-DHT algorithm. As the goal of this work is to compare DQ-DHT with the original DQ algorithm (which works only on unstruc-tured overlays) we extended the original prototype by building also an unstructured overlay among superpeers. In this way, an arbitrary query can be processed using either DQ-DHT over the Chord overlay, or DQ over the unstructured overlay.

For the construction of the Chord overlay we used Open Chord, an imple-mentation of the Chord algorithm by the University of Bamberg [11]. The Open Chord API provides only methods for joining/leaving a Chord network and insert-ing/removing keys from it. To perform DQ-DHT searches over the overlay, we ex-tended that API by adding the functionality to send arbitrary messages among nodes in the system.

The unstructured overlay among superpeers is built using a custom implementa-tion of the Gnutella protocol [3], appropriately extended to implement the original DQ algorithm [7]. DQ works iteratively as described in Sect. 1. In particular, after each iteration, the querying node calculates the total number $H_t$ of hosts to query to reach the desired number of results. Then, it calculates the number $H_n$ of hosts to query per neighbor as $H_t/n$, where $n$ is the number of neighbors that have not yet received the query. Finally, it calculates the minimum TTL to reach $H_n$ hosts through the next neighbor, and sends the query towards that neighbor.

To get a fair comparison of the number of messages generated by DQ and DQ-DHT, the prototype ensures that the average number of connections (i.e., neighbors) in the unstructured overlay is equal to the average number of connections (i.e., unique fingers) in the Chord overlay. As mentioned in Sect. 2.1, this number can be calculated as $\log_2 N$, where $N$ is the number of superpeers in the overlay.

Furthermore, for uniformity purposes, while queries are distributed using either the Chord overlay or the unstructured overlay, results are sent directly to the query initiator. That is, if a peer contains resources that match the query criteria, it issues a query hit message directly to the superpeer that initiated the search (i.e., the superpeer to which the client/peer that issued the query is connected).

## 3.2 Experimental results

The goal of our experiments is to evaluate the efficiency of DQ-DHT by comparing the amount of traffic generated by it with that generated by the original DQ algorithm. The comparison has been performed by executing the two algorithms in the same network scenario (i.e., same number of superpeers and peers) and with the same query parameters (desired number of results and probability of match). The amount of traffic has been measured as the number of messages exchanged across the superpeer overlay to complete a search process. The experiments have been performed by deploying our Grid information service prototype on the Grid'5000 platform [9].

We used hosts from four Grid'5000 sites (Rennes, Sophia, Nancy, and Orsay) for a total of around 400 hosts across those sites. Each host has been used to execute a number of independent superpeer and peer applications. To distribute the load across sites, superpeers and peers have been uniformly and randomly distributed across all hosts. In order to build the largest possible infrastructure, we first fixed $P_S = 10$ as the number of peers per superpeer, and then we performed some experiments to find the maximum number of superpeers (with associated peers) that was possible to deploy using all the available hosts, based on the memory availability of the hosts. Based on the results of these experiments, we managed to build a network including $S = 8500$ superpeers, each one connected to $P_S$ peers, on average. Each superpeer in the unstructured overlay has been connected to $\log_2 S \simeq 13$ other superpeers, in order to obtain approximatively the same number of connections that superpeers have in the Chord overlay, as explained in Sect. 3.1.

After initializing the overlays, we started several clients, each of which submitted the same batch of queries. Each query had a different probability to match the resources available in the network. Given a query, we define the probability of match, $P$, as the ratio between the total number of resources that match the query criteria, and the total number of peers in the network. When submitting the query, each client specifies the desired number of query hits $R_d$, i.e., the number of resources to be located that match the query criteria. Notice that, for the purpose of our experiments, the only relevant information associated to a query is its probability of match. Thus, in our prototype, each query carries its value of $P$ and each node receiving that query will reply with a query hit with probability $P$.

All the searches have been performed in the same network with $S = 8500$ super-peers and $P_S = 10$ peers per superpeer. Each query submitted to the system had a probability of match, $P$, that varied in the following values (expressed as percentages): 0.0125, 0.025, 0.05, 0.1, 0.2, 0.4, 0.8 and 1.6. The desired number of results, $R_d$, was varied in the following values: 10, 20, 40 and 100.

The parameters of the original DQ algorithm are: the number of neighbors contacted during the probe phase, $N_p$, and the TTL used for the probe query, $TTL_p$. We used the following values: $N_p = 3$ and $TTL_p = 2$, as suggested in [7]. After the probe query, the maximum allowed value of $TTL$ is increased to 5, to ensure complete network coverage.

The parameter of DQ-DHT is the set of fingers to contact during the probe query, $V$. We used $V = F_8$ and set consequently the value of $L$ to 7, to reach all superpeers under finger $F_8$. Since the number of nodes reachable through the $i^{th}$ finger is likely to be $2^{i-1}$, the number of superpeers reached during the first iteration was $2^7 = 128$ on average.

Table 1 lists the main parameters introduced above and all the values used to carry out the experiments.

**Table 1** Parameters values used to carry out the experiments

| Symbol | Definition | Values |
|---|---|---|
| $S$ | Number of superpeers | 8500 |
| $P_S$ | Number of peers per superpeer | 10 |
| $P$ | Probability of match (%) | .0125, .025, .05, .1, .2, .4, .8, 1.6 |
| $R_d$ | Desired number of results | 10, 20, 40, 100 |
| $N_p$ | Neighbors contacted during probe phase (DQ) | 3 |
| $TTL_p$ | TTL used during probe phase (DQ) | 2 |
| $V$ | Fingers contacted during probe phase (DQ-DHT) | $\{F_8\}$ |

The graphs in Fig. 4 show the number of messages generated by DQ and DQ-DHT to process queries with different probabilities of match, for increasing values of $R_d$. Each value in the graphs is calculated as an average of 25 search executions, where at each search the same query is submitted to a randomly chosen superpeer.

As expected, for all values of $R_d$, the number of messages decreases when the probability of match increases, with both DQ and DQ-DHT. This is due to the fact that both DQ and DQ-DHT are able to reduce the query propagation when the popularity of the resource to be located increases. In particular, for the highest probabilities of match (i.e., 0.8-1.6%) the lines associated to DQ and DQ-DHT are always superimposing, since with both algorithm it is possible to obtain the desired number of results by contacting just a small number of superpeers.

The behaviors of DQ and DQ-DHT diverge significantly in presence of low probabilities of match. For example, with $R_d = 10$ and $P = 0.0125\%$ (see Fig. 4a), DQ-DHT generates around 8200 messages, while DQ generates almost 14000 messages.

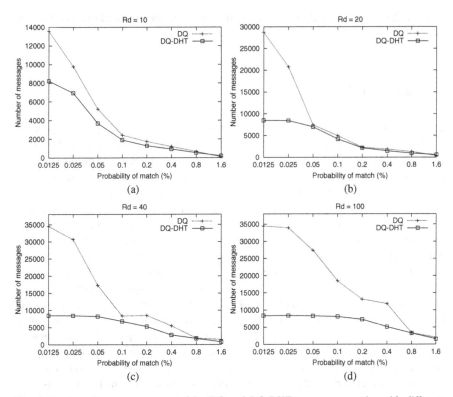

**Fig. 4** Number of messages generated by DQ and DQ-DHT to process queries with different probabilities of match, with increasing values of $R_d$. (a) $R_d = 10$; (b) $R_d = 20$; (c) $R_d = 40$; (d) $R_d = 100$

This difference can be explained taking into account that with DQ-DHT each superpeer is contacted at most once (i.e., there is not messages duplication), while in DQ a message can reach a superpeer more than once due to the randomness of connections.

The difference between DQ and DQ-DHT in presence of low probabilities of match increases when the total number of resources matching the query criteria is lower than $R_d$. In our experiments this happens in three cases: 1) $R_d = 20$ and $P < 0.025\%$; 2) $R_d = 40$ and $P < 0.05\%$; 3) $R_d = 100$ and $P < 0.8\%$. In all these cases, both DQ and DQ-DHT cannot find the desired number of results even if they have distributed the query to all superpeers. Therefore, DQ-DHT generates exactly $S$ messages (i.e., each superpeer is contacted exactly once), while DQ generates a high number of unnecessary (duplicated) messages.

As a final remark, all the experimental results presented above demonstrate the ability of DQ-DHT to control the number of messages generated by the search in function of the probability of match and the number of desired results, also compared to the original DQ algorithm implemented on an unstructured overlay built on top of the same nodes.

## 4 Related work

The most related work to DQ-DHT is the Structella system designed by Castro et al. [12]. Structella replaces the random graph of Gnutella with the structured overlay of Pastry [13], while retaining the content placement and discovery mechanisms of unstructured P2P systems to support complex queries. Two discovery mechanisms are implemented in Structella: constrained flooding and random walks.

Constrained flooding is based on the algorithm of broadcast over Pastry presented in [14]. A node $x$ broadcasts a message by sending the message to all the nodes $y$ in the Pastry's routing table. Each message is tagged with the routing table row $r$ of node $y$. When a node receives a message tagged with $r$, it forwards the message to all nodes in its routing table in rows greater than $r$. To constrain the flood, an upper bound is placed on the row number of entries to which the query is forwarded.

Random walks in Structella are implemented by walking along the ring formed by neighboring nodes in the identifier space. When a node receives a query in a random walker, it uses the Pastry's leaf set to forward the query to its left neighbor in the identifier space. It also evaluates the query against the local content and sends matching content back to the query originator. A random walker is terminated when it finds matching content. Multiple concurrent random walkers can be used to improve search time.

DQ-DHT and Structella share the same goal of supporting complex queries in structured network. However, DQ-DHT has been designed to find an arbitrary number of resources matching the query criteria, while Structella is designed to discover just one of such resources. In Structella in fact, with both constrained flooding and random walks, a node stops forwarding a query if it has matching content.

A few other research works broadly relate to our system for their combined use of structured and unstructured P2P techniques. Loo et al. [15] propose a hybrid system in which DHT-based techniques are used to index and search rare items, while flooding techniques are used for locating highly-replicated content. Search is first performed via conventional flooding techniques of the overlay neighbors. If not enough results are returned within a predefined time, the query is reissued as a DHT query. This allows fast searches for popular items and at the same time reduces the flooding cost for rare items.

A critical point in such system is identifying which items are rare and must be published using the DHT. Two techniques are proposed. A first heuristic classifies as rare the items that are seen in small result sets. However, this method fails to classify those items that have not have been previously queried and found. Another proposal is to base the publishing on well-known term frequencies, and/or by maintaining and possibly gossiping historical summary statistics on item replicas.

Another example is the work by Zaharia and Keshav [16], who focus on the problem of selecting the best algorithm to be used for a given query in a hybrid network allowing both unstructured search and DHT-based lookups. A gossip-based algorithm is used to collect global statistics about document availability and keyword popularity that allow peers to predict the best search technique for a given query.

Each peer starts by generating a synopsis of its own document titles and keywords and labels it as its "best" synopsis. In each round of gossip, it chooses a random neighbor and sends the neighbor its best synopsis. When a node receives a synopsis, it fuses this synopsis with its best synopsis and labels the merged synopsis as its best synopsis. This results in every peer getting the global statistics after $O(\log N)$ rounds of gossip.

Given a query composed by a set of keywords, a peer estimates the expected number of documents matching that set of keywords using the information in its best synopsis. If this number is over a given threshold, many matches are expected, so the peer floods the query. Otherwise, it uses the DHT to search for each keyword, requesting an in-network join, if that is possible. The flooding threshold is dynamically adapted by computing the utility of both flooding and DHT search for a randomly chosen set of queries.

It is worth noticing that the last two systems do not support arbitrary queries, since information about resources is published and searched using DHT-based mechanisms. DQ-DHT, on the contrary, supports arbitrary queries in an easy way since content placement is unrelated from the DHT overlay and query processing is performed on a node-by-node basis.

# 5 Conclusions

Providing efficient resource discovery mechanisms in Grids, Clouds and large-scale distributed systems is fundamental to build and execute distributed applications involving geographically dispersed resources. In this paper we experimentally evaluated the efficiency of DQ-DHT, a resource discovery algorithm that combines the Dynamic Querying (DQ) technique used in unstructured P2P networks with an algorithm for efficient broadcast over a Distributed Hash Table (DHT). Similarly to DQ, DQ-DHT dynamically controls the query propagation on the basis of the desired number of results and the popularity of the resource to be located. Differently from DQ, DQ-DHT exploits the structural constraints of a DHT to avoid message duplications, thus reducing the amount of network traffic generated by each query.

This paper experimentally evaluated the amount of traffic generated by DQ-DHT compared to the original DQ algorithm in a large-scale Grid infrastructure. A prototype of a Grid information service, which can use both DQ and DQ-DHT as resource discovery algorithm, has been implemented and deployed on the Grid'5000 infrastructure for evaluation. The experimental results presented in this paper showed that DQ-DHT significantly reduces the amount of network traffic generated during the resource discovery process compared to the original DQ algorithm. These results confirm that combining unstructured search techniques with structured overlays is a simple but effective way to support both DHT-based lookups and arbitrary queries using a single overlay.

## Acknowledgement

We would like to thank the Grid'5000 team for providing us the platform for deploying and experimenting our system.

## References

1. Trunfio, P., Talia, D., Papadakis, H., Fragopoulou, P., Mordacchini, M., Pennanen, M., Popov, K., Vlassov, V., Haridi, S.: Peer-to-Peer Resource Discovery in Grids: Models and Systems. Future Generation Computer Systems 23(7), 864-878 (2007)
2. Stoica, I., Morris, R., Karger, D., Kaashoek, M. F., Balakrishnan, H.: Chord: A Scalable Peer-to-peer Lookup Service for Internet Applications. SIGCOMM'01, San Diego, USA (2001)
3. Gnutella Protocol Development. http://rfc-gnutella.sourceforge.net. Cited 24 Sep 2009
4. Castro, M., Costa, M., Rowstron, A.: Debunking Some Myths About Structured and Unstructured Overlays. 2nd Symposium on Networked Systems Design and Implementation (NSDI'05), Boston, USA (2005)
5. Chawathe, Y., Ratnasamy, S., Breslau, L., Lanham, N., Shenker, S.: Making Gnutella-like P2P Systems Scalable. SIGCOMM'03, Karlsruhe, Germany (2003)
6. Talia, D., Trunfio, P.: Dynamic Querying in Structured Peer-to-Peer Networks. 19th IFIP/IEEE International Workshop on Distributed Systems: Operations and Management (DSOM 2008), Samos Island, Greece, LNCS 5273, 28-41 (2008)
7. Fisk, A.: Gnutella Dynamic Query Protocol v0.1. http://www9.limewire.com/developer/dynamic_query.html. Cited 24 Sep 2009
8. El-Ansary, S., Alima, L., Brand, P., Haridi, S.: Efficient Broadcast in Structured P2P Networks. 2nd Int. Workshop on Peer-to-Peer Systems (IPTPS'03), Berkeley, USA (2003)
9. Bolze, R., Cappello, F., Caron, E., Dayd, M., Desprez, F., Jeannot, E., Jgou, Y., Lantri, S., Leduc, J., Melab, N., Mornet, G., Namyst, R., Primet, P., Quetier, B., Richard, O., Talbi, E-G., Touche, I.: Grid'5000: a large scale and highly reconfigurable experimental Grid testbed. Int. Journal of High Performance Computing Applications 20(4), 481-494 (2006)
10. Papadakis, H., Trunfio, P., Talia, D., Fragopoulou, P.: Design and Implementation of a Hybrid P2P-based Grid Resource Discovery System. In: Danelutto, M., Fragopoulou, P., Getov, V. (eds.) Making Grids Work, pp. 89-101. Springer, USA (2008)
11. Open Chord. http://open-chord.sourceforge.net. Cited 24 Sep 2009
12. Castro, M., Costa, M., Rowstron, A.: Should we build Gnutella on a structured overlay? Computer Communication Review 34(1), 131-136 (2004)
13. Rowstron, A., Druschel, P.: Pastry: Scalable, Decentralized Object Location, and Routing for Large-Scale Peer-to-Peer Systems. Middleware 2001, Heidelberg, Germany (2001)
14. Castro, M., Jones, M. B., Kermarrec, A.-M., Rowstron, A., Theimer, M., Wang, H., Wolman, A.: An Evaluation of Scalable Application-Level Multicast Built Using Peer-to-Peer Overlays. IEEE INFOCOM'03, San Francisco, USA (2003)
15. Loo, B.T., Huebsch, R., Stoica, I., Hellerstein, J.M.: The Case for a Hybrid P2P Search Infrastructure. 3rd Int. Work. on Peer-to-Peer Systems (IPTPS'04), La Jolla, USA (2004)
16. Zaharia, M., Keshav, S.: Gossip-based Search Selection in Hybrid Peer-to-Peer Networks. 5th Int. Workshop on Peer-to-Peer Systems (IPTPS'06), Santa Barbara, USA (2006)

# Reducing traffic in DHT-based discovery protocols for dynamic resources

Emanuele Carlini, Massimo Coppola, Domenico Laforenza and Laura Ricci

**Abstract** Existing peer-to-peer approaches for resource location based on distributed hash tables focus mainly on optimizing lookup query resolution. The underlying assumption is that the arrival ratio of lookup queries is higher than the ratio of resource publication operations. We propose a set of optimization strategies to reduce the network traffic generated by the data publication and update process when resources have dynamic-valued attributes. We aim at reducing the publication overhead of supporting multi-attribute range queries. We develop a model predicting the bandwidth reduction, and we assign proper values to the model variables on the basis of real data measurements. We further validate these results by a set of simulations. Our experiments are designed to reproduce the typical behaviour of the resulting scheme within large distributed resource location system, like the resource location service of the XtreemOS Grid-enabled Operating System.

Emanuele Carlini
Institute of Information Science and Technologies CNR-ISTI "A. Faedo", Pisa, Italy, and Institutions Markets Technologies IMT, Lucca, Italy e-mail: emanuele.carlini@isti.cnr.it

Massimo Coppola
Institute of Information Science and Technologies CNR-ISTI, Pisa, Italy
e-mail: massimo.coppola@isti.cnr.it

Domenico Laforenza
Institute of Information Science and Technologies CNR-ISTI and Institute of Informatics and Telematics CNR-IIT, Pisa, Italy e-mail: domenico.laforenza@isti.cnr.it

Laura Ricci
Università di Pisa, Pisa, Italy e-mail: ricci@di.unipi.it

# 1 Introduction

The issue of controlling and organizing a large number of computing resources in performing information-related tasks naturally arises and leads to the exploitation of distributed and peer to peer (P2P) techniques.

Many approaches in the literature exploit structured P2P systems, in particular Distributed Hash Tables (DHT). Popular works are based on Space Filling Curves [1, 2], and tree-based structures [3]. The main issue of these approaches is the insufficient scalability in the space dimension (the number of independent attributes). Systems based on *locality preserving hash functions* [4, 5] try to cope with the dimensionality problem as well.

Resource location and directory services in very large distributed systems have to provide multi-attribute range-search capabilities. Our reference case is the XtreemOS [6] platform. XtreemOS is a Grid-enabled Operating System, based on Linux, which aims at scalable management of large computational platforms extending across federated Virtual Organizations. In order to provide system scalability and fault resiliency, XtreemOS employs a P2P approach in providing the resource location services. We reproduce in this work XtreemOS typical conditions, where resources with dynamically varying features congregate into a very large platform (thousands of nodes) and have to be selected according to their instantaneous state.

Existing P2P proposals in the field of resource location focus on optimizing the performance of lookup queries, rather than the data publication phase. They are designed with the assumption that the number of queries submitted to the system is much greater than the amount of publications of resources. In this paper we explore the case where this assumption does not hold. We deal with dynamic attributes of resources and data publications must occur frequently, in order to provide a fresh view of the system to the end-user.

We propose REMED (REduce MEssage on Dht), an enhanced algorithm for the publication process in multi-attribute MAAN-like DHTs. The method is suitable for DHT-based approaches using locality preserving hashing functions, and combines two different optimizations.

In REMED, the base optimization technique exploits a small-size soft-state cache that, in each node, contains the most frequent routing results completed during the publication steps. Results are cached in order to achieve one-hop publication where possible, bypassing the native DHT routing algorithm. We study the cache utilization value and we show that the closer are the published values the better are the performance we achieve. Following the measurements presented in [7] we try to exploit the short-term stability of attributes in spite of their long-term dynamic behaviour.

A second, complementary optimization exploits the concept of attribute *popularity* in order to selectively reduce the update frequency. Resources associated with an attribute which is seldom used in queries are updated less frequently.

Each DHT node maintains its own popularity estimates, which depend on the query history of the system, and are exploited in an adaptive and completely distributed manner. To evaluate the network traffic reduction achieved by our algorithm, we discuss an analytical model describing the behaviour of a single node during the publication process, and evaluate both its parameters and the overall network behaviour by simulation, also considering the impact of churn over the network.

The rest of the paper is organized as follows. Section 2 briefly discusses the most popular approaches used to resolve range queries and others proposals related to our work. Section 3 describes how the range query are resolved in our approach, the optimization of publication process. Section 4 presents the model. Section 5 presents the data used for the evaluation of the model, describes how the model is used in a real context and shows the results of our simulations. Finally, Sect. 6 concludes and discusses open issues for future work.

## 2 Related Work

Many approaches have been suggested to automate the resource discovery process using P2P techniques. Our work is based on popular solutions like SWORD [5] and MAAN [4] that focus on data replication over different *logical* DHT spaces identified by attributes properties.

Other popular solutions such as Baton [3], the work of Caron et al. [8] and Gao [9] make use of DHTs as a building block for solution based on tree data structures. Although studies on hierarchical structures and different indexing schemes may be effective, we consider this kind of approaches as a different research line.

Caches are widely used in many P2P approaches for different purposes. Rodriguez et al. [10] studied the bandwidth consumption of different caching strategies to manage maintenance operation (i.e. peer join and leave). The CUP approach [11] exploits a cache to optimize query resolutions over P2P overlay networks. It also introduces the idea of node popularity, where the popularity of a node $N$ is related to the number of nodes depending on $N$ to resolve a query. Similarly, the ShortCuts algorithm [12] uses soft state caches to improve the look-up performance of DHTs. Like [10, 11, 12], REMED exploits caching, but besides reducing the routing cost, it also caches information needed to reduce the overhead for publishing data. Works like Kelips [13] and the approach of Gupta et al. [14] extend the standards DHTs routing tables to achieve one-hop routing, tolerating non-trivial overhead of memory usage and bandwidth consumption. Contrary to these approaches, REMED has well bounded memory and bandwidth requirements.

The approach of Liben-Nowell et al. [15], suggested us a model based on the concept of half life to estimate the churn frequency over a peer to peer overlay. Finally, Cheema et al. [7] examine the attributes variability of workstations in a Grid context. We exploit as a fundamental assumption what they experimentally observed, that several dynamic attributes (i.e cpu load, memory usage) show a good degree of temporal locality.

## 2.1 MAAN Range Query Implementation

The MAAN [4] approach builds up a mechanism over a Chord DHT [16] to resolve range multi-attribute queries.

A resource is defined by a collection of attribute-value pairs. Each one of these attribute values is coupled with a key that maps that value in the DHT space. Unlike classical DHTs, the key is obtained using a *static locality-preserving hash function* in order to resolve lookup range queries more effectively. Following [4], a mapping function $H(v)$ preserves locality if it has the following properties: (i) $H(v_i) < H(v_j)$ if and only if $v_i < v_j$ and (ii) if an interval $[v_i, v_j]$ is split into $[v_i, v_k]$ and $[v_k, v_j]$, the corresponding interval $[H(v_i), H(v_j)]$ must be split into $[H(v_i), H(v_k)]$ and $[H(v_k), H(v_j)]$. The function is static since it does not change during the system execution.

The MAAN publication process (depicted in Fig. 1 and pseudocode in Fig. 2), works as follow. A node, called *provider*, publishes periodically its attributes-values set $(a_1, v_1)..(a_k, v_k)$, by sending a PUT message with the whole resource description for each different $a_i$. The messages in general reach other nodes, called *recipients*, identified by $H(v_i)$; each recipient responds in turn with a REPLY message. The same resource descriptor is spread and replicated into the overlay by a factor equal to the number $K$ of attributes.

A generic multi-attribute range query is structured like a set of pairs attribute-constraint, where a constraint is the range of values in which an attribute must belong to in order to satisfy the query. Given an attribute constraint $[l, u]$, all the resources that satisfy it lie in the contiguous portion of DHT space bounded by $H(l)$ and $H(u)$. The constraint corresponding to the smallest portion of DHT space is called the most *selective*, and its attribute is called *dominant*.

In order to resolve a lookup query, a QUERY_REQUEST message is sent to the node managing $H(l)$ (the lower bound value) of the most selective constraint. The request is forwarded to the following node in the DHT space, accumulating on the way the identifiers of resources that satisfy *all* query constraints. When the query reaches the node handling $H(u)$, the computed answer is returned to the query initiator.

## 3 REMED

MAAN resolves look-up queries with a number of hops that does not depend on the number of attributes used to describe a resource. However, data is heavily replicated, causing high overhead especially when the data change frequently. Our proposal REMED reduces the traffic generated by publications, in particular when dealing with dynamic resources. We reduce the bandwidth consumption by cutting down the number of messages that spread over the system during the publication process (see Fig. 1).

In the rest of the paper, the generic term *message* refers to the information unit sent using the transport layer protocols (TCP or UDP).

## 3.1 Reducing the Routing Overhead

In various DHT implementations the publication may be divided in two different steps. The routing process (which typically has a logarithmic cost with the network size) can be seen as an isolated operation. It is usually followed by the PUT message with the relative REPLY message as response.

The idea behind the first strategy proposed by REMED is to equip a node with a *soft-state* cache of the routing results obtained during the publication phase. The cache allows to reuse the routing results already discovered in the previous iterations, and consequently to deploy less messages over the network. By using a soft-state cache, we ignore the need to update or synchronize data among the different caches (e.g. we do not explicitly cope with peer arrivals and departures), at the expense of some occasional retry. As we will see later on, this does not impair the other optimization strategy. Refreshing of cache contents is fully hidden inside the optimized publication algorithm.

Consider two generic but sequential resource publications, both relative to the attribute *A*. If the value of *A* does not change between the two steps, the recipient node remains the same (here we do not consider the churn impact on the cache; section 5.4 evaluates and describes in more details the issue). Even if the value of *A* does not change, it is still necessary to publish the resource descriptor if other resource attributes have changed. It is not necessary that *A* keeps a constant value, as long as the difference between consecutive values remains small enough to let the recipient node stays the same. A publication which does not require the routing process is referred as a *direct publication*.

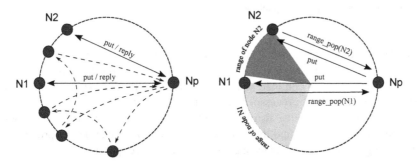

**Fig. 1** (left) Without caches, routing is always performed with the implementation of CHORD, in order to locate N1 and N2. (right) In REMED, routing is skipped if N1 and N2 are found in cache, i.e. values mapped to N1 and N2 were used recently. Reply messages update the cache of the provider node Np with managed range and popularity information.

```
1: resource = monitor.state()
2: for all attribute in resource do
3:    key = hash(attribute.value)
4:    routing = do_routing(key)
5:    reply = put(routing, key, attribute)
6: end for
```

**Fig. 2** Pseudo code of standard MAAN publication. Monitor is a process running on the provider node, which periodically probes the attribute values.

| Peer Information | | | Popularity | |
|---|---|---|---|---|
| ID | Range | IP | A | B |
| N1 | Range(N1) | x.y.z.10 | 70% | 30% |
| N2 | Range(N2) | x.y.z.20 | 50% | 50% |

Provider cache

| Attr. | Pop. |
|---|---|
| A | 70% |
| B | 30% |

Node N1

| Attr. | Pop. |
|---|---|
| A | 50% |
| B | 50% |

Node N2

**Fig. 3** Routing cache and popularity information in REMED, case with two attributes.

```
 1: resource = monitor.state()
 2: for all attribute in resource do
 3:    key = hash(attribute.value)
 4:    info = cache.resolve(key)
 5:    if info contains information then
 6:       if popularity is high then {the put has to be done}
 7:          reply = put(info.routing, key, attribute)
 8:          if reply is an error then {routing has to be done due churn}
 9:             routing = do_routing(key)
10:             reply = put(routing, key, attribute)
11:          end if
12:       end if
13:    else {no data into the cache about key}
14:       routing = do_routing(key)
15:       reply = put(routing, key, attribute)
16:    end if
17:    Update the cache with the newest information
18: end for
```

**Fig. 4** Pseudo code of optimized publication

Although some attributes have a dynamic behaviour, a good chance for a direct publication to happen does exist, as shown in [7]. Their observations reveal that dynamic attributes like cpu load and memory usage exhibit properties of temporal locality. For example, a processor that is idle for a relatively long period of time, maybe at night, is likely to also remain idle in the near future. Following these last considerations, we found that even with a small-size cache the hit probability remains high enough to guarantee a good number of direct publications.

## 3.2 Skipping Publication

The second strategy exploits the implementation of range queries in REMED, as described in section 2.1. Like in the MAAN approach, we resolve queries using the *dominant* attribute. We define the *popularity* of an attribute as the frequency with which it is chosen as dominant.

The popularity depends either on the contents of the published resource and on the queries submitted to the system. In general, attribute popularity may vary over the lifetime of the system, hence we need a dynamic and adaptive solution to exploit this information.

The idea is to update at a low frequency the resource associated with low popularity attributes (i.e. rarely used in query resolution), so to perform only the minimum numbers of publications. For example, if we consider a scenario where an unique attribute is dominant for all the queries, updates for all the other non-dominant attributes become useless. In practice, we can often afford to refresh less often those attributes that do not belong to the narrow set of continuously used ones, but we want to automatically tune the update frequencies according to the current history of publication and queries.

Computing a global measure of attribute popularity, for instance using a logical data structure where nodes in the overlay read and write popularity information, besides being complex to implement and heavy to update, it has the crucial drawback that global popularity values can be misleading.

An example can show why a global view of the system can lead to inaccurate choices. Consider the case of attribute $A$ in a network with 100 nodes, where 30 nodes observe popularity 80%, and 70 nodes observe a value of 10%. Since the global popularity of $A$ is 31%, the consequent update frequency would be too low for resources assigned to the former 30 nodes, which are frequently searched for, while it would be unnecessarily high for the latter nodes.

We thus chose to compute popularity as a *local* value. Every node has a table to keep popularity value for attributes, measured by counting how many times the attribute is dominant in queries that traverse the portion of DHT space handled by the node. Information about popularity is needed by provider nodes, but is gathered by queried nodes. Therefore, we use REPLY messages to carry popularity estimates to the provider (Figure 1). This approach is completely distributed and works without introducing any new message in the existing protocol. Information obtained this way may be used to skip some following publications, throttling the update frequency, whenever a resource is published on the same destination node because of that attribute. How many publications are skipped, and when, can be decided exploiting the popularity value.

Figure 4 shows the pseudo code of an optimized publication. For each of attribute that we want to publish, a key in the DHT space is generated by using the proper hash function on the attribute value, then the cache is searched for the node owning that key. If the popularity value associated to the (key, attribute) pair by the cache is low enough, the publication can sometimes be skipped. Otherwise, the node performs a direct publication. Only if the cache does not contain useful information the publication is done in the standard way. After every iteration, the cache is updated with popularity information from the REPLY message.

# 4 Cost model

We model both the standard and the optimized publication process, according to the algorithm presented. In the following, $N$ is the number of peer participating to the overlay, and $K$ is the number of attributes composing a resource. The publication is logically divided into three different steps: routing, put and reply, associated with the relative messages ROUTING, PUT and REPLY. According to Chord [16] analysis, $O(logN)$ messages correspond to each routing step, while $O(1)$ are needed for both the put and the reply steps.

## 4.1 The Standard MAAN Model

In the standard publication, where no optimization are applied, the number of messages spreading in the system is given by

$$(2KN) + (KNlog(N)) \qquad (1)$$

where the first term evaluates the messages required by put and reply and the second term deals with the routing messages. If $dP$, $dRP$ and $dRT$ are the respective sizes of put, reply and routing messages, we obtain that $P = dP \cdot NK$ is the cost in bytes relative to a put, $RP = dRP \cdot NK$ relative to a reply and $RT = dRT \cdot NK \cdot log(N)$ relative to routing. The total traffic $T$ in bytes for a publication is thus

$$T = P + RP + RT \qquad (2)$$

## 4.2 The REMED Optimized Model

We introduce three boolean variables, in order to model the optimizations according to the algorithm (Figure 4). Variable $X$ states if an item has been found in cache (line 5), $Y$ tells us if an attribute has a low popularity (line 8) and $Z$ is true when a publication is executed without being affected by churn (line 6).

Table 1 shows the expected publication costs depending on these boolean variables. When $X$ is false, we have to follow the standard algorithm. When both $X$ and $Y$ are true, the publication can be completely skipped. If $X$ is true and $Y$ is false, the cost depends on $Z$. If $Z$ is true, we only pay the cost of put and reply operations; if it is false, we waste a put and reply couple by trusting the cache, and a new complete publication is needed thereafter.

Along with the boolean variables, we define also the probability that such variables are true as $P_x$, $P_y$ and $P_z$. The value of $P_x$ essentially depends on the cache size and on its management policies. We evaluate this parameter by simulations in Section 5.3. $P_z$ value expresses the degree of churn within the system, but it also depends on the cache size. We rely on an already known model and we have run simulations to devise a proper value for $P_z$ (Section 5.4). The $P_y$ value depends on the hash functions used and the history of queries in the system.

For each one of the three phases of the publication, these probabilities affect the relative cost. We derive from Table 1 three coefficients, *modifiers* for routing ($M_r$), put $M_p$ and reply ($M_{rp}$) that affect the expected publication cost.

$$\begin{aligned} M_r &= 1 + P_x P_y P_z - P_x P_z - P_x P_y \\ M_p = M_{rp} &= 1 + P_x + P_x P_y P_z - P_x P_z - 2(P_x P_y) \end{aligned} \tag{3}$$

Finally, the traffic of the optimized publication is given by the integration of the equation 2 with the modifiers.

$$T = M_p P + M_{rp} RP + M_r RT \tag{4}$$

# 5 Simulations

The model behaviour depends on a few parameters such cache dimension, level of churn in the network and queries submitted to the system. In order to evaluate the model in a real context, we assign a value to these parameters exploiting a real-world data-set sample. We thus assume to work in a large Grid platform, and let the network size range from 500 to 5000 nodes.

## 5.1 Tools and Implementation

To perform experimental evaluation we use Overlay Weaver (OW, [17]) as our main software development framework. OW also embeds very powerful test tools that we

**Table 1** Different optimizations cases in REMED

| X | Y | Z | REMED cost | MAAN standard cost |
|---|---|---|---|---|
| false | - | - | routing + put + reply | routing + put + reply |
| true | true | - | 0 | routing + put + reply |
| true | false | true | put + reply | routing + put + reply |
| true | false | false | 2(put + reply) + routing | routing + put + reply |

used extensively in our simulation. The OW emulator allows to run a large number of nodes on a single machine, exploiting the very same code that would run on a real platform.

OW has a layered architecture, and aims at separating high level services such as DHT, multicast and anycast from the underlying *key-based routing* (KBR) [18] level. The OW routing layer architecture follows the KBR concepts but leaves behind the monolithic approach, decomposing the routing layer in a set of independent modules, (e.g. communications, routing and query algorithms). The routing module is defined by three layers: the routing layer (bottom), the service layer and the application layer (top). Decoupling of *put(routing.addr)* from *put(key)* allows us to cache the result of each routing operation.

The implementation of REMED within OW belongs to the service layer, providing an alternative to the classical DHT services. The main development effort has been focused on redesigning DHT basic functions like put and get to allow the resolution of multi-attribute range queries. The basic put operation present in Overlay Weaver has been extended to support the needs of the MAAN range query resolution, along with the optimizations we have designed. The pseudo code of the optimized algorithm is shown in Fig. 4.

The *monitor* process takes care of the publication of resources, and in our tests it runs on every node of the overlay. It periodically measures the interesting values of the workstation where it is running, and eventually sends the information to the underlying DHT system. Successive measurements are taken $T = 150$ seconds apart.

In order to estimate attribute popularity, every node maintains a counter $P_i$ for each attribute $i = 1..K$. Counter $P_i$ is incremented whenever a query is processed in which $a_i$ is dominant. Whenever a provider node publishes a resources for attribute $y$, the recipient node $N$ includes the value of $P_y$ in its REPLY message. The provider caches this information. Each cache entry stores more values of popularity, one for each different attribute, since the same resource may be indexed by different attributes (see Fig. 3). Eventually the provider node checks its cache to find attribute popularity regarding $N$ during a successive publication. When the node finds only routing information, it proceeds with a direct publication, otherwise it considers the possibility to skip the publication at all.

## 5.2 Data Analysis

We simulate the behaviour of resources with real-life measurements from Planet-Lab [19], a heterogeneous platform open to public experiments. Services like the content distribution network CoDeeN [20] are available on the platform. One of CoDeeN's sub projects is CoMon [21], whose goal is monitoring the state of PlanetLab machines. Each of these services is running over a *slice*, a set of resources distributed on a subset of nodes; each workstation may handle more active slices at the same time, making the measurements both heterogeneous and realistic for our tests. CoMon every 5 minutes records the measurements on all nodes of PlanetLab. From the whole database we selected six dynamic attributes: available memory, available swap space, bits per second received and sent on the network, CPU load and usage. CPU load differs from usage, load measures the average number of threads currently in the run queue, the way the UNIX command *uptime* does, while CPU usage is the time not spent in the idle state by the processor. Available memory is the output of a daemon that periodically tries to allocate 100MB of memory on the node, with high values meaning that the node is not under memory pressure.

## 5.3 Cache Evaluation

The cache (Figure 3) stores information about other nodes: (i) the range in the ID space each node handles, (ii) the communication address (IP address), (iii) information about attribute popularity at the node. The size of a single cache line grows linearly with K. The overall cache size obviously influences the hit probability, but a large cache is more vulnerable to peer churn.

In order to evaluate the tradeoff on the cache size we exploited two different measurements. Both tests emulate 5000 nodes that join and publish CoMon data over a single DHT for 200 consecutive iterations (about 4 hours).

The first test measures the number of accesses to each cache position during the computation. We consider an optimal situation where an unlimited dimension cache is used and thus we do not apply any cache policy replacement. The results in Fig. 5(a) show that only a few positions are heavily used, leaving most of the cache barely used. The hit count per position follows a power-law trend, it belongs to the *zipf* family [22] with an $\alpha$ value of 1.26. Such a behaviour suggests that even a relatively small cache may allow significant savings.

The second test, in Fig. 5(b), measures the percentage of cache hits as a function of cache size. The total number of accesses is the sum of two numbers: (i) the times every cache position has been used successfully to avoid a routing process, and (ii) the times that a node has been added to the cache. This test confirms that we can obtain good results even with a small size cache and allows to estimate such size. According to our simulation data, when $N = 5000$ a realistic cache size can be range from 40 to 60 lines, e.g. a 50 lines cache provides a 78% hits for in 75% of the attemps (quartile of 0.25).

## 5.4 Churn Evaluation

We study REMED behaviour under churn to evaluate $P_z$, that measures the negative impact of churn on cached routing information. Higher and higher churn values reduce cache accurateness and lower the hit ratio. To model churn, we use the half life model [15]. In a network of size $N$, the *doubling time* is the arrival time for further N nodes, and the *halving time* is the time required for $N/2$ nodes to leave

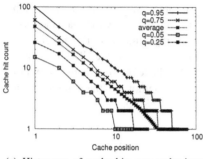

(a) Histogram of cache hits per cache item, sorted by hit count, and plotted with logarithmic scales.

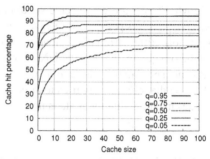

(b) Percentage of cache hits as a function of cache size.

**Fig. 5** Cache behaviour in a a network of 5000 nodes with session of 4 hours (about 100 publications). Results are aggregated in quantiles. No optimization enabled.

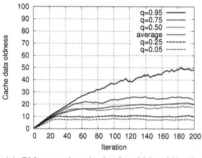

(a) Oldness values in the first 200 publication cycles, with cache size 50 and network size 5000.

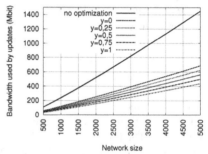

(b) Analytical model: average traffic generated by publication, unoptimized and optimized behavior w.r.t. network size, with $P_x = 0.7, P_z = 0.9$ and varying $P_y$.

**Fig. 6** Effectiveness of the soft-cache approach in reducing the routing traffic overhead.

the network. The *half life* is defined as the smaller of the doubling time and halving time, and represent the time needed for half the nodes in a network to be replaced by new arrivals.

We define $H$ as half life measured in seconds, and the *decay factor* as

$$D = \sqrt[H]{1/2} \qquad (5)$$

According to the model, the cache builds up a proportion of (1-D) of obsolete data per second. As a simple example let $H = 2$; after one second the cache still has $\sqrt{1/2}$ of valid data, that is, about 30% of its data is obsolete.

In a peer to peer overlay, half life $H$ is evaluated as 14400 seconds (4 hours) [23]. This value is related to a world-size content sharing P2P network like Overnet, where a somewhat higher churn is expected than in a Grid environment. We can safely use this value as a worst-case bound. To adapt this value to our context, we define a publication *cycle* as the interval between two publication, which in our case are $T = 150$ seconds apart. We derive from formula 5 the definition of *decay factor per iteration*.

$$D' = \sqrt[H/T]{1/2} \approx 0.9928 \qquad (6)$$

In other words, at each following publication, the probability for each cached item of becoming obsolete is slightly less than 1%.

We define as *oldness* the average time spent in cache by all its elements, normalized with $T$. The higher the oldness, the higher the probability that churn affects cache entries. Oldness value distribution has been evaluated experimentally, Fig. 6(a) reports result over 200 cycles in a network of 5000 nodes, with a cache size of 50. The average oldness tends to a maximum value near to 20, which means an expected churn probability of $1 - D'^{20} \approx 0.135$, and is below 28 in 75% of the cases (expected churn 0.183). On the ground of this analysis, in the optimized model we assume that a cache line is affected by churn with a probability of 10%, which corresponds to $H \approx 19800s$ and to $P_z = 0.9$.

## 5.5 Model Evaluation

In the previous sections we evaluate the cache probability hit ($P_x$) and the probability of low churn ($P_z$) with a series of simulations using a real data-set of measurements. Since we have only preliminary results as far as popularity is concerned, we proceed with the evaluation of the model using sample values for $P_y$. The graph in Fig. 6(b) shows the average bandwidth in Mbits used up by publication, for the MAAN and the REMED optimized model ($P_x = 0.7$, $P_z = 0.9$ and various values $P_y \in [0, 1]$). The analytic results show that the saving in network traffic ranges from 53% to 71% of the MAAN needs, depending on the value of $P_y$. Figure 7 shows the number of messages needed to cope with some combinations of different churn levels and

**Fig. 7** Number of messages on the network with and without REMED optimizations, with different churn probability and cache size (50, unbounded), on a network of 5000 nodes.

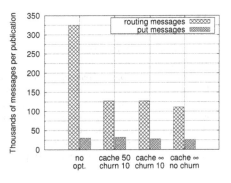

cache sizes, without consider popularity optimizations. From this graph it is already clear that a routing cache saves up to 70% routing messages, that a small cache is already sufficient, imposing no hard memory constraint, and that the estimated level of churn is well tolerated by REMED.

## 6 Conclusion and Future Work

We presented the REMED strategy to reduce network use when publishing dynamic valued resources in a resource discovery P2P system, based on a MAAN approach and on saving routing effort, as well as on reducing the number of actual publication messages. The approach allows consistent savings in term of network bandwidth and number of messages exchanged, allowing the overlay a faster query response and increased scalability. We plan to refine our approach in several directions, starting from a deeper study of popularity-based optimizations, one that exploits real-life query distributions to evaluate $P_y$. In this direction, XtreemOS Resource Location Services will be both an application case and an evaluation platform for REMED.

Another interesting issue is related to load balancing in the DHT space. Discrete valued attributes with low cardinality tend to concentrate keys in a small set of nodes, and unevenly distributed attributes cause a similar behaviour. When many resources are focused on few nodes, in a large DHT there are many nodes between two highly-loaded ones. The query resolution process is affected, as focused queries find a bottleneck at the most loaded nodes, while other queries have to traverse many nodes containing little useful data. Key distribution balancing can be improved by customising the Hash functions used, and we will investigate the relationships among key distribution, query constraint distribution, and local popularity estimates, in order to assess their impact on REMED optimizations.

**Acknowledgements** The authors acknowledge the support of Project FP6-033576, Building and Promoting a Linux-based Operating System to Support Virtual Organizations for Next Generation Grids (2006-2010).

## References

1. C. Schmidt and M. Parashar, "Flexible Information Discovery in Decentralized Distributed Systems," in *HPDC '03: Proceedings of the 12th IEEE International Symposium on High Performance Distributed Computing.* IEEE Computer Society, 2003, p. 226.
2. D. Spence, J. Crowcroft, S. Hand, and T. Harris, "Location based placement of whole distributed systems," in *CoNEXT '05: Proceedings of the 2005 ACM conference on Emerging network experiment and technology.* ACM, 2005, pp. 124–134.
3. H. V. Jagadish, B. C. Ooi, and Q. H. Vu, "BATON: a balanced tree structure for peer-to-peer networks," in *VLDB '05: Proceedings of the 31st International Conference on Very Large Data Bases.* VLDB Endowment, 2005, pp. 661–672.

4. M. Cai, M. Frank, J. Chen, and P. Szekely, "MAAN: A Multi-Attribute Addressable Network for Grid Information Services," in *GRID '03: Proceedings of the 4th International Workshop on Grid Computing*. IEEE Computer Society, 2003, p. 184.
5. D. Oppenheimer, J. Albrecht, D. Patterson, and A. Vahdat, "Distributed resource discovery on PlanetLab with SWORD," in *WORDLS'04: Proceedings of First Workshop on Real, Large Distributed Systems*, 2004.
6. G. Pierre, T. Schütt, J. Domaschka, and M. Coppola, "Highly available and scalable grid services," in *WDDM '09: Proceedings of the Third Workshop on Dependable Distributed Data Management*. New York, NY, USA: ACM, 2009, pp. 18–20.
7. A. S. Cheema, M. Muhammad, and I. Gupta, "Peer-to-Peer Discovery of Computational Resources for Grid Applications," in *GRID '05: Proceedings of the 6th IEEE/ACM International Workshop on Grid Computing*. IEEE Computer Society, 2005, pp. 179–185.
8. E. Caron, F. Desprez, and C. Tedeschi, "A Dynamic Prefix Tree for Service Discovery within Large Scale Grids," in *P2P '06: Proceedings of the Sixth IEEE International Conference on Peer-to-Peer Computing*. IEEE Computer Society, 2006, pp. 106–116.
9. J. Gao, "A distributed and scalable peer-to-peer content discovery system supporting complex queries," Ph.D. dissertation, Carnegie Mellon University, 2004.
10. R. Rodrigues and B. Liskov, "High Availability in DHTs: Erasure Coding vs. Replication," in *IPTPS '05: Proc.s of the 4th Intnl. Workshop on Peer-to-Peer Systems*, Ithaca, New York, 2005.
11. M. Roussopoulos and M. Baker, "CUP: Controlled Update Propagation in Peer-to-Peer Networks," *CoRR*, vol. cs.NI/0202008, 2002.
12. K. Tati and G. M. Voelker, "ShortCuts: Using Soft State to Improve DHT Routing," in *WCW'04 : Proceedings of 9th International Workshop on web content caching and distribution*. Springer, 2004, pp. 44–62.
13. I. Gupta, K. Birman, P. Linga, A. Demers, and R. van Renesse, "Kelips: Building an efficient and stable P2P DHT through increased memory and background overhead," in *IPTPS '03: Proc.s of the 2nd International Workshop on Peer-to-Peer Systems*, 2003.
14. A. Gupta, B. Liskov, and R. Rodrigues, "Efficient routing for peer-to-peer overlays," in *NSDI'04: Proc.s of the 1st Symposium on Networked Systems Design and Implementation*. USENIX Association, 2004, pp. 9–9.
15. D. Liben-Nowell, H. Balakrishnan, and D. Karger, "Observations on the Dynamic Evolution of Peer-to-Peer Networks," in *IPTPS '01: Revised Papers from the First International Workshop on Peer-to-Peer Systems*. Springer, 2002, pp. 22–33.
16. I. Stoica, R. Morris, D. Liben-Nowell, D. R. Karger, M. F. Kaashoek, F. Dabek, and H. Balakrishnan, "Chord: a scalable peer-to-peer lookup protocol for internet applications," *IEEE/ACM Trans. Netw.*, pp. 17–32, 2003.
17. K. Shudo, Y. Tanaka, and S. Sekiguchi, "Overlay Weaver: An overlay construction toolkit," *Computer Communications*, vol. 31, pp. 402–412, 2008.
18. F. Dabek, B. Zhao, P. Druschel, J. Kubiatowicz, and I. Stoica, "Towards a Common API for Structured Peer-to-Peer Overlays," in *Peer-to-Peer Systems II*. Springer, 2003, pp. 33–44.
19. A. Bavier, M. Bowman, B. Chun, D. Culler, S. Karlin, S. Muir, L. Peterson, T. Roscoe, T. Spalink, and M. Wawrzoniak, "Operating System Support for Planetary-Scale Network Services," in *NSDI'04: Proceedings of the 1st conference on Network Systems Design and Implementation*. USENIX, 2004, pp. 253–266.
20. L. Wang, K. S. Park, R. Pang, V. Pai, and L. Peterson, "Reliability and security in the CoDeeN content distribution network," in *ATEC '04: Proceedings of the annual conference on USENIX Annual Technical Conference*. USENIX Association, 2004, pp. 14–14.
21. K. Park and V. S. Pai, "CoMon: a mostly-scalable monitoring system for PlanetLab," *ACM SIGOPS Operating Systems Review*, vol. 40, pp. 65–74, 2006.
22. M. E. J. Newman, "Power laws, Pareto distributions and Zipf's law," *Contemporary Physics*, vol. 46, p. 323, 2005.
23. R. Bhagwan, S. Savage, and G. Voelker, "Understanding Availability," in *IPTPS '03: Proc. of the 2nd Int. Workshop on Peer-to-Peer Systems*. Springer, 2003, pp. 256–267.

# Autonomic management of multiple non-functional concerns in behavioural skeletons

Marco Aldinucci, Marco Danelutto and Peter Kilpatrick

**Abstract** We introduce and address the problem of concurrent autonomic management of different non-functional concerns in parallel applications build as a hierarchical composition of behavioural skeletons. We first define the problems arising when multiple concerns are dealt with by independent managers, then we propose a methodology supporting coordinated management, and finally we discuss how autonomic management of multiple concerns may be implemented in a typical use case. Being based on the behavioural skeleton concept proposed in the CoreGRID GCM, it is anticipated that the methodology will be readily integrated into the current reference implementation of GCM based on Java ProActive and running on top of major grid middleware systems.

**Key words:** Behavioural skeletons, autonomic computing, multi-concern autonomic management.

## 1 Introduction

Efficient implementation of parallel/distributed applications requires solving several problems related to the handling of different non-functional concerns. A *non-functional concern* is a concern not related to *what* is computed by the application, but rather to *how* the results of the application are computed [9]. Typical examples

Marco Aldinucci
Dept. Computer Science, University of Torino, Italy e-mail: `aldinuc@di.unito.it`

Marco Danelutto
Dept. Computer Science, University of Pisa, Italy, e-mail: `marcod@di.unipi.it`

Peter Kilpatrick
Dept. Computer Science, Queen's University Belfast, UK, e-mail: `p.kilpatrick@qub.ac.uk`

of non-functional concerns include performance tuning, fault tolerance, security and power efficiency.

In [1] we discussed a framework based on the concept of *behavioural skeleton*, aimed at supporting the programming of parallel/distributed applications. A behavioural skeleton is a co-designed and optimized implementation of a parallel algorithmic skeleton modelling a well-known parallelism exploitation pattern, *together* with an autonomic manager taking care of one of the non-functional concerns related to the execution of that algorithmic skeleton. The complete behavioural skeleton framework has been experimented with in the GCM context [7]. Simple managers, each taking care of a non-functional concern in a single behavioural skeleton have been designed and implemented [1], as well as hierarchies of autonomic managers, each taking care of a single non-functional concern relative to a single skeleton in a hierarchy of skeletons [2, 4]. In both cases experimental results demonstrated the feasibility of the behavioural skeleton approach and the efficiency of the GCM implementation of behavioural skeletons in its application to real use cases.

However, the autonomic management of *multiple* non-functional concerns has not yet been considered in this framework, although it is clear that it would be a very useful and powerful tool to address non-functional issues.

When dealing with autonomic management of multiple non-functional concerns several distinct issues arise, in addition to those for a single non-functional concern. In particular, *coordination* of the autonomic managers taking care of the different concerns is needed to avoid conflicting decisions being taken that eventually impair the whole autonomic management framework. This coordination represents a significant challenge.

In this paper we consider autonomic management of several different non-functional concerns in a distributed system. We address the problem in a structured programming framework (Sec. 2), we consider the issues related to coordination of autonomic managers each dealing with a different concern (Sec. 3), and we discuss the methodology proposed in Sec. 3.1 applied to a typical use case (Sec. 4). Related work and conclusions sections end the paper.

## 2 Parallel framework

We assume here that parallel applications are programmed according to *structured parallel programming principles* [6]. In particular, we assume a parallel application is built as a composition of *behavioural skeletons* [1] and sequential portions of code modelling pure functions. A behavioural skeleton (BS) models a well-know parallelism exploitation pattern. We assume here the existence of a set of BS including: *pipeline* modelling computations in stages processing streams of tasks; *task farm* modelling embarrassingly parallel computations processing streams of tasks; *data parallel* modelling different kinds of data parallel patterns (embarrassingly parallel, with stencil, with shared read-only data structures, etc.); and *sequential* wrapping pure functional sequential code in such a way that it can be used within other BS. Each BS implements a known parallelism exploitation pattern *and* an autonomic manager taking care of some non-functional concern. A parallel application is thus built as a composition of BS. The user provides the sequential portions of code wrapped in the sequential BS, the input data *and* a QoS contract. The BS run time system executes the application in such a way that the (hierarchy of) application manager(s) takes care of ensuring the QoS contract provided by the user.

As an example, in [2] we discuss an application which is a pipeline whose first and third stages are sequential, whose second stage is parallel (a task farm with sequential workers) and whose autonomic manager deals with performance tuning. The structure of the resulting application is shown in Fig. 1.

Restriction of the parallelism patterns the programmer can exploit by the use of behavioural skeletons makes it possible to achieve better performance and efficiency while implementing the application, and allows effective autonomic management to be programmed in the autonomic managers while preserving the possibility to model all (or most) of the commonly used patterns in parallel and distributed computing.

## 3 Autonomic management of multiple concerns in structured parallel computations

When dealing with multiple non-functional concerns, we have to consider that, in the most general cases, distinct autonomic management strategies may exist for each of the non-functional concerns under consideration. More precisely, we may assume that a collection of (possibly hierarchical) autonomic managers exist $\mathscr{AM}_1, \ldots, \mathscr{AM}_m$ that can independently and autonomically take care of non-functional concerns $\mathscr{C}_1, \ldots, \mathscr{C}_m$. For example, the managers *AMpipe*, *AMseq* (two instances) and *AMfarm* of Fig. 1 constitute a single, hierarchically structured collection of autonomic managers. If more concerns are to be considered, we will assume more managers will be associated with the single behavioural skeleton. Fig. 2 shows how these managers will be organized when two non-functional concerns are involved: $\mathscr{C}_P$ (performance tuning) and $\mathscr{C}_S$ (security).

We will use the term $\mathscr{AM}_i$ to refer to the top level manager of a hierarchy of managers handling non-functional concern $\mathscr{C}_i$, if not otherwise specified.

Our approach to handling multiple non-functional concerns is based on a five-pronged attack: identifying an overall strategy for coordinating the managers' activities; finding a common currency by which managers may interact; finding means of reaching consensus on decisions; determining how the management activity can be initialized; and devising a means to implement autonomic management. We now consider each of these in turn.

## 3.1 Centralized vs. distributed autonomic management of multiple concerns

When considering autonomic management of *multiple* non-functional concerns, we must identify a general strategy to coordinate the autonomic management activities performed by the different managers (or manager hierarchies). In general, it may be the case that manager $\mathscr{AM}_i$ takes a decision affecting the global application that is in contrast with the strategies of manager $\mathscr{AM}_j$. For example, $\mathscr{AM}_P$ (a manager taking care of ensuring performance contracts) may clearly take decisions that are in contrast with the policies ensured by $\mathscr{AM}_W$ (a manager taking care of ensuring power management contracts).

To resolve these conflicts a means must exist by which managers may reach mutually acceptable positions. Two strategies can be identified for this purpose:

SM    a *Super Manager* $\mathscr{AM}_0$ can be introduced, positioned hierarchically above managers $\mathscr{AM}_1$ to $\mathscr{AM}_m$, coordinating the decisions taken locally by these autonomic managers and relating to different, possibly interfering concerns; or

CM    the managers $\mathscr{AM}_1$ to $\mathscr{AM}_m$ can be modified so that *before* actuating any decision, they reach agreement with the others.

Both solutions share a common concept, which is the idea of building a *consensus* on the decisions taken. In the former case (SM) the consensus has to be sought by $\mathscr{AM}_0$, upon communication from one of the $\mathscr{AM}_i$ of a proposed decision. Upon consensus, $\mathscr{AM}_0$ may give the green light to $\mathscr{AM}_i$ so that the decision is actuated. If consensus is not reached, eventually $\mathscr{AM}_0$ will communicate to the $\mathscr{AM}_i$ that the decision is to be aborted. In the latter case (CM), the $\mathscr{AM}_i$ that proposes to

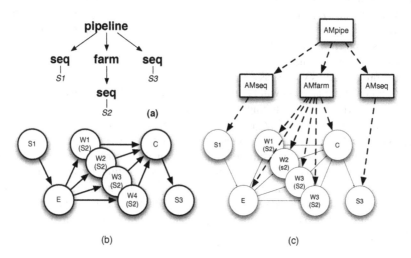

**Fig. 1** Sample parallel application with behavioural skeletons: logic view (a), process view (sample, (b)) and autonomic manager view (c)

take a decision should contact all the other managers and behave as the SM in the former case to build a consensus on this decision. So, the two strategies considered differ only in the way they will build the manager network, but thereafter most of the coordination algorithms and strategies should be the same, or very similar.

As a matter of fact, in solution CM the coordination among managers may happen at any level of the autonomic manager hierarchy. Fig. 2 shows how managers dealing with different concerns within the same behavioural skeleton can be naturally paired in such a way they can coordinate locally taken decisions.

## 3.2 Shared knowledge among different autonomic managers

The second area to be addressed when reasoning about multi-concern management is the common knowledge necessary across different concern managers to make possible agreement on global application management. Different manager hierarchies should agree on a common view of the parallel/distributed application at hand

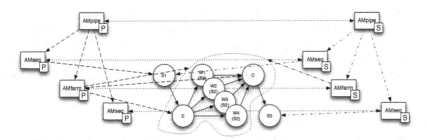

**Fig. 2** Multiple manager hierarchies (S=security managers, P=performance tuning managers) in behavioural skeletons

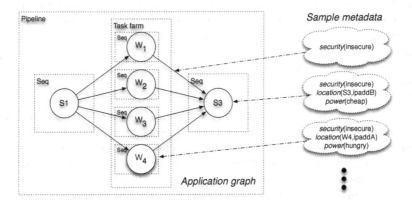

**Fig. 3** Sample application graph

in order to be able to share decisions and, where appropriate, obtain consensus on local decisions before actuating them.

The main common concept across the different managers is the *application graph* whose nodes represent the parallel/distributed activities and whose arcs represent communications/synchronizations among these activities. Each node and arc can be labelled with suitable *metadata*. For example, the node metadata could represent *mapping* information (which processing element(s) host the parallel activity, what are its features in terms of CPU, memory, disk, network bandwidth, etc.); the arc metadata may represent features of the corresponding communication channel (kind of protocol used, bandwidth and latency, whether it can be regarded as a secure channel or not, etc.).

We do not address here general parallel/distributed applications. Rather, we target only those applications build by composing behavioural skeletons. Therefore the application graph we will deal with is the graph representing a *well-formed composition* of parallel/distributed patterns modelled by the behavioural skeleton library at hand. Fig. 3 shows the application graph (with sample associated metadata) corresponding to our sample application: a three-stage pipeline with parallel second stage (task farm with 4 workers).

The application graph represents the minimal information that can be shared among managers to implement multi-concern autonomic management.

Consider a typical example, involving autonomic management of performance, security and power saving options in an application such as that of Fig. 3. A typical decision taken by the $\mathscr{AM}_P$ consists in varying the number of workers in the farm representing the second stage of the pipeline. For example, the number of workers can be increased to increase the throughput of the second stage and thus guarantee the user supplied performance contract. In this case, the decision of the $\mathscr{AM}_P$ will eventually lead to a different application graph. The new worker allocated will be labelled with some metadata representing, among other information, the resource where it will be mapped or the set of resources where the actual resource to host the worker will be taken from. The agreement with the other managers must be obtained in this case before committing the decision. $\mathscr{AM}_W$ may provide some priorities among the potential target resources for allocation of the new worker, in such a way that low consumption options are preferred. On the other hand, $\mathscr{AM}_S$ (an autonomic manager taking care of security concerns) may provide a binary mapping of the resources distinguishing those that are secure (i.e. those that can be reached using only private and trusted network segments) from those that are not. Eventually, $\mathscr{AM}_P$ may decide to allocate the new worker on a low consuming, secure resource (with no additional effort), on a low consuming, insecure resource (with provision for encryption of communications) or on a high consuming, insecure resource (again, providing for encryption). In all cases, the common level of agreement with the other managers will be on the final application graph. Even where no consensus can be reached among the different managers (e.g. no secure resources found, user contract asking for completely secure computations, impossibility to use alternative secure protocols) the eventual agreement will be on retaining the original graph, thus representing the fact that the decision by $\mathscr{AM}_P$ has been aborted.

## 3.3 Impact of local decisions on global application management

Having stated that a consensus has to be reached on the resulting application graph (with metadata) *before* committing any decision, we now consider how such consensus may be built. In particular, we discuss how the consensus process can be established and implemented; and the possible results of the consensus process.

### 3.3.1 Consensus building

Consensus building must be implemented as a two-phase process. In the first phase, the autonomic manager whose control cycle has identified that a decision has to be implemented as a consequence of some triggering event (here we assume it will be $\mathscr{A}\mathscr{M}_1$) must initiate the consensus building, either by interacting with $\mathscr{A}\mathscr{M}_0$ (SM case) or with all the other managers ($\mathscr{A}\mathscr{M}_2$ to $\mathscr{A}\mathscr{M}_m$, CM case). In the second phase, $\mathscr{A}\mathscr{M}_1$ should await for the consensus results and, depending on their nature, either commit the decision (i.e. execute the actions in the plan associated with the decision) or abort it.

The intent of the two-phase protocol for consensus building is clear: no decision may be taken locally if the management of other concerns may be affected by the results of the decision. This in turn has two consequences:

1. decisions can be assigned to one of two classes: *independent* decisions, i.e. those not affecting the behaviour of other autonomic managers handling different concerns, and *interfering* decisions, i.e. those (potentially) having an impact on contract maintenance by other concern managers. For example, a decision to change the implementation of a parallel activity already mapped to a given processing resource, from single to multi-threaded, will most likely be an *independent* decision. On the other hand, a decision to migrate an already mapped parallel activity or to start a new parallel activity will be *interfering* decisions. In this case, new processing resources have to be recruited and that will typically affect contract maintenance by managers concerned with security, power management, etc.

2. decisions taken by $\mathscr{A}\mathscr{M}_1$ could have several alternative equivalent implementations (i.e. plans and sequences of actions implementing the decision at $\mathscr{A}\mathscr{M}_i$) including

   - plain implementation of the decision, i.e. no modification is made with respect to the implementation plan prepared by $\mathscr{A}\mathscr{M}_1$ as a consequence of the answers provided by the other managers, and
   - "adjusted implementation" of the decision, i.e. an implementation whose actions have been modified according to the requirements gathered from the $\mathscr{A}\mathscr{M}_j$ ($j \neq i$) in order to ensure maintenance of the whole set of contracts provided to the different managers rather than taking into account only concern $\mathscr{C}_1$.

Typically, *independent* decisions will lead to the execution of unmodified implementation plans, whereas *interfering* decisions will lead to *adjusted* implementations.

Clearly, the necessity to provide "adjusted" implementation plans at manager $\mathcal{AM}_i$ raises a compositionality issue: if $\mathcal{AM}_i$ only had to take care of concern $\mathcal{C}_i$, no adjustment would be needed to its implementation plans. Adjustments are only needed when other concerns ($\mathcal{C}_j$, $j \neq i$) are taken into account. It is therefore clear that adjustments will depend on the nature of the $\mathcal{C}_j$. Thus $\mathcal{AM}_i$ will be no longer independent of the other managers/concerns.

In order to solve this issue, we propose the following methodology:

- A decision $\mathcal{D}_j$ taken by a manager $\mathcal{AM}_i$ is implemented with an ordered list of actions $a_{j1}, \ldots, a_{jk_j}$. This ordered list of actions is the implementation *plan* of decision $\mathcal{D}_j$.
- The granularity of the actions is the finest possible preserving the independence of each of the actions themselves.
- Actions are labelled as *independent* or *interfering* as above.
- Taking into account the overall set of concerns $\mathcal{C}_j$, $j \neq i$ considered in addition to $\mathcal{C}_i$, for each *interfering* action $a_k$ (or for each sequence of actions $a_{k-m}, \ldots, a_{k+n}$ containing at least one interfering action $a_k$) one or more substitute plans $a_{k1}, \ldots, a_{ki_k}$ are prepared that have the same effect as $a_k$ with respect to the concern $\mathcal{C}_i$ but that also accomplish some property required by other managers $\mathcal{AM}_j$, $j \neq i$.
- Finally, the consensus building phase will be modified as follows: the managers informed of decision $\mathcal{D}_k$ by manager $\mathcal{AM}_i$ will eventually report back to $\mathcal{AM}_i$ either an *ACK* message or a *needProperty(propName$_j$)* message, where *propName$_j$* is one of the "other concern" properties $\mathcal{AM}_i$ is able to deal with. If no suitable *propName* is available at $\mathcal{AM}_i$ to deal with what is required by the other manager, a *NACK* message will be returned that will serve to block the execution of $\mathcal{D}_k$ by $\mathcal{AM}_i$.

### 3.3.2 Consensus results

The smoothest outcome is the one where $\mathcal{AM}_i$, seeking consensus on decision $\mathcal{D}_k$, gets from other managers (CM case) or from $\mathcal{AM}_0$ (SM case) only *ACK* messages. This will be the result both in the case of an *independent* $\mathcal{D}_k$, and of an *interfering* $\mathcal{D}_k$ which at the moment does not cause any conflict with the policies implemented by the other managers.

The second case is in a sense the opposite of the first: $\mathcal{AM}_i$ gets at least one *NACK* message back from one of the other managers. In this case the decision $\mathcal{D}_k$ will be *aborted* and manager $\mathcal{AM}_i$ must attempt to determine some other strategy (if any) to address the situation that triggered decision $\mathcal{D}_k$.

The last, and most interesting (and challenging) case, is that where $\mathscr{AM}_i$ gets only *ACK* or *needProperty* messages back from the other managers. Here we should distinguish two further sub-cases:

- There is a single *needProperty(propName$_i$)* message. In this case, $\mathscr{AM}_i$ should simply implement the substitute plans for the interfering actions in the original $\mathscr{D}_k$ plan corresponding to *propName$_i$*.
- There are multiple *needProperty* messages from the other managers. In this case $\mathscr{AM}_i$ should first determine which substitute implementation plans should be used and then consider whether the simultaneous usage of all of these substitute plans is still consistent. If it is consistent, the resulting new implementation plan will be executed. If not, $\mathscr{D}_k$ will be aborted.

Once the final plan implementing $\mathscr{D}_k$ has been determined (consensus having been achieved), the execution of the plan (i.e. the execution of the sequence of actions $a_1, \ldots, a_n$ in the plan) involves a modification of the application graph (the structure of the graph and/or the associated metadata). This modification has to be notified to all the other managers so that they can maintain a consistent view of the system. Moreover, the execution of the plan $a_1, \ldots, a_n$ has to be implemented as an *atomic* procedure. This means that any further decision taken by other managers should be processed only after finishing action $a_n$ and releasing the atomic action lock. In turn, all of this process obviously requires a distributed coordination mechanism. To avoid running a complicated and costly distributed coordination protocol, we can consider here to have the application graph controlled by $\mathscr{AM}_0$ in a SM implementation of the multiple concern management, and to have the single $\mathscr{AM}_i$ communicating the actions in the agreed plan to $\mathscr{AM}_0$ in such a way that these actions can be executed directly by $\mathscr{AM}_0$.

## 3.4 Initialization of the $\mathscr{AM}$ hierarchy

We assume that the user submits QoS contracts to the different $\mathscr{AM}_i$ provided with the behavioural skeleton framework. These contracts describe the user's (non-functional) requirements that have to be guaranteed by the behavioural skeleton implementation of the user application.

We assume the user provides these contracts in such a way that:

- The order of the contracts establishes a priority among the managers. Thus, if the user provides contracts $QoS_1, \ldots, QoS_k$ (in order), only the managers dealing with concerns $\mathscr{C}_1$ to $\mathscr{C}_k$ will be activated and the decisions of manager $i$ will have precedence over the decisions of manager $i + h$. The relative ordering among managers and, consequently, among manager decisions can be used to resolve conflicts when multiple decisions are communicated for consensus or even to impose an ordering on the substitute plan implementations when multiple *needProperty* messages have been directed to the $\mathscr{AM}_i$ seeking consensus on $\mathscr{D}_j$.

- The first contract $QoS_1$ determines which manager is in charge of establishing the initial application implementation configuration. This is particularly important as multiple concern management needs a starting configuration to initiate the autonomic management activities. Consider the case where performance, security and power saving concerns are of relevance. The same application will be configured to use the maximum number of powerful nodes if run under the sole control of $\mathscr{A}\mathscr{M}_P$, on a number of secure nodes if run under the control of $\mathscr{A}\mathscr{M}_S$, or on a number of low consumption nodes if run under the control of $\mathscr{A}\mathscr{M}_W$. In the three cases, the number of processing elements used may vary as well as the overall performance of the application.

## 3.5 Rule-based multi-concern autonomic manager implementation

In earlier work we demonstrated the suitability of business rule management frameworks for implementing autonomic managers handling a single concern [1]. A business rule framework implements a system of pre-condition ($P$) action ($a_i$) rules in the form $P(x_1, \ldots, x_n) \to a_1; \ldots; a_k$. When executed, the precondition part of all the rules is evaluated. Those rules that have a precondition holding true are fired (possibly using some ordering based on priorities); that is, the corresponding action part is executed.

In particular, the classical control loop (monitor→analyze→plan→execute) implemented by each manager may be implemented in such a way that:

- the monitor phase is implemented by gathering the current values of the variables used in the pre-condition parts of the rules;
- the analyse and plan phases correspond to evaluating which pre-conditions are satisfied and choosing one of the corresponding rules, possibly using some priority-based ordering;
- the execute phase is implemented by simply executing the action set (the implementation plan) in the right hand side of the rule identified in the previous step.

This was shown to work well when a single manager is considered. Now the idea can be adapted to the multi-concern management as follows:

- each rule originally present in the rule set implemented by $\mathscr{A}\mathscr{M}_i$ *in isolation* is transformed into two distinct (classes of) rules: 1) a rule with the same precondition hosting as action part the consensus building start-up actions; 2) one or more rules with a pre-condition evaluating the responses of the other managers in the consensus building phase, and as the action part the original implementation plan or one of the *adjusted* plans.
- specific rules are added to deal with *NACK* answers. These rules may include priority reordering within the manager rules, as well as new rules exploiting the available accumulated knowledge to deal with the new situation (we assume here that some "learning" technique is used).

# 4 Sample case study

We consider here a case study, to illustrate the concepts and the methodology discussed above. A more complete version of this use case may be found in [3]. Consider the application whose schema is depicted in Fig. 1, and assume two distinct non-functional concerns are handled by two autonomic manager hierarchies associated with the BS used: security and performance tuning. Let us assume that the QoS contracts provided by the user are:

1. `secureData()`, directed to $\mathscr{A}\mathscr{M}_S$ and specifying that all the data transfers involving remote nodes must be secured, and
2. `minThroughput(1 task/sec)`, directed to $\mathscr{A}\mathscr{M}_P$ and specifying that the parallel application is expected to deliver at least one result per second.

As the first contract is directed to $\mathscr{A}\mathscr{M}_S$, the autonomic manager dealing with security will handle the initial configuration of the program, i.e. it will define the initial application graph. Not being concerned with performance, $\mathscr{A}\mathscr{M}_S$ will set up a graph using the default values for all those parameters that have been not been specified by the user. In this case, the parallelism degree of the task farm will be set to some default value (say 4) and there will be no grouping of pipeline stages. Thus, the application graph will be a graph $\mathscr{G} = \langle N, A \rangle$ with:

$$N = \{n_{s1}, n_e, n_{w_1}, \ldots, n_{w_4}, n_c, n_{s3}\}$$
$$A = \{(n_{s1}, n_e), (n_e, n_{w_1}), \ldots, (n_e, n_{w_4}), (n_{w_1}, n_c), \ldots, (n_{w_4}, n_c), (n_c, n_{s3})$$

$\mathscr{A}\mathscr{M}_S$ will try to select nodes $n_i$ that belong to trusted domains (i.e. domains that can be reached through trusted interconnections and hosting trusted nodes). If this is not possible, nodes from untrusted domains will be selected and metadata will be inserted in the application graph to state that the arcs leading to the untrusted nodes should be secured.

Once the initial application graph has been produced by $\mathscr{A}\mathscr{M}_S$, it will be mapped onto the target architecture and the application will be started. After application start, metadata will be added to the application graph modelling node placement (e.g. *location($n_i$, ip_address$_j$)*), resource characterization (e.g. *nodeProp($n_i$, opSys(Linux), procType(dualcore), ...)*), etc. This metadata will be used to derive variables and values used in the pre-conditions as well as in the action part of the manager rules. Metadata also represent *de facto* the actual mapping of the abstract application graph to real resources.

Both $\mathscr{A}\mathscr{M}_S$ and $\mathscr{A}\mathscr{M}_P$ will start their control loops. $\mathscr{A}\mathscr{M}_S$, being solely responsible for the initial allocation, will have no rules triggered and therefore will not execute any action affecting the system. On the other hand, $\mathscr{A}\mathscr{M}_P$ will immediately evaluate the performance achieved by the program and this, in turn, will make some rules fireable if the performance is not consistent with the supplied QoS contract. Sample rules used in a hypothetical stand-alone $\mathscr{A}\mathscr{M}_P$ should include the following rules for farms:

| Name | Rule |
|------|------|
| $Farm_{inc}$ | $priority(x)$, |
|  | $instanceof(farm)$ & $T_{arr} > QoS$ & $Throughput < QoS$ |
|  | $\rightarrow findNewResource, allocateNewWorker,$ |
|  | $connectNewWorker$ |
| $Farm_{dec}$ | $priority(x)$, |
|  | $instanceof(farm)$ & $Throughput \gg QoS$ |
|  | $\rightarrow removeWorker$ |

($priority(x)$ denoting the fact that the rule has priority $x$, $T_{arr}$ being the inter-arrival time of tasks to the farm and QoS being the throughput contract issued by the user). These two rules will be different in an $\mathscr{AM}_P$ that is aware of the fact that it is managing performance while some other manager ($\mathscr{AM}_S$) is managing another concern. In this case they should be of the form:

| Name | Rule |
|------|------|
| $Farm_{inc}{}^{PH1}$ | $priority(x)$, |
|  | $instanceof(farm)$ & $T_{arr} > QoS$ & $Throughput < QoS$ |
|  | $\rightarrow findNewResource, askConsensus(G', R')$ |
| $Farm_{inc}{}^{PH2}$ | $priority(x)$, |
|  | $ackFromAll \rightarrow allocateNewWorker, connectWorker$ |
| $Farm_{inc}{}^{PH2}$ | $priority(x)$, |
|  | $ackFromAll$ & $needProperty(security)$ |
|  | $\rightarrow allocateNewWorker, connectSSLWorker$ |
| $Farm_{inc}{}^{PH2}$ | $priority(x)$, |
|  | $nackConsensus \rightarrow lowerPriority(Farm_{inc})$ |
| $Farm_{dec}$ | $priority(x)$, |
|  | $instanceof(farm)$ & $Throughput \gg QoS$ |
|  | $\rightarrow removeWorker$ |

(where $G'$ is the new application graph resulting from the decision taken in the rule, $R'$ is the newly recruited resource).

In this case we assume the use of priorities to smooth the effect of aborted rules. Consider the example above. For the sake of simplicity, we omit other rules relating to autonomic management of performance in the task farm behavioural skeleton. However, it would be probable that other rules exist that also happen to be fireable when rule $Farm_{inc}{}^{PH1}$ is fireable, i.e. when we have sufficient tasks to compute but still do not meet the QoS contract. For example, a rule whose effect is to move a farm worker from a slow resource to a faster resource may exist, or a rule changing the kind of task-to-worker scheduling adopted in the farm to speed up computation. Now, if a rule has been selected and eventually aborted (as in $Farm_{inc}{}^{PH2}$ third item), by lowering the priority of the rule aborted we make fireable (at the next control loop iteration) an alternative rule firing on the same pre-condition but previously ignored due to its lower priority. This is a mechanism for ensuring fairness in rule selection in the presence of NACKs during the consensus building phase.

In classifying actions as being *independent/interfering* (Sec. 3.3) we consider actions such as *allocateNewWorker, findNewResource, askConsensus* to be *independent* while actions such as *connectWorker* are regarded as being *interfering*. In fact, the way we connect a worker (e.g. the way we implement the communications between $n_e$ and $n_{w_{new}}$ and between $n_{w_{new}}$ and $n_c$) impacts the security (confidentiality and integrity) of the communicated data or code. Indeed, if $\mathcal{AM}_W$ (power management) is also included, the *allocateNewWorker* action must be considered *interfering*: the choice of a resource from those available will lead to a particular power consumption that in turn will eventually affect the power management concern managed by $\mathcal{AM}_W$. Notice that *allocateNewWorker* actions could have been considered to be interfering actions when taking into account only the existence of $\mathcal{AM}_S$. However, the choice of an insecure node in place of a secure one can be tolerated provided the actions and plans used by $\mathcal{AM}_P$ can be "adjusted" as outlined in Sec. 3.3. This is actually what happens in the rules above where the plan *findNewResource, allocateNewWorker, connectWorker* is substituted (after consensus) by the plan *findNewResource, allocateNewWorker, connectSSLWorker*.

In general, the decision to label an action as *interfering* depends on the set of concerns $\mathcal{C}_j$ ($i \neq j$) involved in addition to the concern $\mathcal{C}_i$ of the manager executing the actions. Also, it is worth pointing out that metadata associated with the element of the application graph may influence handling of *interfering* actions. If the metadata associated with the application graph allows $\mathcal{AM}_S$ to conclude that the node added by $\mathcal{AM}_P$ is a secure node, no "adjustment" will be necessary to the *interfering* action *connectWorker*, for example.

# 5 Related work

The IBM blueprint paper on autonomic computing has already established, in a slightly different context, the need to orchestrate independent autonomic managers [10]. In [8] strategies to handle performance and power management issues by autonomic managers are discussed. However the approach is much more oriented to the generic combination of target functions relating to the two non-functional concerns considered, rather than to the constructive coordination of the actions planned by the two managers.

A framework that can be used to reason on multiple concerns was introduced in [11]. Based on the concepts of state and action (i.e., state transition) adopted from the field of artificial intelligence, this framework maps three types of agenthood concepts (action, goal, utility-function) into autonomic computing policies. Action policies may produce and consume resources, which are used by a *resource arbiter* (i.e. a super manager) to harmonize conflicting concerns. The framework, however, does not provide any specific support for policy design and distributed management overlay.

A similar approach was followed in [5], which also exploits the same policies (action, goal, utility-function) defined on the (Cartesian product of) *state* and *configuration* space of the system. These policies are extended with *resource-definition* policies, which specify how the autonomic manager exposes the system to its environment; this makes it possible to dynamically extend manager knowledge with

other resources/parameters, possibly coming from other managers, thus supporting
management overlay.

# 6 Conclusions

In this work we discussed a general methodology that can be used to support autonomic management of multiple non-functional concerns in a behavioural skeleton
framework. The methodology is based on coordination of decisions taken by mostly
independent autonomic managers (each taking care of a single non-functional concern) through a two-phase consensus protocol. We also discussed how the methodology can be applied to a typical use case.

While protocols and policies may be established to coordinate the activities of
different concern managers, the main challenge lies in not being overwhelmed by
the sheer complexity of their interactions. To this end, we need to exploit to the full
the fact that the structure of the underlying skeleton is *known* and use this knowledge
in marshalling the activities of the overlaid autonomic management structure.

# References

1. Aldinucci, M., Campa, S., Danelutto, M., Vanneschi, M., Dazzi, P., Laforenza, D., Tonellotto,
   N., Kilpatrick, P.: Behavioural skeletons in GCM: autonomic management of grid components. In: D.E. Baz, J. Bourgeois, F. Spies (eds.) Proc. of Intl. Euromicro PDP 2008: Parallel
   Distributed and network-based Processing, pp. 54–63. IEEE, Toulouse, France (2008). DOI
   10.1109/PDP.2008.46
2. Aldinucci, M., Danelutto, M., Kilpatrick, P.: Autonomic management of non-functional concerns in distributed and parallel application programming. In: Proc. of Intl. Parallel &
   Distributed Processing Symposium (IPDPS), pp. 1–12. IEEE, Rome, Italy (2009). DOI
   10.1109/IPDPS.2009.5161034
3. Aldinucci, M., Danelutto, M., Kilpatrick, P.: Handling multiple non-functional concerns in
   Behavioural Skeletons. Tech. Rep. TR-09-10, Dept. Computer Science, Univ. of Pisa (2009).
   Available at http://compass2.di.unipi.it/TR/
4. Aldinucci, M., Danelutto, M., Kilpatrick, P.: Towards hierarchical management of autonomic
   components: a case study. In: F.S. Didier El Baz Tom Gross (ed.) Proc. of Intl. Euromicro PDP
   2009: Parallel Distributed and network-based Processing, pp. 3–10. IEEE, Weimar, Germany
   (2009). DOI 10.1109/PDP.2009.48
5. Calinescu, R.: Resource-definition policies for autonomic computing. In: Proc. of the 5th Intl.
   Conference on Autonomic and Autonomous Systems (ICAS), pp. 111–116. IEEE (2009).
   DOI 10.1109/ICAS.2009.16
6. Cole, M.: Bringing skeletons out of the closet: A pragmatic manifesto for skeletal parallel
   programming. Parallel Computing **30**(3), 389–406 (2004)
7. CoreGRID NoE deliverable series, Institute on Programming Model: Deliverable D.PM.04
   – Basic Features of the Grid Component Model (assessed) (2007). URL http://www.
   coregrid.net
8. Das, R., Kephart, J.O., Lefurgy, C., Tesauro, G., Levine, D.W., Chan, H.: Autonomic multi-
   agent management of power and performance in data centers. In: Proc. of the 7th Intl. Conference of Autonomic Agents and Multiagent Systems (2008)

9. Glinz, M.: On non-functional requirements. Requirements Engineering, IEEE International Conference on **0**, 21–26 (2007). DOI 10.1109/RE.2007.45
10. IBM Corp.: An Architectural Blueprint for Autonomic Computing (2005). `http://www-01.ibm.com/software/tivoli/autonomic/`
11. Kephart, J.O., Walsh, W.E.: An artificial intelligence perspective on autonomic computing policies. In: Proc. of the 5th Intl. Workshop on Policies for Distributed Systems and Networks (POLICY'04). IEEE (2004)

# Decision Models for Resource Aggregation in Peer-to-Peer Architectures

Mircea Moca and Gheorghe Cosmin Silaghi

**Abstract** As service-oriented systems emerge toward a fully decentralized collaborative environment, resource aggregation becomes one of the important features to study. While previous work investigated the effectiveness of resource aggregation in unstructured peer-to-peer networks with autonomous nodes, in this paper we investigate several sorts of decision models for this task. By extensive experimentation, we find that a good decision model can further enhance the overall user satisfaction and reduce the transaction risks.

## 1 Introduction

As the grid emerges toward fully distributed P2P networks [8], service oriented architectures need to adapt to the new peer-to-peer networked environment. To make the P2P-based SOA pervasive, the challenge is to let all the nodes in the system to play both roles: consumers and providers of services. Such an ideal system should be able to discover and aggregate the suitable resources to supply a consumer query.

In [14] we analyzed the effectiveness of resource aggregation in P2P architectures. We investigated a two-steps resource aggregation mechanism consisting of an initial service discovery, where for each service request available provider peers are identified, and a subsequent partners selection. For the latter phase, we employed a simple decision model, emphasizing the difference between an objective and a subjective partner selection. The subjective partner selection method allows each node to customary modify the decision scheme to accommodate individual or local preferences. We found that unstructured P2P networks equipped with resource discovery mechanisms of some a-priori performance are able to properly fulfill the

Mircea Moca, Gheorghe Cosmin Silaghi
Babeş-Bolyai University of Cluj-Napoca, Str. Theodor Mihali, nr. 58-60, Cluj-Napoca, Romania,
e-mail: \{mircea.moca,gheorghe.silaghi\}@econ.ubbcluj.ro

consumers' queries. If the wealth is heterogeneously distributed on the network, the subjective decision model can bring more global user satisfaction.

In this paper we continue our previous work on resource aggregation, by investigating several more complex decision models. In [14] we employed only the Onicescu decision model [9], focusing on both the objective and the subjective variants of the model. The Onicescu model fits in the non-parametric class of decision models, the literature [1, 7] recommending also other more complex alternatives. In this paper, besides Onicescu, we considered the Global Utility Method [9] from the Multi-Attribute Utility Theory (MAUT) [11] and Promethee [2], covering all spectrum of decision models types. We aim to recommend the decision model class that suits best for a given wealth endowment of the P2P network and a given service request load.

The paper is structured as follows. After a short introduction into related work concerning resource aggregation, section 3 describes the resource aggregation setup in unstructured P2P networks. Section 4 presents the decision models selected for this analysis. Section 5 presents simulation experiments and results, and section 6 concludes.

## 2 Related Work

Resource allocation is widely studied in multi-agent systems [4]. They present various issues of interest we should consider when designing a resource allocation mechanism. Such mechanisms are employed in grid systems for job scheduling [5]. Xiang-Yang L. et al. [12] is concerned in designing mechanisms that provide more trust in intermediate nodes of a transaction. They treat the "moral hazard" (as called in economics) problem in networks with multi-hop routing and design incentive schemes for nodes to eliminate hidden information that stands between end-points of a transaction.

Service composition in the sense of finding the proper instantiation for an orchestration is approached in [3] by employing genetic algorithms. The authors propose a slower (than integer programming) but scalable solution that deals with generic QoS attributes.

In [15], authors present a model for improving cooperation by using reciprocation between immediate neighbors, in decentralized networks. This work tackles the economic concept of "utility-maximizing behavior". Emerging cooperative behavior in P2P networks is mostly based on developing incentive techniques, like the one presented in [6] to confront the problem of "free riding" (lack of cooperation). The basis of their techniques consist in the Generalized Prisoner's Dilemma and the Reciprocative decision function. Jurca & Faltings [10] propose a reputation model to stand as an incentive mechanism.

# 3 The resource aggregation setup

In this section we present our resource aggregation setup, similar with the one considered in [14].

The discussed system comprises a set of $N$ participants, organized in a unstructured peer-to-peer architecture. Each peer owns a certain quantity of resources and it is linked to a subset of other peers, called neighbors. Consequently, our system is a connected graph. This structure is established a-priori, in the sense that it remains stable during one round of experiments. Thus, before each round, we randomly build the graph structure of the system architecture by selecting the neighbors of each peer.

Each peer $p_i$ owns a quantity $q_i$ from some resource $R$. The resource $R$ (which might be a service) is defined by a set of attributes (properties) $\{is_1, ..., is_k\}$ that characterize the resource. These issues might be the price, the resource quality etc. and can hold numerical values $\{v_{i,1}, v_{i,2}, ..., v_{i,k}\}$, specific for the resource provider $p_i$. For the sake of simplicity, we endow the system with only one sort of resource $R$ and we vary the attributes' values.

We consider various endowments of the system with resources. Thus, the wealth can be uniformly distributed among the peers or peers might be unequally equipped with resources (e.g. some peers might own a big quantity and might ask for a higher price in contrast with other peers that can supply only with a small quantity of resource).

Upon this peer-to-peer infrastructure we construct the resource aggregation functionality employing two mechanisms: resource discovery and partner selection. During resource discovery, the process starts at a node - called *initiator* - that demands a quantity $Q_d$ of the resource $R$ for $T_d$ units of time. We assume the network is equipped with some resource discovery mechanism to search the network in order to discover potential resource providers [16]. The discovery mechanism has some intrinsic discovery power in the sense that it is able to investigate a fraction $f$ of the total number of peers. The resource discovery process returns a list of potential partners (providers).

Next, the partner selection mechanism is applied. During this phase, the initiator selects the proper peers to aggregate resources from, by applying a decision model on the list returned by the resource discovery mechanism. Section 4 describes several decision models investigated for the partner selection phase. If the initiator can not aggregate the entire demanded quantity, the query fails.

At the end of the resource aggregation process the initiator holds an optimal list with selected partners as the result of the query injected into the system.

The time $T_d$ related with a resource demand indicates the duration in time units for which the initiator will hold occupied the selected resource, during resource usage.

Models for resource discovery in peer-to-peer architectures are presented in [16]. Among them, we can consider the deterministic simple-flooding broadcasting protocol [13]. With message broadcasting, each resource query is broadcasted by the initiator in the network with a time-to-live (TTL) parameter. The TTL is strongly related with the connection degree of the network. They determine the number of nodes reached by the search - the query horizon. The bigger the TTL, the farther the message is delivered in the network and the query horizon of the resource discovery mechanism increases. The theoretical query horizon can be deduced out of the network size, topology and TTL. The actual horizon is the total number of distinct nodes that actually respond the queries.

In our setup, a round of experiments consists of multiple resource demands, each being delivered at individual time units on the time scale. For a resource demand, a peer $p_i$ is randomly selected and it initiates a query for $Q_d$ quantity of resources with $T_d$. The resource discovery mechanism retrieves a list of potential providers. Next, the initiator applies some decision model in order to select the peers to aggregate resources from. The efficacy of the selection is evaluated and next, the transaction happens in the sense that the selected peers will have the selected quantity of resource unavailable for the next $T_d$ units of time. This resource demand scenario is applied several times and at the end, we report the total efficacy achieved.

During experimentation (section 5), we test several decision models, by changing various inputs, and we report and conclude about how effective each model is for resource aggregation.

User satisfaction is evaluated globally, after each round of experiments. Global user satisfaction is a summation of the individual utility acquired from each resource aggregation process, in response to a service demand. The computation of an individual result is based on the number of selected partners $N_p$, the total prices $P_i$, $i = \overline{1, N_p}$ required by each partner and the quantities $Q_i$ delivered for the prices $P_i$. Initiators are interested in:

- aggregating all the demanded quantity $Q_d$
- minimizing the payments
- minimizing the risks associated with the transaction delivery. In our case, risks increase with the number of partners per transaction.

Eq. 1 describes the individual 'utility' associated with a query.

$$U_d = \frac{1}{N_p} \times \frac{1}{\sum_{i=1}^{N_p} P_i} \times \frac{1}{\sum_{i=1}^{N_p} Q_i} \tag{1}$$

The bigger the utility yielded by a demand $d$, the better. Utilities are aggregated over all demands in a run of experiments to obtain the global utility $U_g$ of a system setup. The global utility $U_g$ characterizes the social welfare concept, presented in [4].

From the consumers' point of view, the objective is to minimize the payments. From the providers' point of view, the objective is to maximize the payments.

Besides the above-described utility, we could also count the number of failures to supply the entire demanded quantity and the total payments. But, as we have seen in [14], for every initial endowment of the network, the system architect can select a TTL big enough to eliminate failures. Thus, in this paper we will not be concerned any more about the number of failures.

# 4 Decision Models for Resource Aggregation

In this section we describe the decision models employed in the partner selection phase.

As indicated by the decision making literature [1, 7], decision makers take action based on various criteria and on their preference among them. Criteria can be qualitative and quantitative and the decision models are parametric or non-parametric as they employ rankings of the alternatives based on their evaluations, or they fully employ the evaluations of the criteria in some more complicated computations.

The ranking produced by a decision model is valuable for us when no single provider can deliver the demanded quantity. Thus, the provider will have a mean to select the top-ranked potential providers in order to aggregate the demanded quantity. If one provider can supply the demand, the initiator will select the first-ranked potential provider.

In this study we apply and evaluate the performances of some representative decision models from both parametric and non-parametric categories. Thus, we employ Onicescu, Global Utility (from MAUT) and Promethee models, presented in the following subsections.

## 4.1 Onicescu

Onicescu model is a non-parametric decision model, presented in [9], developed by the Romanian mathematician Octav Onicescu, which is applicable in the same initial conditions of the ELECTRE method (version with one decision maker) [7]. The key requirements of the method are:

- the decision makers include more criteria in the model;
- actions are evaluated on an ordinal scale;
- a strong heterogeneity related to the nature of the evaluations exists among criteria;
- compensation of the loss on a given criterion by the gain on another may not be acceptable for the decision maker.

The Onicescu algorithm assigns a score to each alternative and ranks the alternatives based on their scores. The score is an evaluation of the decision maker's preference for the evaluated alternative. We present below two variants of the Onicescu's decision criteria algorithm.

Given the set of alternatives $V = \{v_i\}$, $i = \overline{1,n}$, the decision maker uses a set of criteria $C = \{c_j\}$, $j = \overline{1,k}$ to evaluate the alternatives. In our case, potential providers represent the alternatives, and the price and quantity proposed by peers are the criteria.

The Onicescu algorithm starts with a matrix $A$ of size $n \times k$ having a line for each alternative and a column for each decision criteria. Value $a_{i,j}$ represents the actual values of the $i$th alternative for the $j$th criterion. Next, the algorithm builds a matrix $B$ of size $n \times k$ where the value $b_{i,j}$ represents the rank of value $a_{i,j}$ among the values on the column $j$ of $A$. Hence, the $b_{i,j}$ represents the ranking of alternative $v_i$ on criterion $c_j$.

In the objective version of the Onicescu's algorithm, from $B$, we further build a new matrix $C$ of size $n \times n$, where $c_{i,j}$ represents the count of rank $j$ for the alternative $v_i$ on all values on line $i$ of $B$. Thus, matrix $C$ depicts how many times alternative $v_i$ ranked first, second, third etc. among all decision criteria. Equation 2 gives the score for an alternative $v_i$ computed out of C:

$$SC_1(v_i) = \sum_{j=1}^{n} c_{i,j} \frac{1}{2^j} \qquad (2)$$

Next, each alternative is ranked according to the score $SC_1$, the best one being the one that scores highest.

The subjective version of Onicescu's algorithm takes as input the matrix $B$ containing all rankings of alternatives $v_i$ for all criteria. This version allows the decision maker to assign importance weights to each criterion. Assuming that the $k$ criteria are ordered according with the preference of the decision maker (criterion 1 being the most preferred one, next criterion 2 and so on), eq. 3 presents a possible weighting scheme that assigns to each criterion twice as much importance than to the next positioned one:

$$W = \{w_j, w_j = \frac{1}{2^j}, j = \overline{1,k}\} \qquad (3)$$

Using this weighting scheme, the subjective Onicescu's score for each decision alternative is presented in eq. 4:

$$SC_2(v_i) = \sum_{j=1}^{k} w_j \frac{1}{2^{b_{i,j}}} \qquad (4)$$

The variants of Onicescu differ only on the score assigned to the decision alternatives. We note that the subjective variant of Onicescu personalizes the decision making process. Each decision maker is free to consider her own preference order among criteria and this preference order might vary from a resource demand to another. More, the decision maker can use other weighting schemes instead the one described in eq. 3 and recommended in [9]. The subjective approach was envisaged as more realistic, coming close to the real-world decision problems.

## 4.2 Promethee

Promethee [2] is another non-parametric decision model which employs pairwise comparisons to produce a ranking of potential providers. The literature [7] describes this method as representative for a decision maker due to its structure. Hence, it takes into consideration preferences and priorities of the decision maker, providing a *space of freedom* [7] for her. Also, Promethee does not assess an intrinsic absolute utility for an alternative, neither on a criterion nor globally, but makes pairwise comparisons, which provides the decision maker with a thorough perception over the alternatives.

Promethee considers the set of criteria $C$ and the set of alternatives $V$ as defined above for the Onicescu model. Like other multicriteria decision aids, Promethee starts from an evaluation table, then, by making pairwise comparisons of the evaluations within a criterion, assesses a dominance relation. After comparing the evaluations $c_j(a)$ and $c_j(b)$, the dominance relation between alternatives $(a,b) \in V$ can fall into one of the following situations, as defined in [7]:

- $aPb$, meaning that alternative $a$ is strictly preferred to $b$,
- $aIb$, meaning that there is some indifference (equivalence) between $a$ and $b$, and
- $aRb$, meaning that $a$ and $b$ are incomparable.

The practice of the pairwise comparisons can lead to incomparability of the alternatives. Thus, some additional information is required for reducing the incomparability occurrences and turn them into preference relations. The main distinction between different decision models is the additional information they require from the decision maker. Thus, Promethee requires information within each criterion and between criteria. The information within each criterion is represented by a preference function defined as in equation 5.

$$P_j(a,b) = F_j[d_j(a,b)], \; \forall a, b \in V \tag{5}$$

The preference function above takes as input the amplitude of the deviation between two evaluations of the same criteria $j$: $d_j(a,b) = c_j(a) - c_j(b)$ and yields a $P$ or $I$ state. The literature [7] proposes several models for the preference function P:

- Usual criterion: $P(d) = \begin{cases} 0, \; if \; d \leq 0 \\ 1, \; otherwise \end{cases}$

- U-shape criterion: $P(d) = \begin{cases} 0, \; if \; d \leq q \\ 1, \; otherwise \end{cases}$

- V-shape criterion: $P(d) = \begin{cases} 0, \; if \; d < 0 \\ \frac{d}{p}, \; if \; 0 \leq d \leq p \\ 1, \; if \; d > p \end{cases}$

- Gaussian criterion: $P(d) = \begin{cases} 1 - e^{-\frac{d^2}{2s^2}} \; if \; d > 0 \\ 0, \; otherwise \end{cases}$

- Level criterion: $P(d) = \begin{cases} 0, \; if \; d \leq q \\ \frac{1}{2} \; if \; q < d < p \\ 1, \; if \; d > p \end{cases}$

Each decision maker should have in mind a preference function for each criterion $c(\cdot)$, which highly influences the result of Promethee.

The key-facts for adjusting the result yielded by Promethee are the thresholds for some of the preference functions. That means that the decision maker can decide for himself which is the threshold for the amplitude of the deviation to consider the preference relation between the alternatives. In other words, the decision maker is free to establish how significant has to be the deviation to determine the preference relation.

Having the above prerequisites established, the Promethee decision model can be applied. Based on the fact that each alternative is facing $m-1$ other alternatives, Promethee calculates the outranking flows, defined in [7]: the positive outranking flows $\phi^+(a)$ which expresses how many times an alternative outranks all the others and the negative outranking flows $\phi^-(a)$ which expresses how many times an alternative is outranked by all the others. Thus, the higher the $\phi^+(a)$, the better.

At least two versions of the Promethee decision aid exist [7]: Promethee I, which ends by providing the positive and negative outranking flows and Promethee II. This latter version can yield a final ranking, by calculating the *net outranking flow*, $\phi(a) = \phi^+(a) - \phi^-(a)$. Thus, the higher the net flow, the better the alternative. We employ in our study the Promethee II, since we need a complete ranking of the alternatives.

### 4.3 The Multi-Attribute Utility Theory

The Multi-Attribute Utility Theory (MAUT) [11] represents a class of parametric decision aids that fully employ the values scored by each candidate alternative for the various decision criteria. MAUT is based on the preference theory which assumes the existence of a binary preference relation $\succ$ on the choice set of alternatives.

Given that for each criterion a best and worst scored value can be objectively observed and an ordinary relation exists for the criterion values, the binary preference relation can be deducted as follows:

- for each criterion $j$ of an alternative choice $a$, weights the deviation between the scored value $c_j(a)$ and the worst value for the criterion and report it to the deviation between the best and worst evaluations.

Thus, the valuation of an alternative is calculated by summating the relative valuations within each criterion, as in equation 6 [9]:

$$U(a) = \sum_{j=1}^{n} \frac{c_j(a) - worst(c_j(\cdot))}{best(c_j(\cdot)) - worst(c_j(\cdot))} \tag{6}$$

Alternatives $a$ are ranked according with their scored evaluations $U(a)$.

# 5 Experiments and results

In this section we describe the experiments and comment the obtained results. Experimentation is performed on the message-based simulator for a P2P network used in [14] extended with modules for Promethee and MAUT-based decision aids. We employ the P2P system architecture described in section 3 with the broadcasting protocol for resource discovery. Next, we present the set of the main system parameters that guide our experiments:

- the TTL of the broadcasting mechanism employed for resource discovery,
- the query horizon ($H_d$), meaning the number of potential providers that an initiator discovers; this is the practical achieved value for the parameter $f$ - the coverage factor of the resource discovery mechanism,
- the number of selected providers $N_p$,
- the initial endowment $q_i$ of a node,
- the total number of request messages ($N_m$) broadcasted for a particular resource demand (This is a cost measure for the resource discovery mechanism), and
- the demanded quantity $Q_d$ for a query; might be (i) low, (ii) high or can uniformly vary between the low and the high value. Each fulfilled query will hold the committed resources busy for the next $T_d$ queries, with $T_d$ being set up to a random number from 2 to 10. The demanded quantity is in fact the load factor of the network, as employed in [5].

We experiment on three different network setups regarding the distribution of $q_i$ as in [14]: $q_i \approx \frac{1}{QN}$: the welfare is uniformly distributed in the network, $q_i \approx Pois(1)$: very few nodes hold large quantities of resources and $q_i \approx Pois(4)$: only few nodes own large or small quantities of resources. We consider this third scenario closer to the reality.

For the rest of our discussion, a scenario (or a round of experiments) is a set of 100 queries initiated by participants randomly chosen from a network of 500 nodes. The results we present below scales proportionally with the network size and the load in queries, by maintaining the same network topology.

First, we inspect how the different decision models perform in terms of the global utility as a function of TTL (figure 1), as we expect that a higher TTL value would lead to a broader horizon and therefore, a better satisfaction. Thus, for a uniformly distributed load $Q_d$ of the network, we run scenarios for each decision model and a range of TTL values.

We notice that the total utility $U_g$ increases with the TTL, as depicted in figure 1. We also notice that decision aids show similar performances without regard to the distribution of $q_i$, except the MAUT-based decision aid, which performs differently. Hence, this method performs better when the value of $q_i$ has a Pois(1) distribution, nearly equaling the performance of Promethee aid. For the rest of the distribution types of $q_i$ Promethee yields best results in terms of global utility. We also notice that both Promethee and the MAUT-based parametric method yield better results than Onicescu. This means that is worth to investigate more complex decision models when designing the resource aggregation inside a P2P architecture.

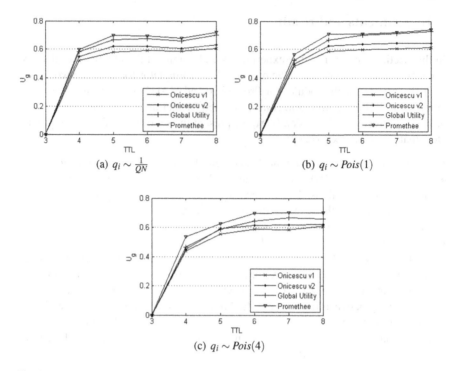

**Fig. 1** Total utility curves for different distributions of $q_i$ value

Next, within the same scenario we highlight the variation of two parameters: the query horizon $H_d$ and number of selected participants $N_p$ (figure 2). In figure 2 we considered the $q_i \approx Pois(4)$ distribution of wealth, corresponding with the situation in figure 1(c). Query horizon and the number of selected partners is almost the same for the rest of decision models. Thus, it means that Promethee succeeds to improve the global user satisfaction not by minimizing the payments and increasing the monetary benefits but, from reducing the risks associated with the aggregation transactions.

Out of figure 2, we extract an interesting conclusion: the Promethee method which supplies with the best user satisfaction achieves it with fewer selected participants in the aggregation (figure 2(b)), which leaves a larger available horizon for the forthcomming queries (figure 2(a))

Further, we inspect the the way in which the network load influences the global utility $U_g$. Thus, for a range of TTL values we run experiments with high as well as low values of $Q_d$. Figure 3 presents the results.

We notice that even for high loads of the P2P network (figure 3(a)), still the Promethee method produces the best results. The low loads of the network (figure 3(b)) shows how weak is a simpler decision model like Onicescu.

In [14] we emphasized that a subjective decision model has the power to lead to better user satisfaction in heterogeneous environments, characterized by medium

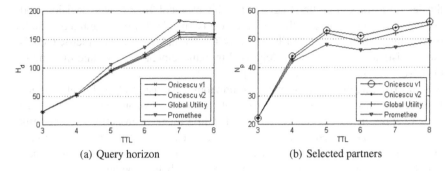

(a) Query horizon                  (b) Selected partners

**Fig. 2** Horizon and selected partners variation

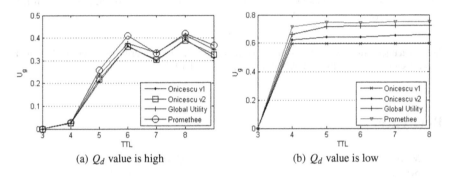

(a) $Q_d$ value is high               (b) $Q_d$ value is low

**Fig. 3** Global utility for high and low loads of network queries

to high network loads and un-evenly distributed wealth. This conclusion is further supported by the evidences extracted out of our experimentation, which put the Promethee method in front of the rest. Promethee is strongly characterized by subjectivity, in the sense of the concept defined in section 4.1. In Promethee, each decision maker has its own (subjective) preference relation among the criteria, similar with the MAUT. We also noticed that the parametric MAUT-based model scored better results than Onicescu.

Another conclusion is the fact that Promethee overpasses MAUT indicates that a ranking extracted from local pairwise comparisons performs better than a ranking computed from a global evaluation.

# 6 Conclusion

In this paper we investigated several decision models in order to achieve an effective resource aggregation in peer-to-peer architectures. We present here the general resource aggregation scenario in a totally unstructured P2P network equipped with the deterministic simple-flooding broadcasting protocol. Investigated decision models were selected to cover all the important decision aids classes: a parametric model originating in the Multiple Attribute Utility Theory and two non-parametric models: the sophisticated Promethee, widely used in management sciences and the simpler Onicescu, previously employed in [14].

Our experiments further support the previous conclusion of [14], that a subjective decision model can bring more user satisfaction in environment, by letting each node to apply its own preferences when deciding for the transaction partners. But, we found out that refined methods like Promethee can further enhance the gains and also reduce the transaction risks by globally reducing the number of selected partners for resource aggregation. Promethee proved to behave better even for difficult conditions, like a high query load. Selecting a proper decision model is important, while both the MAUT-based method and Promethee overpassed Onicescu, even for setups with low network load.

**Acknowledgements** This work is supported by the Romanian Authority for Scientific Research under doctoral scholarship no. 399/2008 and the project IDEI_2452.

# References

1. M. Abdellaoui, J. D. Hey, *Advances in Decision Making Under Risk and Uncertainty*. Springer, 2008.
2. J.P. Brans, M. Mareschal, Ph. Vincke, How to select and how to rank projects: the promethee method. *European Journal of Operational Research*, 24(2):228 – 238, 1986.
3. G. Canfora, M. Di Penta, R. Esposito, M. L. Villani, An approach for qos-aware service composition based on genetic algorithms. In *GECCO '05: Proc. of the 2005 Conf. on Genetic and Evolutionary Computation*, pages 1069–1075. ACM, 2005.
4. Y. Chevaleyre, P. E. Dunne, U. Endriss, J. Lang, M. Lematre, N. Maudet, J. Padget, S. Phelps, J. A. Rodrguez-aguilar, P. Sousa, Issues in multiagent resource allocation. *Informatica*, 30(1):3–31, 2006.
5. L. Chunlin, L. Layuan, Multi economic agent interaction for optimizing the aggregate utility of grid users in computational grid. *Applied Intelligence*, 25(2):147–158, 2006.
6. M. Feldman, K. Lai, I. Stoica, J. Chuang. Robust incentive techniques for peer-to-peer networks. In *Proc. of the 5th ACM Conf. on Electronic Commerce, New York, NY, USA*, pages 102–111, 2004.
7. J. Figueira, S. Greco, M. Ehrgott. *Multiple Criteria Decision Analysis:State of the Art Surveys*. Springer, 2005.
8. I. T. Foster, A. Iamnitchi, On death, taxes, and the convergence of peer-to-peer and grid computing. In *Peer-to-Peer Systems II, Second Intl. Workshop, IPTPS 2003*, volume 2735 of *LNCS*, pages 118–128. Springer, 2003.
9. L. Ilies, M. Mortan, D. Lungescu, I. Lazar, M. Popa, V. Veres, *Handbook of Management (in Romanian)*. Risoprint, 2006.
10. R. Jurca, B. Faltings, Reputation-based pricing of p2p services. In *P2PECON '05: Proc. of the 2005 ACM SIGCOMM Workshop on Economics of Peer-to-Peer Systems*, pages 144–149. ACM, 2005.
11. R. L. Keeney, H. Raiffa, *Decisions with Multiple Objectives: Preferences and Value Trade-Offs*. Cambridge University Press, 1993.

12. L. Xiang-Yang, W. YanWei, X. Ping, C. GuiHai, L. Mo, Hidden information and actions in multi-hop wireless ad hoc networks. In *MobiHoc '08: Proc. of the 9th ACM Intl. Symposium on Mobile Ad Hoc Networking and Computing*, pages 283–292. ACM, 2008.
13. I.-H. Mkwawa, D. Kouvatsos, Broadcasting methods in mobile ad hoc networks: An overview. In *Technical Proc. of the Third Intl. Working Conf. HET-NETs 2005*, pages T9/1–14. Networks UK, 2005.
14. M. Moca, G. C. Silaghi, Resource aggregation effectiveness in peer-to-peer architectures. In *Advances in Grid and Pervasive Computing, 4th Intl. Conf. GPC 2009, Geneva, Switzerland.*, volume 5529 of *Lecture Notes in Computer Science*, pages 388–399. Springer, 2009.
15. M. Rogers, S. Bhatti, Cooperation in decentralised networks. *London Communications Symposium*, 2005.
16. P. Trunfio, D. Talia, H. Papadakis, P. Fragopoulou, M. Mordacchini, M. Pennanen, K. Popov, V. Vlassov, S. Haridi, Peer-to-peer resource discovery in grids: Models and systems. *Future Generation Computer Systems*, 23(7):864–878, 2007.

# Mapping Workflows on Grid Resources: Experiments with the Montage Workflow

Rizos Sakellariou and Henan Zhao and Ewa Deelman

**Abstract** Scientific workflows have received considerable attention in Grid computing. This paper is concerned with the issue of scheduling scientific workflows and, by considering a commonly used astronomy workflow, Montage, investigates the impact of different strategies to schedule the workflow graph. Our experiments suggest that the rather regular and symmetric nature of the Montage graph allows rather simple to implement scheduling heuristics that do not take into account the whole structure of the graph, such as Min-min, to deliver competitive performance in most cases of interest. The results support the view that sophisticated graph scheduling heuristics may not be always a prerequisite for good performance in workflow execution. Instead, mechanisms to deal with uncertainties in execution time may be of comparatively higher importance.

**Key words:** Grid scheduling, DAG scheduling, Montage workflow application

## 1 Introduction

A number of scientific applications consist of individual, standalone application components, each often independently designed and developed, which are then combined in pre-defined ways to perform large-scale scientific analysis. In recent years, *scientific workflows* [9, 22] have been used to refer to the process of bringing the individual components together and specifying their interactions in a systematic

Rizos Sakellariou
School of Computer Science, University of Manchester, Manchester M13 9PL, United Kingdom,
e-mail: rizos@cs.man.ac.uk

Henan Zhao
School of Computer Science, University of Manchester, Manchester M13 9PL, United Kingdom

Ewa Deelman
USC Information Sciences Institute, 4676 Admiralty Way, Marina Del Rey, CA90292, USA

way. Once a scientific workflow (or simply workflow) has been assembled, a key problem that needs to be addressed relates to *mapping* the components of the workflow onto distributed resources, that is, what node of the graph is going to execute on what resource. This problem needs to take into account all constraints (for instance, some components may have to execute on specific nodes) as well as to optimize for various objectives such as the overall completion time of the workflow, resource usage, (monetary) cost of using the resources, etc.

Since most known types of workflows appear to be typically represented by a Directed Acyclic Graph (DAG), there has been a considerable amount of work trying to solve this workflow mapping problem using DAG scheduling heuristics [4, 25, 27]. Such heuristics generally aim at minimizing the cost of running the critical path of the graph. However, it has been argued [12] that such heuristics, although worthwhile, might not be substantially more efficient in the particular context of workflow scheduling on the grid; their benefits might be outweighed by their additional complexity. This argument can be reinforced by the easy to make observation that DAGs representing many real-world workflow applications seem to have a somewhat regular and symmetric structure. As a consequence, simple scheduling approaches, which do not consider the whole structure of the DAG at once, might be a good alternative for workflow scheduling. Following the broad classification in [4, 26], we term the latter approaches as *local* (or task-based), since their decision making strategy relies on locally optimal choices, as opposed to *global* (or *workflow-based* according to [4]) strategies that consider the whole structure of the graph.

To the best of our knowledge, there has been only limited work trying to evaluate and quantify the advantages and disadvantages of local strategies versus global strategies when mapping workflows on the grid. In [4], it has been found that the difference in the makespan between a global and a local strategy using the well-known Montage workflow [2, 17] was less than 0.3%. However, the difference would increase to more than 100% for data-intensive workflows, where the communication cost would dominate computation (see Table 1 in [4]). In contrast, the experimental study in [12] has indicated that a simple local strategy can also cope with data-intensive cases and high communication to computation cost; however, the authors of this study notice limitations for the local strategy in the case of sparse DAGs, which are due to the small degree of parallelism or the small number of dependencies amongst the tasks.

In this paper, we contribute to the quantitative evaluation of the advantages and disadvantages of local versus global strategies by considering the impact of *uncertainty* in workflow mapping, using, in our study, a workflow that implements a widely mentioned astronomy application to build mosaics of the sky, Montage [2, 17]. Since the initial mapping decisions for the workflow are made on the basis of static estimates, a key factor in the evaluation of the performance of local vs global strategies is how well the initial mapping onto resources performs when there are deviations from the estimated execution time of each task.[1] The ability of

---

[1] Such deviations, from the initially estimated execution time, may be due to any reason: wrong prediction, resource load, etc. In principle, these deviations can be corrected at run-time using, for example, rescheduling [21] or adaptive [14] techniques. However, there is also a need to minimize

a scheduling algorithm to produce a schedule that is affected as little as possible by run-time changes is known as *robustness* and, for limited degrees of uncertainty, has been studied elsewhere [7]. In this paper, we use large degrees of uncertainty, which include actual execution times that may be up to 4 times higher than initially estimated (these times can also be shorter than the estimates). Our simulation results validate our hypothesis: when using Montage, variations between local and global workflow mapping strategies are insignificant (at most about 3.5%) and appear to be consistent regardless of the degree of uncertainty with respect to the initial execution times estimates. Instead, by using a tweaked version of the Montage DAG, with a smaller number of edges, and longer parallel paths in the graph, the variation in execution time between local and global workflow mapping strategies becomes more profound, up to about 12%. This indicates some correlation of the performance of these mapping strategies strategies with the type of the DAG they are applied to.

The remainder of the paper is structured as follows. Section 2 provides some background on the problem of DAG/workflow scheduling and relevant heuristics. Section 3 gives a motivating example that highlights the possible differences in performance that some heuristics may exhibit depending on the structure of the graph considered. Section 4 is trying to assess the possible differences in performance between a local, task-based, approach and a global, workflow-based, approach when scheduling Montage [10], a commonly cited application used in astronomy to create a large mosaic image of the sky from many smaller astronomical images. Finally, Section 5 concludes the paper.

## 2 Background

The model used for the representation of a workflow is a Directed Acyclic Graph (DAG), where nodes (or tasks) represent computation and edges represent data or control flow dependences between nodes. A set of machines is assumed to be already available and known. These machines and the network links between them are heterogeneous: tasks may need a different amount of time to execute on each machine and the transmission of data between different machines is not the same. A machine can execute only one task at a time, and a task cannot start execution until all data from its parent nodes is available. The scheduling problem is to assign the tasks onto machines so that precedence constraints are respected and the makespan is minimized.

In order to be able to make sensible scheduling decisions, it is assumed that information about the estimated execution time of each task on each machine is available. In addition, it is assumed that there are estimates about the speed of the links connecting the machines available. This information, used in conjunction with the amount of data that may need to be transferred before a task starts its execution,

---

the overhead associated with rescheduling and/or adaptivity and keep the number of times when such an action occurs small. Our work focuses on how the initial workflow mapping decisions can help in this respect.

can provide an estimate about the earliest possible start time of a task whose parents have finished their execution.

The problem of scheduling DAGs onto parallel resources is well studied in the literature [13]. In recent years, partly as a result of the emergence of Grid systems and applications such as workflows, additional research has focused on DAG scheduling algorithms for heterogeneous systems [20, 23, 27], as well as their performance in the context of the uncertainties typically associated with the actual execution time of tasks [7, 11, 15, 21]. A growing amount of work has also evaluated DAG scheduling algorithms in the context of specific workflow applications [4, 16, 24].

As already mentioned, it is common to classify DAG scheduling algorithms according to whether scheduling decisions are made *locally*, with reference to just a task or a set of tasks, or *globally*, with reference to the whole DAG (workflow) [4, 26]. A commonly used heuristic in the former class (task-based) is *Min-min*, originally developed in the context of scheduling independent tasks [5]. This can also be applied in the context of scheduling DAGs, since, at any point in time, the tasks that are considered to be eligible for scheduling are, by definition, independent. This is because the eligible tasks are tasks whose data is available, hence, their parents have finished execution. The key idea of Min-min is to find, for each eligible task, the machine that gives the earliest completion time for this task. Then, the task with the minimum earliest completion time is chosen for scheduling. The process is then repeated with the remaining task as well as any new tasks that become eligible (as a result of the completion of their parents). As noticed in [4], "the intuition behind this heuristic is that the makespan increases the least at each iterative step, hopefully resulting in a small makespan for the whole workflow".

A commonly cited global heuristic in the context of DAG scheduling for heterogeneous systems is HEFT [23]. HEFT first orders tasks by assigning a value to each task. This value roughly corresponds to the cost to reach the exit node from this task. Then, tasks are scheduled using this order to the machine that gives the earliest completion time. The key idea (of this *list scheduling* based heuristic [18]) is to give higher priority to tasks on the critical path. Several variations to assign weights and prioritize the tasks have been studied in [28]. Following observations about the impact of such variations, HBMCT [20] tries to improve the performance of HEFT by relaxing the requirement to schedule tasks in a strict order of their ranking, considering groups of independent tasks. Among the global heuristics, it is also worth mentioning the workflow-based allocation algorithm (WBA) [4], which compares several alternative workflow schedules before the final schedule is chosen, based on a generalized greedy randomized adaptive search procedure.

Typically, heuristics that make decisions locally (task-based) are simpler and faster, whereas heuristics that make decisions globally, with reference to the whole workflow (workflow-based), have the potential to produce a shorter makespan at the expense of increased complexity. Such a potentially shorter makespan is a consequence of their ability to consider the whole graph at once and, hence, give appropriate priority in execution to tasks in the critical path. The hypothesis considered in this paper, however, is that the regular and symmetric structure of scientific workflows does not stand to benefit from global heuristics. To illustrate the impact that the structure of the graph may have, we present two examples in the next section.

## 3 A Motivating Example

The simplicity of local, task-based approaches as opposed to the shorter makespan expected to be produced by a global, workflow-based approach is the key trade-off to assess when selecting the heuristic that would be more suitable to schedule a certain application. In the context of arbitrary DAGs, global heuristics, which are capable of tracking the critical path, are expected to give better performance. However, it is questionable whether the examples of scientific workflows that exist can be regarded as *arbitrary* DAGs. Instead, all the evidence available seems to suggest that many scientific workflows have a regular and rather symmetric structure. Many appear to consist of sequences of fan-out (where the output of a task is input to several children) and fan-in (where the output of several tasks is aggregated by a child). Typically, the outcome of fan-out procedures is identical tasks that simply operate on different data (indicating the exploitation of data parallelism). For examples, we refer to workflows such as Montage (see Figure 9 in [10]), Chimera (see Figures 6 and 7 in [1]), LIGO (see Figure 4 in [19]), WIEN2k (see Figure 6 in [24]), Invmod (see Figure 7 in [24]) and AIRSN (see Figure 5 in [29]) as well as the workflows studied in [3].

In order to illustrate the possible differences in the schedule resulting from a local heuristic, Min-min, and a global heuristic, HBMCT, and how they are affected by the structure of the graph, consider the examples in Figures 1 and 2. The graph in Figure 1 has a rather regular, symmetric structure. We view it as regular because it consists of a sequence of fan-out and fan-in (repeated twice) and symmetric because the independent subgraphs created during the fan-out procedure are identical (in terms of their structure). In addition, the execution time of the tasks on three different machines, M0, M1, M2, is similar, although not always identical (see the table at the top right of the figure), while the cost of sending data from one task to another (when these tasks are executed on different machines) is set to 8 time units. The schedule produced by Min-min and HBMCT is shown at the bottom of the figure (Min-min is on the left-hand side). Both heuristics produce a schedule of an identical length (130 time units), although task assignments to machines are different (and tasks are not necessarily assigned by HBMCT to the fastest machine for the task).

Conversely, the example in Figure 2 considers a graph with an asymmetric structure (for example, each of nodes 6, 7, and 8, which are at the same layer, has a different number of parents: 1, 2, 3, respectively). Also, the execution time of each task on three different machines shows a higher degree of heterogeneity, while the time needed to send data between different machines varies, with the link between machines M0 and M2 being the slowest. In this case, the makespan of the schedule produced by Min-min (left-hand side at the bottom of the figure) is 143.6 time

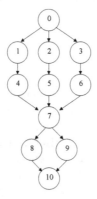

| task | M0 | M1 | M2 |
|------|----|----|----|
| 0 | 25 | 27 | 24 |
| 1 | 24 | 24 | 24 |
| 2 | 25 | 25 | 26 |
| 3 | 24 | 24 | 25 |
| 4 | 16 | 16 | 16 |
| 5 | 16 | 15 | 16 |
| 6 | 14 | 14 | 14 |
| 7 | 10 | 11 | 11 |
| 8 | 12 | 12 | 12 |
| 9 | 11 | 11 | 11 |
| 10 | 15 | 17 | 16 |

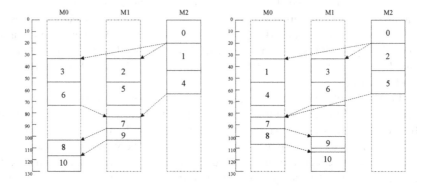

**Fig. 1** Scheduling a regular and symmetric graph using Min-min and HBMCT.

units, while the makespan of the schedule produced by HBMCT (right-hand side) is 124.6, which is approximately 13% better than Min-min. This is because a global approach, such as HBMCT, is capable of giving priority to tasks of those (critical) paths in the graph that have a higher cost (such as the paths consisting of the tasks 0, 1, 7, and 9 and 0, 5, 8, and 9) as opposed to tasks of other paths.

The question that this paper is set to investigate is whether a typical scientific workflow, such as Montage, would stand to benefit significantly from a global, workflow-based approach for scheduling. The hypothesis is that the regular and symmetric structure of the graph in workflows, such as Montage, is the key factor

| task | M0 | M1 | M2 |
|------|----|----|----|
| 0 | 17 | 19 | 21 |
| 1 | 22 | 27 | 23 |
| 2 | 15 | 15 | 9 |
| 3 | 4 | 8 | 9 |
| 4 | 17 | 14 | 20 |
| 5 | 30 | 27 | 18 |
| 6 | 17 | 16 | 15 |
| 7 | 49 | 49 | 46 |
| 8 | 25 | 22 | 16 |
| 9 | 23 | 27 | 19 |

| machines | time for a data unit |
|----------|----------------------|
| M0 - M1 | 0.9 |
| M1 - M2 | 1.0 |
| M0 - M2 | 1.4 |

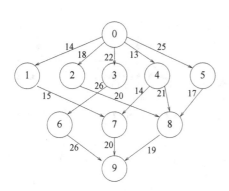

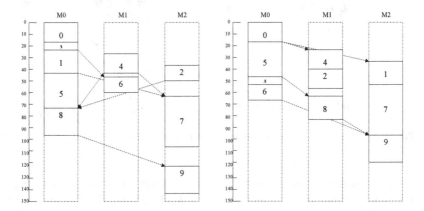

**Fig. 2** Scheduling an asymmetric graph using Min-min and HBMCT.

that makes the performance of local approaches for scheduling equally competitive to the performance of the more complex global strategies.

# 4 Experimental Evaluation

## 4.1 The Simulator and Settings

For the purposes of our evaluation we used a grid simulator built on the top of the network simulator NS-2 [6], which was also used in earlier research [4]. We only briefly describe the grid simulator here; more details can be found in [4]. The

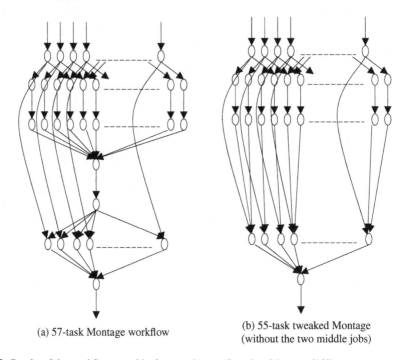

(a) 57-task Montage workflow

(b) 55-task tweaked Montage
(without the two middle jobs)

**Fig. 3** Graphs of the workflows used in the experiments (based on Montage [10]).

simulator models resources, networks connecting different resources, jobs and files. Each file is considered as a separate object. Each resource (i.e., a site) consists of several hosts and each host can run jobs and store files. The simulator can be adapted to include different scheduling algorithms to allocate jobs to sites; as part of this work we adapted it to include HBMCT [20]. Thus, the simulator includes three different approaches for scheduling: one local, task-based, Min-min, and two global, workflow-based, from which one is based on a list scheduling principle, HBMCT, whereas the other, WBA, is not.

The workflow application we considered is Montage [2, 10, 17]. The instance of the workflow we used is shown in Figure 3(a). This contains 57 tasks (adding the tasks of each level from the top the sum is 13+14+14+1+1+13+1). The original version of Montage assumes that tasks at the same level have a similar computation cost. In some of the experiments we considered different types of variation in the execution time of the tasks at each level. In addition, in order to experiment with the structure of the graph, a variant of the Montage graph has also been used; this is shown in Figure 3(b). The latter graph does not contain the middle two tasks of the original graph, thus reducing the degree of synchronization needed and increasing the relative importance of the independent (i.e., parallel) paths in the graph when it comes to the overall makespan.

| QoI | 57-task Montage | | | | 55-task tweaked Montage | | | |
|-----|---------|---------|--------|------|---------|---------|---------|------|
| (%) | Min-min | WBA | HBMCT | % | Min-min | WBA | HBMCT | % |
| 0 | 7802.6 | 7785.4 | 7796.9 | 0.22 | 7302.1 | 7288.5 | 7234.9 | 0.92 |
| 50 | 9146.0 | 9060.4 | 9097.7 | 0.93 | 9750.3 | 9710.6 | 9688.0 | 0.64 |
| 100 | 9949.4 | 9878.8 | 9930.2 | 0.71 | 10293.4 | 9696.1 | 9627.7 | 6.47 |
| 200 | 12562.7 | 12436.4 | 12420.3 | 1.13 | 11949.0 | 11432.3 | 11370.5 | 4.84 |
| 300 | 12763.4 | 12531.3 | 12305.2 | 3.58 | 11273.3 | 10410.1 | 10392.1 | 7.82 |
| 400 | 13125.0 | 12710.7 | 12687.3 | 3.33 | 11287.0 | 10551.1 | 10523.8 | 6.76 |

**Table 1** Overall execution time when tasks at each level have a similar (estimated) execution time.

In order to capture the degree of variation expected between the estimated execution time and the actual execution time of each task, we adopted the notion of the *Quality of Information* (QoI) [8, 21]. This corresponds to an upper bound on the percentage of error that the static estimate may have with respect to the actual execution time. So, for example, a percentage error of 50% indicates that the actual (run-time) execution time of a task will be within 50% (plus or minus) of the static estimate for this task. This value is always positive. In our experiments, we consider values for QoI of 0% (perfect estimates), 50%, 100%, 200%, 300%, and 400%.

## 4.2 Results and Discussion

The objective of our experiments has been to quantify and assess the difference in the performance of the schedule produced by Min-min, HBMCT and WBA, and test our hypothesis that the symmetric and regular structure of the graph does not have much to gain from global scheduling strategies. To achieve our objective, we used:

I Five different values for QoI to check run-time deviations, which are up to four times the estimated execution times of tasks.

II Two different graph structures, one corresponding to a 57-task instance of the original Montage workflow, shown in Figure 3(a), and one corresponding to a 55-task tweaked version of Montage, shown in Figure 3(b), which reduces the degree of synchronization by removing two tasks.

III Three different assumptions about the *estimated* execution time of tasks at each level of the graph. These assumptions are: (a) tasks at each level have a similar execution time; (b) all tasks except the rightmost task at each level have an execution time which is twice the execution time of the rightmost task; and (c) the leftmost task at each level has an execution time which is ten times the execution time of the remaining tasks at the same level.

In the following, we group the results using the three different assumptions for the execution time of the tasks at each level. We also note than, in all cases, the results are averaged over 20 runs and there are always 6 machines available to schedule the tasks of the workflow.

| QoI | 57-task Montage | | | | 55-task tweaked Montage | | | |
|---|---|---|---|---|---|---|---|---|
| (%) | Min-min | WBA | HBMCT | % | Min-min | WBA | HBMCT | % |
| 0 | 14437.2 | 14109.4 | 14120.8 | 2.27 | 14667.2 | 14059.0 | 13527.3 | 7.77 |
| 50 | 16024.3 | 15327.1 | 15545.2 | 4.35 | 15994.0 | 15197.2 | 15068.9 | 5.78 |
| 100 | 18774.0 | 18258.0 | 18223.5 | 2.93 | 17466.2 | 15855.5 | 15356.1 | 12.08 |
| 200 | 33625.5 | 32485.0 | 32448.7 | 3.50 | 28843.6 | 27598.7 | 26832.8 | 6.97 |
| 300 | 39438.9 | 37937.1 | 38066.2 | 3.81 | 39151.8 | 37430.0 | 36557.0 | 6.63 |
| 400 | 51123.0 | 50701.0 | 50278.6 | 1.65 | 50706.6 | 49861.0 | 49211.3 | 2.95 |

**Table 2** Overall execution time when all tasks at each level except the rightmost task have an (estimated) execution time which is twice the (estimated) execution time of the rightmost task.

### 4.2.1 All tasks at each level have a similar (estimated) execution time

Table 1 shows the overall execution time (as provided by the simulator) of the two different variants of Montage considered, when tasks at each level have a similar execution time. The leftmost column shows the upper bound of Quality of Information (QoI) considered in each row. The next three columns show the execution time for each scheduling algorithm used with the 57-task Montage. The fourth column shows the percentage gain of the best global scheduling strategy (that is, the best of WBA and HBMCT) as compared to the task-based Min-min (this value is computed as $100 \times (1 - \min(m_{WBA}, m_{HBMCT})/m_{MinMin}))$, where $m$ is the makespan of the corresponding strategy. From the results, it can be seen that in the case of the 57-task Montage, Min-min has a performance which is comparable to the performance of the workflow-based heuristics. Thus, the gain of global, workflow-based heuristics is less than 1% if the value of QoI is up to 100%, reaching a maximum of just 3.58% in more extreme cases where the value of QoI is higher. The comparatively worse performance of Min-min in the case of high variations in the actual execution time (as opposed to the estimated execution time) may be due to its lower robustness (comparing to HBMCT and WBA), a result also corroborated from [7]. The gain is higher in the case of the tweaked 55-task Montage, due to the higher degree of parallelism, which opens up more opportunities for different schedules. As an aside remark, it is noted that, with the 57-task Montage, WBA has a slightly better performance than HBMCT for small values of QoI, whereas HBMCT tends to perform better as the value of QoI increases (a result also corroborated from [7]). The performance of HBMCT is consistently better than WBA (although not by much) in the case of the 55-task tweaked Montage.

### 4.2.2 All tasks at each level, except the rightmost task, have an (estimated) execution time which is twice the (estimated) execution time of the rightmost task

Table 2 shows the overall execution time when there is some variation in the execution time of the tasks at each level, in particular when the rightmost task has

| QoI | 57-task Montage | | | | 55-task tweaked Montage | | | |
|-----|---------|---------|---------|------|---------|---------|---------|------|
| (%) | Min-min | WBA | HBMCT | % | Min-min | WBA | HBMCT | % |
| 0 | 8213.0 | 8190.6 | 8204.7 | 0.27 | 7685.6 | 7674.8 | 7662.0 | 0.31 |
| 50 | 9297.3 | 9286.6 | 9276.3 | 0.23 | 9311.3 | 9199.4 | 9034.7 | 2.97 |
| 100 | 10105.2 | 10071.0 | 10151.0 | 0.34 | 10323.7 | 10002.8 | 9839.0 | 4.70 |
| 200 | 12946.5 | 12836.4 | 12633.9 | 2.41 | 14181.6 | 12684.3 | 12557.3 | 11.45 |
| 300 | 14277.8 | 14001.6 | 14247.0 | 1.93 | 13926.9 | 12578.5 | 12482.6 | 10.37 |
| 400 | 21896.4 | 21719.1 | 22035.1 | 0.81 | 23462.0 | 21214.3 | 21092.0 | 10.10 |

**Table 3** Overall execution time when the leftmost task at each level has an (estimated) execution time which is 10 times the (estimated) execution time of the other tasks at the same level.

an execution time which is half the execution time of the other tasks at the same level. The impact of this variation is that it creates a particular shorter path as opposed to several longer paths in the graph. The Min-min heuristic still manages to produce reasonably efficient schedules comparing to WBA and HBMCT. Even though these schedules are not as efficient as before, their performance is still only up to 4.35% worse than the performance of the more sophisticated, workflow-based heuristics. We observe the same pattern of behaviour as before; the efficiency of Min-min is worse in the case of the 55-task tweaked Montage. Furthermore, we observe the same pattern of behaviour when we compare the performance of WBA and HBMCT.

### 4.2.3 The leftmost task at each level has an (estimated) execution time, which is 10 times the (estimated) execution time of the other tasks at the same level

Table 3 shows the overall execution time of the workflows when the variation in task execution time is due to an increase in the execution time of the leftmost task at each level, which is 10 times the execution time of the other tasks at the same level. The impact of this variation in execution time is that it creates one relatively long critical path in the graph. It can be seen that in the case of the 57-task Montage the performance of Min-min is clearly comparable to the performance of WBA and HBMCT; it is at most 2.41% worse. In one case (for a value of QoI equal to 400), Min-min even outperforms HBMCT. Same as before, the performance of Min-min worsens in the case of the 55-task tweaked Montage. In fact, interestingly enough, in this case, the deficiency of Min-min is worst comparing to the two previous sets of results.

### 4.2.4 Summary

The results in Tables 1, 2, 3 support our view that in the case of the regular and symmetric Montage application, a local strategy, such as Min-min, does not appear to be inferior to sophisticated global strategies, both when there are large run-time deviations from the actual estimated execution times (i.e., large values of QoI) and when there are differences in the estimated execution time between tasks at each level (as it is the case in Tables 2 and 3). As already hypothesized, this property appears to be a consequence of the structure of the graph. This is supported by our experiments with the tweaked Montage, where Min-min clearly lags behind as a result of its inability to handle efficiently the critical paths. Finally, it is interesting to observe that the introduction of uncertainty in the execution time (which may also cause individual tasks to run faster) on average increases the overall execution time of the workflow by up to more than three times with respect to the statically estimated execution time. This observation suggests that, regardless of the quality of the scheduling heuristic that is used to find an initial mapping for tasks of a DAG, there may be, comparatively, much more to be gained in performance by run-time rescheduling, a finding also supported by the experiments in [14].

# 5 Conclusion

This paper has compared the performance of the schedule produced by three different approaches for scheduling workflows on the Grid. It has been found that scheduling a workflow, such as (a 57-task) Montage, using a simple heuristic that makes only local decisions, Min-min, results in performance which is comparable to the performance obtained with more sophisticated, workflow-based scheduling heuristics such as WBA or HBMCT. The performance of Min-min worsens slightly, but not significantly, when high variations between the estimated and the actual execution time of the tasks of the workflow exist. Min-min also exhibits good performance if the workflow consists of a single critical path with significantly longer execution time. The performance of Min-min drops when there is a single path of shorter length and multiple critical paths in the workflow (cf. Table 2). Its performance worsens even further in the case of a workflow with multiple long parallel paths (cf. the results with the 55-task tweaked Montage). It is noted that this may not be a common case in practice, since, as already mentioned, the structure of several commonly cited workflows consists of alternating fan-out and fan-in phases.

In summary, the results are encouraging in that they suggest that Min-min may be sufficiently efficient in the context of scheduling certain classes of scientific workflows on the Grid even when there are uncertainties in the estimated task execution times. It is noted that the small performance deficits of Min-min can be offset by its inherent simplicity and the ease with which it can be adopted to perform adaptive rescheduling at run-time, options that have been shown to be relatively more important when addressing run-time changes [14, 21]. Future work can expand the preliminary experimental study of this paper. Also, it can try to find out under what circumstances the relative importance of run-time changes dominates the choice of an appropriate heuristic for the initial mapping onto the resources.

# References

1. J. Annis, Y. Zhao, J. Voeckler, M. Wilde, S. Kent, and I. Foster. Applying Chimera virtual data concepts to cluster finding in the Sloan Sky Survey. In: *Supercomputing'02: Proceedings of the 2002 ACM/IEEE Conference on Supercomputing*, Los Alamitos, CA, USA, IEEE Computer Society Press, 2002, pp. 1-14.
2. G. B. Berriman, J. C. Good, A. C. Laity, *et al.* Montage: A Grid Enabled Image Mosaic Service for the National Virtual Observatory. In *Astronomical Data Analysis Software & Systems (ADASS) XIII*, 2003.
3. S. Bharathi, A. Chervenak, E. Deelman, G. Mehta, M.-H. Su, and K. Vahi. Characterization of Scientific Workflows. In *Proceedings of the 3rd Workshop on Workflows in Support of Large-Scale Science* (WORKS 2008), November 2008.
4. J. Blythe, S. Jain, E. Deelman, Y. Gil, K. Vahi, A. Mandal, and K. Kennedy. Task Scheduling Strategies for Workflow-based Applications in Grids. In *IEEE International Symposium on Cluster Computing and the Grid (CCGrid 2005)*, 2005.
5. T. D. Braun, H. J. Siegel, N. Beck, L. L. Boloni, M. Maheswaran, A. I. Reuther, J. P. Robertson, M. D. Theys, and B. Yao. A comparison of eleven static heuristics for mapping a class of independent tasks onto heterogeneous distributed computing systems. *Journal of Parallel and Distributed Computing*, vol. 61, pp. 810-837, 2001.
6. L. Breslau, D. Estrin, K. Fall, S. Floyd, J. Heidemann, A. Helmy, P. Huang, S. McCanne, K. Varadhan, Y. Xu, and H. Yu. Advances in network simulation. *Computer*, vol.33(5), pp.59-67, May 2000. See also http://www.isi.edu/nsnam/ns.
7. L.-C. Canon, E. Jeannot, R. Sakellariou, and W. Zheng. Comparative evaluation of the Robustness of DAG Scheduling Heuristics. In *Grid Computing: Achievements and Prospects* (eds: S. Gorlatch, P. Fragopoulou, T. Priol), Springer, 2008, pp. 73-84. An extended version is available as CoreGRID Technical Report TR-0120, December 2007.
8. H. Casanova, A. Legrand, D. Zagorodnov, and F. Berman. Heuristics for scheduling parameter sweep applications in Grid environments. In *Proceedings of the 9th Heterogeneous Computing Workshop (HCW'00)*, 2000, pp. 349-363.
9. E. Deelman, D. Gannon, M. Shields, and I. Taylor. Workflows and e-Science: An overview of workflow system features and capabilities. *Future Generation Computer Systems*, 25, 2009, pp. 528-540.
10. E. Deelman, G. Singh, M. H. Su, J. Blythe, Y. Gil, C. Kesselman, G. Mehta, K. Vahi, G. B. Berriman, J. Good, A. Laity, J. C. Jacob, and D. S. Katz. Pegasus: A framework for mapping complex scientific workflows onto distributed systems. *Scientific Programming*, 13(3), 2005, pp. 219-237.
11. F. Dong and S. G. Akl. PFAS: A Resource-Performance-Fluctuation-Aware Workflow Scheduling Algorithm for Grid Computing. In *Proceedings of IPDPS 2007*, 2007.
12. R. Huang, H. Casanova, and A. A. Chien. Using Virtual Grids to Simplify Application Scheduling. In *Proceedings of IPDPS 2006*, 2006.
13. Y.-K. Kwok and I. Ahmad. Static scheduling algorithms for allocating directed task graphs to multiprocessors. *ACM Computing Surveys*, 31(4), December 1999, pp. 406-471.
14. K. Lee, N. W. Paton, R. Sakellariou, E. Deelman, A. A. A. Fernandes, and G. Mehta. Adaptive Workflow Processing and Execution in Pegasus. In *3rd International Workshop on Workflow Management and Applications in Grid Environments* (WaGe08) (in *Proceedings of the Third International Conference on Grid and Pervasive Computing Symposia/Workshops*, May 25-28 2008, Kunming, China), 2008, pp. 99-106.
15. M. M. Lopez, E. Heymann, and M. A. Senar. Analysis of Dynamic Heuristics for Workflow Scheduling on Grid Systems. In *Proceedings of the 5th International Symposium on Parallel and Distributed Computing* (ISPDC), 2006, pp. 199-207.
16. A. Mandal, K. Kennedy, C. Koelbel, G. Marin, J. Mellor-Crummey, B. Liu, and L. Johnsson. Scheduling Strategies for Mapping Application Workflows onto the Grid. In *IEEE International Symposium on High Performance Distributed Computing (HPDC 2005)*, 2005.
17. Montage. An Astronomical Image Mosaic Engine. http://montage.ipac.caltech.edu/

18. M. L. Pinedo. *Scheduling: Theory, Algorithms, and Systems*. Springer, 2008.
19. A. Ramakrishnan, G. Singh, H. Zhao, E. Deelman, R. Sakellariou, K. Vahi, K. Blackburn, D. Meyers, and M. Samidi. Scheduling Data-Intensive Workflows onto Storage-Constrained Distributed Resources. In *Proceedings of the 7th IEEE International Symposium on Cluster Computing and the Grid* (CCGrid'07), 2007, pp. 401-409.
20. R. Sakellariou and H. Zhao. A Hybrid Heuristic for DAG Scheduling on Heterogeneous Systems. In *Proceedings of the 13th Heterogeneous Computing Workshop (HCW'04)*, Santa Fe, New Mexico, USA, on April 26, 2004.
21. R. Sakellariou and H. Zhao. A low-cost rescheduling policy for efficient mapping of workflows on grid systems. *Scientific Programming*, 12(4), December 2004.
22. I. J. Taylor, E. Deelman, D. B. Gannon, and M. Schields. *Workflows for e-Science. Scientific Workflows for Grids*. Springer, 2007.
23. H. Topcuoglu, S. Hariri, and M.-Y. Wu. Performance-effective and low-complexity task scheduling for heterogeneous computing. *IEEE Transactions on Parallel and Distributed Systems*, 13(3), March 2002, pp. 260-274.
24. M. Wieczorek, R. Prodan, and T. Fahringer. Scheduling of Scientific Workflows in the ASKALON Grid Environment. In *SIGMOD Record*, volume 34(3), September 2005.
25. M. Wieczorek, R. Prodan, and T. Fahringer. Comparison of Workflow Scheduling Strategies on the Grid. In *Proceedings of the Second Grid Resource Management Workshop* (GRMW'2005), Springer, LNCS 3911, 2006, pp. 792-800.
26. J. Yu and R. Buyya. A Taxonomy of Scientific Workflow Systems for Grid Computing. In *SIGMOD Record*, volume 34(3), September 2005.
27. J. Yu, R. Buyya, and K. Ramamohanarao. Workflow Scheduling Algorithms for Grid Computing. In *Studies in Computational Intelligence*, volume 146, Springer, 2008, pp. 173-214.
28. H. Zhao and R. Sakellariou. An experimental investigation into the rank function of the heterogeneous earliest finish time scheduling algorithm. In *Euro-Par 2003*, Springer-Verlag, LNCS 2790, 2003.
29. Y. Zhao, J. Dobson, I. Foster, L. Moreau, and M. Wilde. A notation and system for expressing and executing cleanly typed workflows on messy scientific data. In *SIGMOD Record*, volume 34(3), September 2005, pp. 37-43.

# A Proposal on Enhancing XACML with Continuous Usage Control Features*

Maurizio Colombo, Aliaksandr Lazouski, Fabio Martinelli, and Paolo Mori

**Abstract** Usage control (UCON) proposed by R. Sandhu et al. [8, 9] is an attribute-based authorization model and its main novelties are mutability of attributes and continuity of control.

OASIS eXtensible Access Control Markup Language (XACML) [10] is a widely-used language to write authorization policies to protect resources in a distributed computing environment (e.g. Grid). The XACML policy specifies before-usage authorization process optionally complemented with obligation actions fulfillment. By now, XACML has insufficient facilities to express continuous usage control afterwards an access was granted and started.

In this paper, we introduce U-XACML, a new policy language, which enhances the original XACML with the UCON novelties. We extend a syntax and semantics of the XACML policy to define mutability of attributes and continuity of control. We introduce an architecture to enforce the U-XACML policy.

**Key words:** Access control, usage control, policy language, XACML, UCON, Grid computing

Maurizio Colombo, Fabio Martinelli, Paolo Mori
Istituto di Informatica e Telematica, Consiglio Nazionale delle Ricerche, via G. Moruzzi 1, Pisa, Italy e-mail: \{maurizio.colombo,fabio.martinelli,paolo.mori\}@iit.cnr.it

Aliaksandr Lazouski
Universita di Pisa, via B. Pontecorvo 3, Pisa, Italy e-mail: lazouski@di.unipi.it

* This work has been partially supported by the EU project FP6-033817 GRIDTRUST (*Trust and Security for Next Generation Grids*).

# 1 Introduction

Over the last decade researchers have shown advantages of attribute-based access control. Access decision is based on attributes of a requesting subject, of an accessing object, and of an environment where the computing system operates. Traditional authorization scenarios assume that attributes remain invariable in time. Therefore, authorization conditions can be checked only once before granting an access and they will also hold when the access is in progress. To express comprehensive usage scenarios R. Sandhu et al. [8, 9] proposed the UCON model and an idea of the attributes mutability occurred as a side-effect of the object usage. This idea goes beyond a before-usage authorization and assumes a continuous evaluation of a security policy before granting an access, and when the access is in progress. Essentially, this is important for long-lived accesses, which are peculiarities of Grid computing, e.g. computational services [6, 7, 11]. During last years, UCON has gathered a lot of attention as the most expressive attribute-based access control model.

XACML [10] is an OASIS standard for expressing, combining and managing access control policies in a distributed environment. XACML was designed for attribute-based access control and it is widely used nowadays in many applications and environments due to its extensibility and interoperability. By now, XACML has facilities to express traditional access control.

Several papers stated that XACML needs extension to capture the concept of access decision continuity [4, 11]. Recently, some attempts were done to implement a continuous policy enforcement using XACML [3, 5, 11]. These approaches introduce events that trigger the policy reevaluation when the access is in progress. Security checks are invoked by changes of subject, object, and/or environmental attributes. The focus of these papers was on an architecture and policy enforcement mechanisms, while a few attention was placed on the policy model expressing the UCON model. Moreover, they consider how the XACML is capable to model the UCON. In contrast, our approach considers how XACML should be extended to capture the UCON model.

The aim of this work is to present a flexible policy language called U-XACML, which enhances the original XACML with the UCON novelties. The policy language is designed towards a service oriented architecture and collaborative computing, e.g. the Grid. We analyzed semantics of the XACML policy and the UCON abstract model. We revised the notion of authorizations, obligations, conditions and attribute update actions to establish a unified semantics for the U-XACML. The U-XACML captures attribute updates, continuous policy evaluation, and places conditions triggering ongoing attribute updates and obligations. The original XACML architecture and authorization dataflow was modified to enforce the U-XACML policy. We studied several architectural approaches and shown their advantages and disadvantages.

This paper is organized as follows. Section 2 gives background on XACML and UCON. In section 3 we introduce syntax and semantics of the U-XACML policy language. Section 4 shows an architecture to enforce a continuous usage control.

Section 5 introduces a usage scenario and informal security policy for Grid computational service. We summarize the paper in Section 6.

## 2 Background

### 2.1 UCON

UCON [5, 8, 9] is a novel access control model that addresses problems of modern distributed environments. UCON has two novel aspects: 1) mutability of attributes, and 2) continuity of policy enforcement. Mutability of attributes means that attributes may change in time. Since attributes are used for access decision evaluation, policy statements should be reevaluated continuously whenever any change of any attribute value occurs. UCON implies security policy enforcement not only when the request for an object should be authorized, but also when the actual usage of the object is in progress. This continuous evaluation is particularly important in the case of long-lived accesses, i.e. accesses that lasts hours or even days (e.g. Grid services). If during the usage attribute change violates a security policy, the access has to be revoked and the resource's usage terminated.

The UCON policy is stated using authorizations, obligations and conditions. Authorization predicates put constrains on subject's and/or object's attributes (e.g. subject's name must be "John"). Obligations are mandatory actions performed by an obligation subject (not always a requesting subject). Conditions are environment restrictions (e.g. object is available during working hours).

Generally, the UCON policy is paired with the following meta information:

- *Access decision factor.* A security policy can be stated using authorizations only, obligations only, conditions only, or any of their combinations. These policy statements are encoded by A, B, and C respectively.
- *Access decision timing* specifies when an access decision is evaluated. If the access decision is made before the usage, these scenarios are encoded with a prefix "pre". Access decisions evaluated during the usage are encoded with "on".
- *Attribute update timing* identifies when attributes are updated by the authorization system. Attributes can be updated before the usage (the pre-update action is encoded by (1)), during the usage (on-update action is encoded by (2)), or when the usage is over (post-update action is encoded by (3)). If no attribute updates are needed, the corresponding models are encoded by (0).

Based on the policy meta-information, the UCON model launches 24 core scenarios - combining "pre" and "on" evaluation of authorizations, obligations and conditions with attribute updates that can be performed before (1), during (2), after (3) the access, or no updates (0). For example, the "preA3" model, called as pre-authorization with post-updates, represents a scenario where an access decision is evaluated only once before the usage starts. The access decision is done by checking authorization predicates only, and one or more attributes are updated after the resource usage ends.

## 2.2 XACML

Although, the UCON proposes a comprehensive access control model, it still remains abstract. In contrast, XACML [10] is a widely-used standard to write and manage security policies. Arbitrary attributes can be expressed which makes XACML application-independent and extensible to accommodate the specific requirements of a specific application and domain. This also encourages an interoperability between components of the authorization system. Currently, the OASIS is working on XACML v3.0 draft, while several implementations of XACML v2.0 have been presented recently by third-party vendors[2].

XACML is facilitated to express the classical access control model, where the access decision is evaluated only once when a request to access a resource comes. The XACML model implies a security policy managed by multiply parties. XACML provides algorithms to build a resulting policy and assumes that many points of enforcement exists in distributed system. Access decision is based on attributes which characterize a subject, object, environment and also the content of the accessing object. A set of mathematical operators can be used over attributes to build authorization predicates. Also, the XACML model expressiveness is enhanced by introducing obligations, a set of actions performed in conjunction with the policy enforcement. XACML v3.0 is enhanced with advices, a supplementary information (not mandatory for execution) for the policy enforcement point (PEP).

XACML standards a policy meta-model, syntax and semantics, and enforcement architecture. The top-level policy elements are `<PolicySet>`, `<Policy>`, and `<Rule>`. The `<Rule>` has three main parts `<Target>` which denotes rule's applicability to the authorization request, `<Condition>`s which are authorization predicates over attributes, and effect is the result of the rule evaluation. It returns either "Permit" or "Deny" if the rule is satisfied and "Non Applicable" if the `<Target>` and/or `<Condition>`s are not satisfied. The XACML `<Policy>` consists of one or more `<Rule>`s and forms an the authorization decision accompanied with a set of `<Obligations>`. The `<Policy>` has a procedure for combining the result of the evaluation of `<Rule>`s it contains. XACML identifies several combining algorithms: deny-overrides, permit-overrides, first-applicable and only-one-applicable. The `<PolicySet>` is an optional element which provides the resulting policy through the combining of several `<Policy>`s applicable to the access request.

XACML realizes the enforcement architecture and abstract dataflow model compliant with IETF and ISO standards. Access request goes through an abstract component PEP. The PEP invokes a policy decision point (PDP) for an access decision. The PDP works as a double "filtering" of the initial access request. First, the PDP

---

[2] http://sunxacml.sourceforge.net, http://mvpos.sourceforge.net

evaluates an applicability of the policy to a given request (`<Target>` element is satisfied). In the second phase, a set of `<Condition>`s is checked. The resulting authorization decision plus set of `<Obligations>` and `<Advice>`s are sent back to the PEP. After fulfilling `<Obligations>`, the PEP grants or denies access to the resource and no further control is provided when the access is in progress. The interactions between the PDP and the PEP are synchronous and state-less.

## 3 U-XACML policy syntax and semantics

In this section, we propose syntax and semantics for U-XACML, an enhancement of the XACML standard that includes facilities to express UCON policies. The U-XACML policy meta-model derived from the original XACML and enhanced with UCON novelties is presented in the Figure 1. The original model was extended to capture attribute updates, continuous policy evaluation, and to place conditions triggering ongoing attribute updates and obligations.

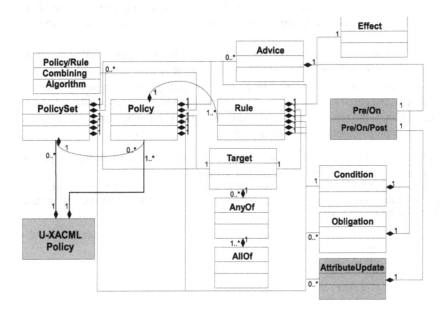

**Fig. 1** U-XACML policy language model.

We start from an authorization request. `Subject`, `object` and `right` of the UCON model are represented in the XACML by `subject`, `resource` and `action` respectively. The `<Target>` element specifies a policy applicability to the authorization request.

Subjects, resources and environment are associated with a set of attributes. Attributes are presented in both models and the XACML identified the following elements to describe attributes: `<AttributeDesignator>` (states to whom and by whom the attribute is issued), `<AttributeSelector>` (states where the attribute can be found), and `<AttributeValue>` (contains an attribute value). In the XACML attributes have static values and are never changed by the policy. In contrary, the UCON model presents an attribute mutability occurred as a side-effect of the policy enforcement. Also, attributes can be changed by the execution environment. We categorizes the U-XACML attributes as follows:

- (i) Immutable, e.g. identity. These attributes are static during the usage and can be change only by the administrative actions.
- (ii) Mutable by the security policy (enforceable mutability). These attributes are changed as the result of the policy enforcement only. As example, the subject attribute could be the number of applications currently running on behalf of the subject in Grid.
- (iii) Mutable by the execution environment (observable mutability). These attributes are mutable by their nature (e.g. environmental attributes), but how they change is not stated explicitly in the policy. As example, consider time-based attributes, e.g. resource usage time, current time value, or location-based attributes, etc.
- (iv) Combination of the last two (observable mutability). These attributes can be change either by the policy, or by the environment (e.g. a reputation). Here, we also consider attributes mutable by the security policy, but the update of this attribute is triggered by the environmental attribute (e.g. in the case study presented in section 5, the time quota is updated by the policy, but when the update occurs depends on the application execution time).

This attribute mutability category is optional and can be useful during the policy enforcement phase (we refer the reader to Section 4).

To represent attribute updates, we defined a new element, `<AttrUpdates>`, that contains a collection of single `<AttrUpdate>` elements to specify update actions in the U-XACML:

```
<xs:element name="AttrUpdates" type="u-xacml:AttrUpdatesType"/>
<xs:complexType name="AttrUpdatesType">
    <xs:sequence>
        <xs:element ref="u-xacml:AttrUpdate"
            maxOccurs="unbounded"/>
    </xs:sequence>
    ...
</xs:complexType>
```

`<AttrUpdate>` element defines a sequence of update functions which can run in `UpdateTime`. In general, each of these functions refers to a distinct attribute, and defines: the name of the attribute to be updated, the mutability category of the attribute, and the update function to compute the new value of the attribute.

`UpdateTime` has values 1, 2, or 3 that denote, respectively, pre-, on- and post-updates:

```
<xs:element name="AttrUpdate" type="u-xacml:AttrUpdateType"/>
<xs:complexType name="AttrUpdateType">
    <xs:sequence>
        <xs:element ref="u-xacml:UpdateExpression"
          minOccurs="0"/>
    </xs:sequence>
    . . .
    <xs:attribute name="UpdateTime" type="xs:integer"
      use="required"/>
    <xs:element ref="TriggerOn"/>
    . . .
</xs:complexType>
```

In the previous definition, <UpdateExpression> is a specific update function.

The U-XACML policy inherits the policy structure from the XACML. The U-XACML policy contains a set of <Rule>s and each <Rule> besides update actions includes a set of decision factors. Authorizations and conditions proposed in the UCON are modeled in the XACML by means of the <Target> and <Condition>s elements. In the U-XACML, we assume that the <Target> element puts constraints on the immutable attributes only, while the <Condition>s element covers other attributes of the subject, object and environment.

*Obligations.* In the UCON model, obligations are actions that have to be performed by obligation subjects over obligation objects. In XACML, instead, obligations have different semantics, and are considered as duties that will be performed by the PEP enforcing the access decision.

XACML obligations can easily be exploited to implement UCON obligations when the obligation subject and object are under the control of the protection system, and the PEP can assure the obligation fulfilment. In U-XACML, we also extended XACML obligations to model UCON obligations whose subject or object reside outside the protection system. However, in this case, the PEP can only observe the obligation fulfilment by checking some conditions. Such UCON obligations are modelled as two U-XACML obligations. The first asks the obligation subject to fulfil the obligation, and the second one checks the fulfilment. This check is triggered when some conditions hold (e.g. deadline to fulfil the obligation is over or some attributes changed). XACML obligations take a set of attributes as input parameters. Due to XACML extensibility, these parameters can state a UCON obligation subject and object.

*Continuous policy enforcement.* In the UCON access decision should be evaluated not only before granting the access but also continuously when the access is in progress. The U-XACML policy specifies when the access decision is made by the DecisionTime in the <Obligation> and <Condition> elements. For example, the <Condition> element in the U-XACML should include the following:

```
<xs:element name="Condition"/>
<xs:complexType name="ConditionType">
    . . .
    <xs:attribute name="DecisionTime" type="xs:string"
      use="required"/>
```

```
    . . .
</xs:complexType>
```

DecisionTime has values pre and on. For the pre models, the conditions are evaluated only once, while for the on-going models they have to be valid permanently. Meanwhile, the obligations are duration-less in both scenarios. For the on model, obligations invocation is triggered by some conditions (e.g. in the case study presented in section 5, if application's execution time is 1 hour to reach the quota value, the ongoing obligation is triggered). The same observation applies for on-going attribute updates, they are duration-less and triggered when some conditions hold. <ObligationExpression> and <AttrUpdate> elements contains a <TriggerOn> element:

```
<xs:element name="ObligationExpression"/>
<xs:complexType name="ObligationExpressionType">
    . . .
    <xs:element ref="TriggerOn"/>
    . . .
</xs:complexType>
```

The element <TriggerOn> states conditions which trigger the update and obligation actions. As a matter of fact, the <TriggerOn> has the same syntax as the <Condition>.

# 4 U-XACML architecture

This section presents an architecture to enforce the U-XACML policy and a data-flow between its main components (see Figure 2). The U-XACML extends the functionality of authorization components of the XACML to handle continuous policy enforcement. The policy enforcement can be separated in two parts: pre-authorization, and ongoing usage.

For pre part, we have authorization/condition predicates evaluation, attributes update and obligations fulfilment. All this actions are duration-less and executed in the order as stated above: first predicates evaluation, than updates and finally obligations. We fix this order whether the UCON assumes any possible combination. We will address this issue in the future work presenting the formal model of the U-XACML policy. The data-flow in pre-authorization is the same as in the original XACML excepting the attribute updates. The PDP invokes an Attribute Manager to update attributes before sending the access decision and obligations to the PEP.

In the ongoing model, we assume that authorization and condition predicates should be valid during all the usage, while obligation and update actions still remain duration-less. Obligations and updates are conditioned by attributes and are triggered when they change appropriately. The U-XACML ongoing policy can be represented by the sequence of states and the state is specified by attribute values. The policy state transition and decision reevaluation are driven as the result of attributes mutability. This schema is similar to the run-time monitoring of applications where the PEP intercepts security-relevant actions performed by applications and triggers the PDP for the policy reevaluation. In usage control, instead of security-relevant actions there are security-relevant events, i.e. the change of an attribute value. The U-XACML architecture should be enhanced with a component (the Attribute Manager) which captures all security-relevant events and keeps fresh values of attri butes. Whenever an attribute is changed the PDP performs a policy check.

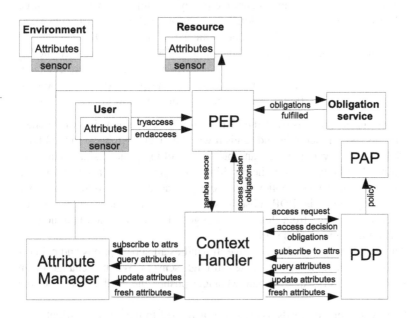

**Fig. 2** U-XACML architecture and data flow.

As shown in the Figure 2 the U-XACML architecture consists of the following components (we omit the explanation of components if they functionality coincide with the original XACML):

- PEP is responsible for the enforcement of the access decision and the obligations fulfillment. The PEP can also manage meta-information associated with the usage session, e.g. session id and the current state of the policy.
- PDP receives as an input the policy, a current policy state, a set of fresh attributes. The PDP evaluates the policy associated with the current policy state. If the policy is violated the PDP return "Non applicable". Otherwise, it returns "Permit" and makes a state transition if needed. The PDP may also invoke attribute update and/or obligation actions.
- Attribute manager has fresh values of attributes. It enforces update actions triggered by the PDP and is capable to capture any change of attributes done by the execution environment and/or the policy administration point (PAP). The Attribute Manager exploits sensors to collect attributes.

- Sensors are plugged into subject, object and environment attribute repositories. They are activated every time when attributes are changed. The new value is forwarded to the Attribute Manager.
- Context handler converts messages circulating in the system to the proper format.

Depending on how fresh attributes are acquired and security-relevant events are detected in the system, and who triggers the policy reevaluation, we assume three possible data-flow models: (i) active Attribute Manager; (ii) passive Attribute Manager with active PEP; (iii) passive Attribute Manager with active PDP.

*Active Attribute Manager* (push attribute model). This is an event-based model. It assumes that sensors are activated every time whenever attributes are changed. This information is forwarded to the active Attribute Manager who invokes the PDP for the policy reevaluation. It more details the ongoing data-flow goes as follows:

- When a pre-usage phase is over, the PEP starts a usage session. The PEP generates a usage session identifier and sends it with the ongoing request to the PDP;
- The PDP loads relevant policies, and builds a resulting policy using combining algorithms. The PDP analyzes the resulting policy and selects a set of mutable attributes that can change a policy state, i.e trigger access revocation, obligations or attribute updates. The PDP subscribes to the Attribute Manager be notified whenever any attribute from this set is changed. The subscription is done only once when the usage session starts.
- The Attribute Manager is always active. It handles all subscriptions and collects information about requested attributes through sensors. When a change of an attribute value occurs, the Attribute Manager pushes the attribute value to the PDP.
- The PDP wakes up and loads usage sessions related to the pushed attribute and reevaluates the policy. If no change in the access decision, the PDP awaits for the next invocation. Otherwise, the PDP performs state transition and triggers either access revocation, or attribute update, or obligation actions request to the PEP.
- The usage session is over, when either the endaccess() action is forwarded from the user, or the PDP recognizes a violation of a policy and returns "Non applicable" access decision to the PEP. Afterwards, the PDP initiates post-updates and unsubscribes from the Attribute Manager for attributes which are no longer used. All the relevant information to the usage session is deleted.

The model with active Attribute Manager is the most appropriate and intuitive for the usage control needs but it has pros and cons. The main advantage is that policy reevaluation is run immediately when a security-relevant event occurs. Unfortunately, in distributed system it is costly to discover and broadcast every attribute change from possible repositories. Frequent secure communications between authorization components provide a meaningful overhead. Further, communications between the PEP and the PDP are asynchronous and state-full. The PEP invokes the PDP only when a usage session starts or is ended by a user. The PDP calls the PEP when the access should be revoked or every time when ongoing obligations should be fulfilled. The support of the asynchronous communication requires the usage session identifier shared between the PDP and the PEP.

The alternative approach assumes *passive Attribute Manager* (pull attribute model). In this approach, fresh attributes are pulled to the PDP and the policy reevaluation in triggered periodically when a certain time interval elapsed.

*Passive Attribute Manager with active PEP* imposes that the PEP during the usage session periodically sends access requests to the PDP. The PDP pulls the required attributes from the Attribute Manager. The Attribute Manager questions the sensors to obtain fresh values and returns them to the PDP. The PDP makes access decision and replies to the PEP. Notice, that it is not necessary, that attribute values and/or the access decision will change between two adjacent invocations. The procedure is repeated iteratively until the usage session is ended or revoked. In this model the interactions between the PEP and the PDP are synchronous. For every request the PEP receives the response from the PDP. The PEP also manages the usage session meta-information. The current policy state is included into the access request. As the result, the PDP can be state-less and is capable to recover the policy state from the access request. After the policy reevaluation, the PDP ins erts the current policy state to the response message. The *passive Attribute Manager with active PEP* puts too much functionality on the PEP side which is usually application depended. We consider this as a limitation of the model.

*Passive Attribute Manager with active PDP* imposes that the PDP during the usage session periodically pulls fresh attributes values from the Attribute Manager and reevaluates the access decision. In contrast to the previous model, the PDP is active now and manages the usage session meta-information. The interactions between the PDP and the PEP are asynchronous in this case and are the same as in the case of *active Attribute Manager*.

Although the models with the passive Attribute Manager are easier to implement, they have some limitations. The most crucial issue is that a choice of a big time slot leads to a security breach. The access can not be revoked immediately when the policy is violated due to change of attributes. The access will be revoked only after the scheduled invocation. On the other side, too frequent invocations will produce a time-overhead. To minimize this shortcoming, a several adoptive checks can be used. The idea is to adapt the next scheduled policy reevaluation to the current values of the attributes depending on how far attribute values are from the critical value which triggers an obligation, or update actions, or the access revocation. As closer the values are as more frequently the policy should be reevaluated and vice versa [2]. We consider as a future work an appropriate model for the periodic policy checks.

The preferable data-flow model also depends on the attributes used in the policy. If the policy based on immutable attributes, the model with the passive Attribute Manager and active PDP is the best solution. In this case, only PDP is a responsible for all attribute updates and triggers security-relevant events. In contrast, if the policy exploits attributes mutable rarely by the PAP, environment and third parties, the model with active Attribute Manager is more appropriate.

# 5 A case study

We chosen an access to and usage of Grid computational services as a case study. Computational services (e.g. GRAM service in Globus Toolkit) are designed to execute remote user's applications at the resource provider side.

The traditional authorization model, where an authorization decision is taken only once before granting an access to a service, is insufficient for long-lived computational services. Initial conditions can change during the application execution due to attributes change. This requires continuous access reevaluation. The policy violation can lead to the access revocation and service termination.

We follow the XACML philosophy and impose a security policy combining many policies from distinct parties, e.g. a policy written by a VO (virtual organization) administrator and a policy written by a provider of a computational service. The VO administrator might want to implement the following policy containing 2 rules:

- Grid user should present his/her VO membership certificate with the initial request (pre-authorization). This rule refers to "preA0" model;
- No more that 10 applications in the whole VO can run on behalf of the user. If the number exceeded 10, than the access should be denied (pre-authorization). The update of the number of running applications is required before starting a service (pre-update) and when the usage is over (post-update). This rule refers to "preA13" model.

The resource provider policy contains 5 rules:

- Grid user's reputation should be higher the threshold value before the usage (pre-authorization). If it is below the threshold during the execution, the access should be revoked and the application terminated (on-authorization). After the usage, the resource provider updates Grid user's reputation (post-update). If the service was ended normally by the user, the reputation should be increased, while if the access was revoked by the system, than the reputation should be decreased. This rule refers to "onA3" model;
- No more that 5 applications can run on behalf of the user on the resource provider node. If the number exceeded 5, than the access should be denied (pre-authorization). The update of the number of running applications is required before starting a service (pre-update) and when the usage is over (post-update). This rule refers to "preA13" model;
- Grid user has to sign an agreement, e.g. that application is not malicious, before submitting it to the execution. This rule refers to "preB0" model;
- The application submitted for execution can exploit computational resources for a particular time quota. If during the usage, application's execution time is 1 hour to reach the quota value, the ongoing obligation is triggered. This obligation informs the user, that allowed execution time is elapsing and the credit is required to proceed the execution. This rule refers to "onB0" model;

- If application's execution time exceeded the quota and no credit was submitted by the user, the system should terminate the execution of the application (on-authorization). Otherwise, if the credit is presented, the system triggers attribute updates (on-update). It doubles the execution quota time limit and sets the credit value to zero. The iterative prolonging of the usage quota can be performed unbounded number of times. This rule refers to "onA2" model;

The policies given above fit to the UCON abstract model but can not be expressed in the XACML. Actually, they contain features which are not presented in the XACML, e.g. the policies have continuous checks of authorization predicates, have ongoing obligations and attribute updates. Some obligations and updates are conditioned using the application execution time attribute.

The resulting policy is the combination of the VO and the resource provider policies. Before the usage, the system first checks the VO certificate of the user, the number of running applications in the VO on the behalf of the user, the number of running applications on the local host on the behalf of the user. If these conditions are satisfied, the PDP invokes the Attribute Manager to update number of running application in the VO and on the local host. Further, the grant access and obligation to sign an agreement is sent to the PEP. The PEP enforces the obligation. If the user signs the agreement, the PEP starts the user's application execution and initializes a new usage session. During the usage, the system follows that the time quota does not exceed and a user's reputation is over a threshold. When the usage time is in hour to the time quota value, the system enforces ongoing obligation and proposes the user to obtain a credit to prolong the usage session. If the user acc epts and presents the credit, the time quota is doubled. The time quota can be prolonged unbounded number of times. Eventually, when the usage session is over, the system performs post-updates - decreases the number of running applications and updates the user's reputation appropriately.

# 6 Conclusions

In this paper, we introduced the U-XACML policy language which extends the XACML to capture the UCON features. We outlined the syntax and semantics and the enforcement architecture for the U-XACML. XACML has been extended to capture attribute updates, continuous checks of authorization predicates and obligations fulfilment, and conditions over ongoing attribute update and obligation actions. We studied the enforcement architecture with the event-based and a push attribute model and periodic invocation with a pull attribute model of the policy reevaluation. All approaches shown advantages and disadvantages.

Our future step will be an implementation of the U-XACML policy engine which can be exploited for the usage control over Grid resources. This work is in progress and currently we implemented the Grid service revocation mechanism [1] which can be considered as a part of the U-XACML PEP. Afterwards, we intend to give a formal model and the analysis of the U-XACML policy.

# References

1. Colombo, M., Lazouski, A., Martinelli, F., Mori, P.: On Usage Control for Grid Services. In: The 2009 IEEE International Workshop on HPC and Grid Applications. Sanya, China (2009)
2. Damiani, M.L., Bertino, E., Silvestri, C.: Approach to supporting continuity of usage in location-based access control. In: FTDCS '08: Proceedings of the 2008 12th IEEE International Workshop on Future Trends of Distributed Computing Systems, pp. 199–205. IEEE Computer Society, Washington, DC, USA (2008)
3. Feng, J., Wasson, G., Humphrey, M.: Resource usage policy expression and enforcement in grid computing. IEEE/ACM International Workshop on Grid Computing pp. 66–73 (2007)
4. Hafner, M., Memon, M., Alam, M.: Modeling and enforcing advanced access control policies in healthcare systems with Sectet. In: Models in Software Engineering: Workshops and Symposia at MoDELS, pp. 132–144. Springer-Verlag, Berlin, Heidelberg (2008)
5. Katt, B., Zhang, X., Breu, R., Hafner, M., Seifert, J.P.: A general obligation model and continuity: enhanced policy enforcement engine for usage control. In: SACMAT '08: Proceedings of the 13th ACM symposium on Access control models and technologies, pp. 123–132. ACM, New York, NY, USA (2008)
6. Martinelli, F., Mori, P., Vaccarelli, A.: Towards continuous usage control on grid computational services. In: Proceedings of Joint International Conference on Autonomic and Autonomous Systems and International Conference on Networking and Services (ICAS-ICNS 2005), IEEE Computer Society, p. 82 (2005)
7. Naqvi, S., Massonet, P., Aziz, B., Arenas, A., Martinelli, F., Mori, P., Blasi, L., Cortese, G.: Fine-Grained Continuous Usage Control of Service Based Grids - The GridTrust Approach. In: ServiceWave '08: Proceedings of the 1st European Conference on Towards a Service-Based Internet, pp. 242–253. Springer-Verlag, Berlin, Heidelberg (2008)
8. Park, J., Sandhu, R.: Towards usage control models: Beyond traditional access control. In: SACMAT '02: Proceedings of the seventh ACM symposium on Access control models and technologies, pp. 57–64. ACM, New York, NY, USA (2002)
9. Park, J., Sandhu, R.: The $UCON_{ABC}$ usage control model. ACM Transactions on Information and System Security **7**(1), 128–174 (2004)
10. XACML: eXtensible Access Control Markup Language (XACML). Www.oasis-open.org/committees/xacml
11. Zhang, X., Nakae, M., Covington, M.J., Sandhu, R.: Toward a usage-based security framework for collaborative computing systems. ACM Transactions on Information and System Security **11**(1), 1–36 (2008)

# Self-* and Adaptive Mechanisms for Large Scale Distributed Systems

P. Fragopoulou, C. Mastroianni, R. Montero, A. Andrjezak, D. Kondo

**Abstract** Large-scale distributed computing systems and infrastructure, such as Grids, P2P systems and desktop Grid platforms, are decentralized, pervasive, and composed of a large number of autonomous entities. The complexity of these systems is such that human administration is nearly impossible and centralized or hierarchical control is highly inefficient. These systems need to run on highly dynamic environments, where content, network topologies and workloads are continuously changing. Moreover, they are characterized by the high degree of volatility of their components and the need to provide efficient service management and to handle efficiently large amounts of data. This paper describes some of the areas for which adaptation emerges as a key feature, namely, the management of computational Grids, the self-management of desktop Grid platforms and the monitoring and healing of complex applications. It also elaborates on the use of bio-inspired algorithms to achieve self-management. Related future trends and challenges are described.

Paraskevi Fragopoulou
FORTH-ICS, N. Plastira 100, Vassilika Vouton, GR 71003 Heraklion-Crete, Greece, e-mail: fragopou@ics.forth.gr

Carlo Mastroianni
ICAR-CNR, Via P. Bucci 41C, 87036 Rende (CS), Italy, e-mail: mastroianni@icar.cnr.it

Ruben Montero
Departamento de Arquitectura de Computadores y Automática, Universidad Complutense, 28040 Madrid, Spain, e-mail: rubensm@dacya.ucm.es

Artur Andrjezak
Zuse-Institute Berlin, Takustr. 7, 14195 Berlin, Germany, e-mail: andrzejak@zib.de

Derrick Kondo
Laboratoire LIG, ENSIMAG - antenne de Montbonnot, ZIRST 51, Av. Jean Kuntzmann, 38330 Monbonnot Saint Martin, France, e-mail: dkondo@imag.fr

# 1 Introduction

Many current large-scale distributed computing systems and infrastructure, such as Grids, P2P systems and desktop Grid platforms, have the characteristic of being decentralized, pervasive, and composed of a large number of autonomous entities. The complexity of these systems is such that human administration is nearly impossible and centralized or hierarchical control is highly inefficient. Moreover, often these systems need to run on highly dynamic environments, where content, network topologies and workloads are continuously changing. These systems are also characterized by the high degree of volatility of their components and the need to handle efficiently large amounts of data. Thus, design for adaptation becomes a key feature.

Self-directing and self-managing systems are emerging in response to these issues. Novel approaches for the construction of scalable and efficient Grid systems need to have the following properties: "self-organization" (Grid components are autonomous and do not rely on any external supervisor), decentralization (decisions are to be taken only on the basis of local information) and adaptive nature (mechanisms must be provided to cope with the dynamic characteristics of hosts and resources). Having these characteristics, these systems become naturally robust, because they adapt to the environmental changes, scalable, because they do not depend on any centralized control or information, and dependable, as they are able to ensure their own maintenance or repair.

Current Grids present a number of obstacles that prevent their efficient use, namely: high degree of heterogeneity; difficult isolation and partition of the resource contributed to the Grid; specific environment requirements by each Virtual Organization; and high operational costs. Recently virtualization technologies have emerged as a promising solution to overcome these barriers. The challenge is to devise efficient methods based on virtualization to dynamically shape and adapt large scale Grid infrastructures. Additionally this challenge includes the study of heuristics to adapt the computational capacity of the Grid using Cloud providers.

Self-organizing and adaptive systems often involve a social dimension, since entities within such systems can engage in interactions, discover suitable other participants, negotiate, and perform transactions. These characteristics are similar to those that can be observed in self-organizing systems we see in nature, such as physical, biological and social systems. In such systems, a number of entities perform simple activities in an autonomous fashion, but as a whole such systems are able to carry out much more complex tasks. Such behavior, in some cases referred to as "swarm intelligence", emerges in a coherent way through the local interactions of the various components. There is no wonder that bio-inspired algorithms as well as evolutionary processes, are emerging as powerful techniques for the design and implementation of self-organizing systems.

The remaining of this paper is organized as follows: Following the introduction to the subject, Section 2 is devoted to the elastic management of Grid infrastructure. Section 3 elaborates on the topic of bio-inspired algorithms to achieve self-adaptation. In Section 4, the topic of monitoring and healing of complex applications to deal with the volatility of the infrastructure is presented. Section 5 of this paper is devoted to desktop Grids and the methods to increase availability. We conclude in Section 6.

## 2 Elastic management of computational Grid resources

In spite of their success, current Grids suffer from several obstacles that limit their efficiency, namely: (i) increase in the cost of the application development cycle; (ii) a limitation on the effective number of resources available to each application; and (iii) increase in the operational cost of the infrastructure. This situation often leads to a struggle between the users, who need more control on their execution environments, and Grid operators, who want to limit the heterogeneity of the infrastructure. As a result several alternatives to reconcile both positions have been explored in the past [1, 2].

However, virtualization, has emerged as the most promising technology to provide both the users with custom execution environments and Grid administrator with a powerful tool to manage the infrastructure. The first works in this area integrated resource management systems with Virtual Machines (VMs) to provide custom execution environments on a per-job basis (see for example [3]). A more general approach that involves the use of virtual machines as workload units combined with public Cloud providers is proposed in [5, 7].

A computing cluster can be easily virtualized by putting the front-end and worker nodes into VMs, see Fig. 1. This separation of resource provisioning from job execution provides the following benefits: (i) elastic cluster capacity; (ii) cluster partitioning; and (iii) support for heterogeneous configurations [9]. We have evaluated the performance of this approach in a physical infrastructure that consists of five hosts interconnected by a Gigabit Ethernet LAN; and Amazon EC2 small instances. Fig. 1 shows the dynamic performance (jobs per second or throughput) of three different cluster configurations in the execution of the ED, NAS Grid Benchmark.

As expected, the EC2 cluster presents a lower performance, about half of the performance of the local cluster. This lower throughput is due to the lower performance profile of the EC2 instance compared to the local nodes. Additionally, these results show a sustained increment in the performance of the cluster with a growing number of EC2 nodes.

Current results show that virtualization and Cloud computing can be effectively used to manage Grid Resources. The decoupling of the infrastructure from the application layer enables an elastic management of the resource, and opens up a whole new framework for the self-adaptivity of Grid infrastructures. In this way, these technologies establish the basis for self-adapting Grid resources not only in terms of their capacity but also in their type, cost or power consumption in three basic ways:

- *Self-adapting Grid sites.* Virtualization and Cloud technologies enable the dynamic *re-shaping* of Grid services. In particular, a Grid site will be able to self-adapt its computational capacity and the number and type of its computational services to the dynamic demands of the Grid users. This would require the development of load-driven algorithms to adapt the underlying computational facility, that may include Cloud resources, to the Grid workload.

- *Self-configuring Grid services.* The use of central repositories would make possible to easily distribute security patches or new versions of a given software component. The use of VO-specific images (appliance) will ease the development and porting of Grid applications.
- *Self-adapting Grid Applications.* The ability to request Grid resources on-demand would allow applications to adapt the underlying computational infrastructure to their particular control flow and parallelism level.

# 3 Bio-inspired algorithms for self-organizing distributed systems

The large-scale and dynamic nature of Grids makes human administrative intervention difficult or even unfeasible and centralized information services are proving unsuitable to scale to hundreds or thousands of nodes. To tackle these issues, the scientific community has proposed to design information services according to the P2P paradigm, which offers better scalability and adaptivity features [10]. A similar trend can be envisioned for the recently emerged Cloud paradigm [11], which is switching computation and storage responsibilities from the client size to the "Clouds", i.e., to unseen computers on the server side, possibly scattered across continents. Grid and Cloud issues are similar in many aspects [12], especially in the need to assure scalability in a dynamic environment, therefore P2P techniques are very likely to be adopted in Clouds as they are today in Grids.

Along with the P2P approach, another interesting and recent trend is the design of *self-organizing Grids* [13], often inspired by biological systems such as ant colonies and insect swarms. Complex functionalities are achieved by mobile agents that perform simple operations at the local level, but at the global level engender an advanced form of intelligence that would be impossible to obtain with centralized or human-driven strategies [14]. For example, the Anthill system [15] is tailored to the design, implementation and evaluation of P2P applications based on multi-agent and evolutionary programming. It is composed of a collection of interconnected *nests*. Each nest is a peer entity that makes its storage and computational resources available to swarms of *ants*, mobile agents that travel the network to satisfy user requests.

Recently, ant algorithms have been proposed to design "self-structured" P2P systems, in which the association of keys with hosts is not pre-determined but adapts to the modification of the environment [16, 17, 18]. In So-Grid [16], Grid resources are assumed to be pre-categorized in classes, and their descriptors are spatially clustered by ant-inspired mobile agents, thus facilitating the discovery of a cluster containing a large number of resources that belong to the desired class. Antares [18] extends this concept by using a locality preserving hash function, which guarantees that similar resources are assigned similar key values. Keys are spatially sorted by mobile agents according to their key values. In this way, a search message can be driven towards the desired descriptors by following the gradient of resource keys: at each step the message is forwarded to the neighbor peer that minimizes the distance between the keys stored there and the target key. Anthill, So-Grid and Antares are all unstructured P2P systems. Indeed, structured P2P systems have always been considered not compatible with self-organizing properties and adaptive behaviors. Recently, however, it was shown that self-organization can also be provided to structured systems. Self-Chord [19] is a P2P system that inherits from Chord the ability to construct and maintain a structured ring of peers, but features enhanced functionalities achieved through the activity of ant-inspired mobile agents. As opposed to Chord, Self-Chord decouples the naming of resources and peers, resulting in two sets of keys/indices that can have different cardinalities. Resource keys are organized and managed by self-organizing mobile agents through simple local operations driven by probabilistic choices. Self-Chord features enhanced functionalities deriving from ant-inspired algorithms, such as autonomous behavior, self-organization and capacity to adapt to a changing environment.

One of the objectives of future research is the application of self-organizing algorithms to other structured systems. For example, in CAN [20], resource keys are placed in a toroidal multi-dimensional structure: the position of a key over each dimension is equal to the value of a corresponding numerical parameter. An ant-inspired algorithm can be devised also in this case: a centroid can be defined to represent the keys stored in a restricted region of the multi-dimensional space. The keys will be moved by agents through adjacent peers, by comparing their values with the values of peer centroids, with the objective of sorting the keys over the multi-dimensional structure. The reordering of keys will allow the efficient execution of queries, without requiring a rigid association among resource keys and peer codes. Similar techniques can be devised for Pastry and other structured systems: a general approach can be defined to retain the advantages of self-organization behavior in structured P2P systems.

Another research trend concerns the use of bio-inspired algorithms for the efficient discovery and composition of services. The ICT market is experiencing an important shift from the request/provisioning of products toward a service-oriented view where everything (computing, storage, applications) is provided as a network-enabled service. It often happens that a solution to a problem cannot be offered by a single service, but through a proper composition of multiple basic services in a "workflow" [21, 22]. The problem of service composition involves issues such as the design and execution of a workflow and the discovery of its basic components on the network.

A line of research is the definition and design of an ant-inspired framework that facilitates "collective" discovery requests, issued to search a peer-to-peer network for all the basic services that will compose a specific workflow. The basic idea would be to reorganize the services so that the descriptors of services that are often used together are placed in neighboring peers. This would help a single discovery request to find multiple basic services, in order to decrease the number of needed discovery requests and, consequently, to reduce the search time and the network load.

# 4 Non-intrusive monitoring and healing of complex applications

As computers continue to invade all areas of human activities ranging from work to entertainment, keeping systems running is the major challenge as more and more applications require non-stop computing - frequently with real time requirements [28]. Yet a negative effect of this growing proliferation and functionality of computer systems is their increasing complexity, mostly due to larger number of (heterogeneous) software components, hardware distribution, configuration dependencies, and others. Coupled with fact that many of the components are black-boxes (e.g. COTS or legacy applications), resolving faults or performance bottlenecks in complex (especially enterprise and distributed) systems become an extremely challenging and costly task, making the above-mentioned requirement for high dependability even harder to fulfill [29]. A related phenomenon is the increasing rate of changes in systems due to software updates, reconfiguration or infrastructure replacement. All these maintenance actions are likely to induce service outages or cause (in worst-case long-term) functionality or performance degradation, creating a further challenge to ensure reliable, uninterrupted system operations. The amount of such maintenance is illustrated by the fact that major high-tech companies, e.g., SAP get more than 40% of their income from software maintenance, and many others simply "live" from maintenance cost. The result is soaring system management costs and increased likelihood of failures. Especially difficult and expensive is maintenance, fixing of errors and introducing changes in "post-release" software and in complex productive systems:

- Some systems can be taken off-line only for a brief period of time or not at all.
- Application-level debugging and code changes are frequently impossible due to legacy, COTS or complexity issues.
- Configuration and update errors can be catastrophic for availability and user experience.
- Some problems e.g. related to software updates or aging occur only in the deployment scenarios and cannot be replicated in a "sandbox".
- The difficulties and costs grow with larger complexity and heterogeneity, as e.g. fault diagnosis and performance modeling becomes increasingly difficult.

All above problems require solutions and practices which can handle partially "black-boxed" systems and eliminate or minimize the risk of service outage or functionality degradation due to system maintenance or changes. It is important to device self-* techniques for system monitoring, resolution of faults and performance problems, software updates and other maintenance, paying particular attention to aspects such as overhead, cost, and practicability. A further goal is to help in identifying and popularizing a consolidated set of tools and practices for non-intrusive, low-risk maintenance and healing of software systems. More specifically, the development of realistic and cost-effective solutions which take into account constraints imposed by working with productive systems, include:

- Overhead of fault and performance monitoring has to be minimal.

- Debugging and error fixing on code level is in many cases impractical or impossible.
- Software/configuration changes or updates might cause degradation of performance or functionality.

The methods and fields which are relevant span a variety of areas, rougly to be divided into monitoring/analysis, system healing, and software maintenance. Within the monitoring/analysis area, the most interesting approaches appear to be: low-overhead and DTrace-based monitoring [25]; analysis and modeling of COTS and legacy components; statistical performance and fault modeling [24], and proactive fault management [28]. Concerning the healing part, topics of root cause analysis (RCA) [26], automated debugging, software aging and rejuvenation [23], and (self-) healing support in operating systems and middleware [29] should be considered. To solve the problems related to application and software maintenance, attention should be devoted to approaches including reversible software updates [27], virtualization-based replication [29], and studies of maintenance practices in Grids and enterprise / heterogeneous software systems.

# 5 Self-management in desktop Grids

Recent work on self-managing desktop Grids focuses on availability prediction and modeling. Increasingly services are being deployed over large-scale computational and storage infrastructures. To meet ever-increasing computational demands and to reduce both hardware and system administration costs, these infrastructures have begun to include Internet resources distributed over enterprize and residential broadband networks. As these infrastructures increase in scale to hundreds of thousands to millions of resources, issues of resource availability and service reliability inevitably emerge. Recent work [32, 33], determines and evaluates predictive methods that ensure the availability of a collection of resources. More specifically, prediction models are developed that ensure a set of resources is continuously available for a period of time.

In addition to online predictive models, statistical distributions and properties of availability in desktop Grid resources are analyzed [30]. This in turn can be used for automated stochastic scheduling. In particular, it is investigated in recent work the stationary versus non-stationary behavior of resource availability and fit different models (for example Exponential, Weibull, or Pareto probability distributions) to the observed availability. It is believed that this characterization is fundamental in the design of automated stochastic scheduling algorithms across large-scale systems where host availability is uncertain.

Three critical areas for future research have been identified, namely automated resource co-allocation, automated green computing, and automated integration of distributed systems such as desktop Grids and Clouds. With the trend of many-core processors in consumer desktops, the likelihood of idle cores increases. This brings the research question of how to co-schedule automatically multiple desktop Grid applications on the same host. The difficulty of this problem lies in the scheduling of applications that minimizes resource contention. One approach is to automatically develop application signatures that indicate which resources (for example CPU, memory, disk) the application uses and when. These signatures of desktop Grid applications can then be used for automated co-allocation on multi-core processors.

The second critical research challenge is automated energy management on desktops. Desktop Grid applications often run without considering energy consumption. At the same time, the additional energy consumption of running such applications can incur significant environmental and monetary costs to the PC owner. Thus automated methods that limit energy consumption, i.e., energy throttling, are vital. One approach again is to use application signatures as a way of proactivelly estimating energy consumption. Then one can use methods such as dynamic voltage scaling or limiting core-usage to reduce energy consumption as needed.

The third critical research challenge is the integration of distributed systems such as desktop Grids and Clouds [31]. Clouds have emerged as a cost-effective platform for many applications, in particular web services. The advantages of Clouds include the ability to pay for resources as one uses them and the ability to scale up or down the number of resources used. The disadvantages include the cost of transferring data to and from the Cloud, and the potential for lock-in to a particular Cloud when using a specific platform API. By contrast, the advantage of desktop Grids is that their amortized cost is orders of magnitude lower than Clouds, and the potential computing power is higher. The disadvantage is that desktop Grids require nontrivial system administration and application development costs. Moreover, the time to construct a platform can be significant, and resources have higher volatility and heterogeneity.

Thus, given a scientific or industrial workload, the challenge is to partition the workload to use both Clouds and desktop Grids in a way that minimizes costs and maximizes application turnaround. Self-management methods must be developed to predict which platform type is more advantageous or whether the application execution should be split to use both platforms. These decision will certainly leverage our previous work on availability prediction in desktop Grids.

# 6 Conclusions

This paper presented some of the areas for which adaptation emerges as a key feature, namely, the management of computational Grids and of desktop Grid platforms and the monitoring and healing of complex applications. Finally, the use of bio-inspired algorithms to achieve self-management was presented. Future trends and challenges related to each one of these issues were described. Self-adapting and self-configuring Grid sites and applications through virtualization will lead to a real elastic management of computational Grid resources. Self-adaptation also emerges as a key feature in desktop Grids, for example to efficiently partition workloads to desktop Grids and Clouds, using prediction algorithms, for most efficient utilization. In another approach bio-inspired algorithms are devised for efficient service discovery and composition.

## Acknowledgements

We would like to thank Ignacio M. Llorente and Rafael Moreno-Vozmediano for their contribution in Section 2 of this paper.

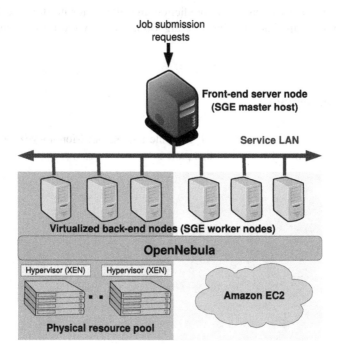

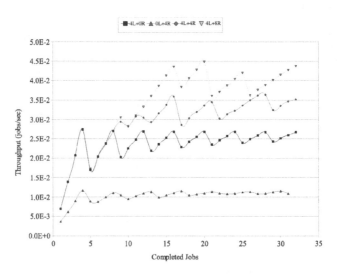

**Fig. 1** Upper chart: Virtual computing cluster infrastructure. Lower chart: Experimental performance of the ED benchmark for a local cluster (4L0R), an EC2 cluster (0L4R), and for a hybrid cluster configuration (4L4R and 4L8R).

# Network Monitoring in the age of the Cloud

Augusto Ciuffoletti

**Abstract** Network virtualization plays a relevant role in provisioning an Infrastructure as a Service (IaaS), implementing the fabric that interconnects virtual components. We identify the standard protocol IEEE802.1Q [1] , that describes Virtual LAN (VLAN) functionalities, as a cornerstone in this architecture.

We distinguish two aspects of virtual networking: one related to the user of the virtual connectivity, the other related to the provider that implements virtual connectivity. We describe these aspects, and put them into relation with commercial products considered typical: Amazon EC2[2] and VMware[3].

Next we devise network monitoring features that are appropriate in the user and in the provider environments. It turns out that there are significant differences between the two, and we conclude with directions for future research in the field.

## 1 Introduction

One of the reasons that sustain the peak of popularity reached by the *cloud computing* concept, is that it aggregates a number of extremely effective techniques into a unique abstraction, which is intuitively understandable also without a technical background.

The pieces that come to implement the concept of cloud computing are many, and come from all fields of information technology: from the point of view of the software architecture it is a descendant of Web Services, from that of processing resources it inherits from cluster computing, from the point of view of storage man-

Augusto Ciuffoletti
Dipartimento di Informatica Università di Pisa e-mail: `augusto@di.unipi.it`

[1] IEEE and 802 are registered trademarks of The Institute of Electrical and Electronics Engineers, Inc.

[2] Amazon Elastic Compute Cloud (Amazon EC2) [2] is a trademark of Amazon.com

[3] VMware is a trademark of VMware, Inc.

agement it takes from distributed storage architectures, to name the more evident, and we find a first crosspoint of all these technologies in the concept of *Grid computing*.

*Cloud computing* adds another ingredient into the melting pot: resource virtualization. The result is a concept quite effective for the company dedicated to the management of large IT infrastructures, impressive for the manager that doesn't want to invest in the volatile IT technology.

From the point of view of the infrastructure management, the implementation of a Service that offers *on demand* a virtual infrastructure means the maintenance of a unique technology throughout the whole infrastructure, with every available Mips usable to satisfy the next request. There is no resource specialization, since user needs are met when configuring the virtual infrastructure onto generic hardware.

From the point of view of the user, an Infrastructure as a Service (IaaS) provider makes available reliable, low cost resources with unlimited scalability. The know-how needed to exploit an IaaS resource is minimal.

Other aspects are less transparent: from *green* aspects related to energy savings reached optimizing resource utilization (e.g, processing units), to the technological *lock in* deriving from the dependency from a given *IaaS provider* in order to carry on a productive activity.

The same aspects that are now evident from the point of view of the computing activity, are also present from the networking point of view. In this paper we want to give a perspective of how networking issues emerge in a framework that offers IaaS.

We argue that the role played by the hypervisor in computing resources domain is here taken by the VLAN, implemented using networking facilities compliant with the ad-hoc standard IEEE802.1Q [5].

This standard regulates the functionalities offered by VLAN-aware switches, which enable the implementation of VLANs over a switched network: frames originated within the virtual LAN are transparently delivered to every other interface registered in the VLAN. Its history begins in 1998, and a revision has been released in 2005: there is an intense activity around this standard, and several substandards[4] are being developed.

One consequence of the IEEE802.1Q protocol is the introduction of a sort of "two tiers" networking, that hardly fits into the layered ISO/OSI architecture: the Data Link layer is decomposed into two tiers, the *server* implementing an abstraction for use of the *client*.

In figure 1 we see a popular example (see Cisco white paper [3]): a network decomposed into three distinguished physical subnetworks for logistic reasons (the network spans three floors in a building), is rearranged into three VLANs reflecting distinguished offices.

Note that the level 3 router controls routing among the VLANs, and traffic in one VLAN is not visible to interfaces attached to other ones.

---

[4] http://standards.ieee.org/cgi-bin/status?802

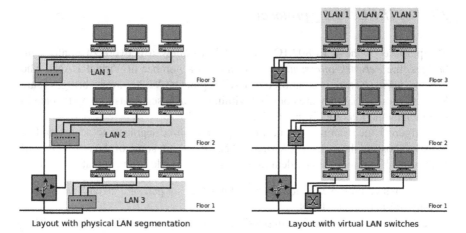

Layout with physical LAN segmentation          Layout with virtual LAN switches

**Fig. 1** Two tiers view through using LAN virtualization

The effect of the introduction of VLANs in a complex network is of decoupling the needs of infrastructure management, worried by logistic issues and load balancing, and of network-aware applications, that are usually happy with a flat network abstraction.

The role of network monitoring is different in the two tiers: on client's side the user is mainly concerned by the compliance to the agreed quality of service, within the infrastructure its role is to verify the expected performance of the network and help the diagnosis in case of deviation.

The next section is dedicated to an insight of the IEEE802.1Q protocol, in order to introduce some basic concepts for use. Later we proceed analyzing the kind of network abstraction offered by popular cloud providers, and finally we give an outlook of the role of network monitoring in that framework.

## 2 LAN virtualization

The infrastructure that supports virtual networking is a traditional, geographically extended network, that includes diverse technologies in order to adapt to different demands: distant computer centers, connected by long haul links, segmented into a number of LANs, connected by switches [3].

The technology used to implement virtual networks over a real network is based on a specific protocol, the IEEE802.1Q, and a specific device, the VLAN-aware bridge.

## 2.1 The IEEE802.1Q protocol

The purpose of the IEEE802.1Q protocol is to allow a network of conformant bridges, the *network infrastructure*, to emulate a number of Virtual LANs. The *network infrastructure* is composed of LAN segments: VLAN-aware bridges route MAC frames so that they are confined within the LAN segments that participate in the implementation of a given VLAN.

In figure 1 the example of a network split into three segments to accommodate logistics, hosting three distinct Virtual LANs. Although some of the advantages of LAN virtualization are not evident in that simple example, we note that:

- performance improves, since physical links that are part of a given VLAN carry only traffic on that VLAN;
- security improves, since it is impossible to interfere (e.g. sniff) traffic on a different VLAN;
- network configuration (e.g., move a host onto a different VLAN) becomes easier since VLAN reconfiguration does not require intervention on cabling.

At this point of our description, each physical link is associated to a single VLAN. To simplify the cabling, IEEE902.1Q defines bridge ports that exchange frames belonging to several VLANs, while ensuring that each VLAN is isolated from the others. This introduces the presence of *trunks* that aggregate the traffic for several VLANs.

The IEEE802.1Q protocol confines communication within one single VLAN: there is no provision for inter-VLAN routing using VLAN-aware bridges. This must be done by a level 3 router: for instance a router with one trunking interface attached to the network infrastructure supporting IEEE802.1Q is split into several virtual interfaces (or sub-interfaces in Cisco jargon) attached to distinct VLANs: packets from one VLAN to the other will cross the router.

The extra functionalities of VLAN-aware bridges are supported by an extra field added to the Ethernet frame header (see figure 2), whose presence is announced by an Ethernet Type specific for the IEEE802.1Q (0x8100).

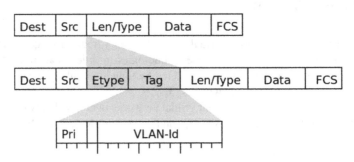

**Fig. 2** Frame header with IEEE802.1Q tagging

The tag contains a subfield to indicate a priority (3 bits), and another (12 bits) to indicate the VLAN, using an identifier (or color) unique for a specific VLAN.

The Priority is used by a VLAN-aware bridge in order to select the appropriate outbound queue associated with the output port of the bridge. In its turn, each queue is associated to a given class of service, corresponding to a determined quality of service.

As a consequence, each VLAN is separately manageable, and VLAN-aware bridges are informed about the quality of service associated to a given VLAN. In particular, this can be used to differentiate expedited traffic, like VoIP, from other classes.

A LAN segment that has been selected by network management to receive frames assigned to a given VLAN is said to be a member of the VLAN. Similarly, end stations that are attached to those LAN segments and that can receive frames assigned to the VLAN are said to be attached to that VLAN.

One relevant consequence of the introduction of the IEEE802.1Q protocol is that part of the routing activity is moved from layer 3 (network) to level 2 (data link), using the VLAN identifier recorded in each frame: routing aims at multicasting the frames only within segments that belong to the destination VLAN. Routing activity in IEEE802.1 materializes in a *filtering activity*.

The information for taking the decisions needed to drive the filtering activity are contained in a database, the *Filtering Database*. In principle its content might be compiled by network administrators. In practice this task is delicate and difficult, so that a specific protocol has been designed to gather informations from manager requests, and automatically diffuse Filtering Database updates to the concerned VLAN switches. A standard specification for such protocol has been given (called Multiple VLAN Registration Protocol (MVRP) defined in IEEE802.1ak-2007), and there are also proprietary solution (Cisco[5] VTP [4]).

It is important to note that the presence of these facilities makes practically feasible the *on demand* management of a VLAN aware network.

One of the *caveats* in the configuration of the filtering database contents that implement a VLAN is the presence of loops: the packets originated at an interface attached to a VLAN should be propagated in a tree rooted in the originating interface. An algorithm that conforms to this requirement is embedded in the same standard document. The Multiple Spanning Tree (MSTP) is based on an algorithm found by R. Perlman [7], modified in order to take into account the existence of VLANs.

---

[5] Cisco is a trademark of Cisco Systems, Inc

# 3 The VLAN-cloud connection

The VLAN technology is quite powerful, and has a number of potential applications. The point for us is that it converges towards the concept of cloud computing in the IaaS sense.

In fact,

- VLAN trunking allows a single interface to serve several VLANs through virtual interfaces;
- a protocol exists to automatically reconfigure VLANs by managing the filtering databases of the involved switches;
- distinct VLANs run in isolation, without the possibility of leaking, thus ensuring an adequate level of security.

These facts allow to introduce the abstract concept of a virtual host, attached to a virtual LAN through a virtual interface: the building block of a virtual infrastructure. All this can be arranged dynamically, on demand, using the VLAN management protocol.

Here we want to note that the result is that the management of a complex infrastructure is rendered with a very simple metaphor, with the effect of making the infrastructure usable with limited background, without even knowing the name of the IEEE902.1Q protocol, reaching an extremely wide platea of users.

Although appealing, this concept exhibits a potential problem given by the limited scalability. In fact, the number of VLANs in a network is necessarily limited by the length of the VLAN-Id field: 12 bits allow not more that 4096 VLANs to be specified.

In the next section we consider two cases of commercial products that offer virtualization benefits. The two cases are quite different in nature, although they fall in the IaaS category: their study is a way to understand different approaches to virtualization from the point of view of networking, and thus give the basis for our discussion of network monitoring issues.

Amazon EC2 offers a service to the end user wishing to exploit the IaaS technology for its own purpose. VMware is capable of implementing the IaaS service using available technologies, including VLANs. We briefly summarize their characteristics, before proceeding in our discussion on network monitoring.

## 3.1 Amazon EC2

EC2 gives a minimal control over networking issues, which are almost completely hidden from the user. The user is provided with one pair of IP addresses assigned to the Virtual Machine (VM) when it is created: one accessible only from inside the cloud, the other accessible from outside. The user has no control on how these IPs are generated. In addition, the client may reserve a few additional IP numbers exposed to the Internet.

The user has some possibility to indicate the logistics of a given VM. With this, Amazon wants to meet the practical needs of an enterprise wishing to delocalize computational activities: legal issues concerning the place where processing takes place, and reliability concerns, related to avoiding the loss of data as a consequence of a single failure.

The two aspects are coped with using two distinct abstractions: the *region*, which specifies the geographical region where the computation will take place, and the *availability zone*, that allows to allocate instances so to minimize the possibility that a single failure hits more than one instance.

The *security group* may indirectly serve to implement a sort of VLAN, intended as a set of VMs sharing the same reachability constraints. There are no guarantees of efficiency in the communication, and such tool is primarily intended to simplify the management of security issues.

We note that such abstractions are mostly oriented to a solid and specific market: 3-tiers web servers. Offering a restricted number of functionalities the resulting interface is easy to use, and hides most of the complexities inherent to provisioning an IaaS.

Here we consider EC2 as the representative of a larger class of products with similar characteristics: from our point of view, they share an opaque approach to networking. The service provider may make efforts in order to optimize network utilization, but this is totally out of control from the point of view of the client.

The Open Grid Forum OCCI Working Group [1] is currently pursuing the standardization of an interface for Cloud Computing. The concepts reflected in the interface, for what is concerning networking, are quite similar to those implemented by EC2.

## 3.2 VMware

VMware offers a quite complete set of tools oriented to exploiting various virtualization technologies; when we focus on networking, we see that the VLAN concepts descending from the standard IEEE802.1Q are easily integrated in VMware infrastructures [10].

Both *virtual adapters* and *virtual switches* [8] are present as abstractions in the toolset. Trunking between ports on virtual switches and adapters is supported as well. However, VMware introduces a notable limitation: within a single host there is no possibility to interconnect two virtual switches.

This option is justified by the improved reliability obtained by forcing the network into a flat structure; on the other hand, complex hierarchical structures are mainly justified by logistics, but a virtualized environment removes such kind of concerns.

In essence, a Virtual Switch can be connected to a number of virtual hosts arranged into distinct VLANs within the server, and to physical adapters or switches outside the server. The typical networking internal to a server is depicted in figure 3.

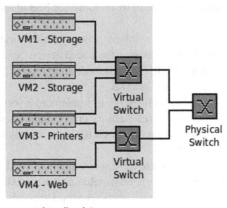

Virtualized Server

**Fig. 3** Typical internal networking of a VMware server

This option makes useless running the cumbersome spanning tree protocol inside the server: the single-tier structure enforced by VMware simply does not allow the introduction of loops, whose avoidance is the main reason for the existence of the spanning tree protocol.

The flexibility inherent to a virtual infrastructure allows the introduction of some limits to the utilization of the traffic trunking technology: these restrictions contribute to a more efficient operation of the server. The recommended organization envisions virtual switches exposing trunking links to the outside (uplinks, in VMware terminology), and untagged communications on ports directed to virtualized hosts within the VMware server.

Overall, the VMware framework allows the exploitation of the VLAN advantage in a virtualized environment: for instance, a virtual server can be moved from one VLAN to another just by reconfiguring switches.

The perspective of a cloud computing facility offering elastic services is envisioned as one of the potential applications, using the *Lab Manager* application. Within this framework the possibility of managing network configuration is retained.

## 4 Network Monitoring in the age of the Cloud

In order to find the concepts that should guide the design of an effective network monitoring activity in an environment that makes use of virtualization techniques, we need to identify which kind of data do we need to obtain from this activity. We discover that they are different, depending on the layer where the monitored activity takes place: we distinguish, and examine separately, the user layer and the cloud infrastructure layer.

Further, network monitoring activity may be directed to fulfill two distinct purposes: on one side, to detect networking problems and thus improve fault tolerance, on the other to optimize network utilization. Here we mostly focus on the second alternative: the typical scenario is a network intensive application that has alternative ways to carry out its activity. Network availability may bias the decision process.

## 4.1 Network monitoring on the user side

The user is typically presented with an unstructured set of processing units with no clues about the network infrastructure that binds them together, as seen inspecting the EC2 framework. We may envision two scenarios for the requirements of an end client to a network monitoring infrastructure:

- verify the conformance of the provided service with respect to the Quality of Service (QoS) or for accounting;
- optimize its operation depending on network performance.

We note that the Cloud Service provider may dynamically interfere with both aspects, as seen studying the VMware toolset.

The conformance to QoS is accommodated using passive monitoring tools that inspect traffic across virtual interfaces: being implemented in software, a tempting idea is that such interfaces might be easily instrumented with code used to extract traffic patterns and characteristics. However, the implementation of virtual interfaces turns out to be rather out of control from the point of view of the user, who should rely on features implemented by the IaaS provider.

Network Monitoring tools running in the user space appear to be more appropriate for the task: for instance, inside a virtual server used for load balancing purposes of a number of virtual data servers. In this case, traffic and connections monitoring can be used, for instance, to measure the data transfer rate within the cloud between data servers and the load balancer, or to bill the user accounts according to the quantity of data transferred.

One relevant aspect is that, since one of the major benefits of the cloud computing concept is dynamic adaptation, network monitoring configuration must be dynamic as well. For instance, in the data server example above, when one data server is added or removed to respond to load changes, the network monitoring activity must be adapted accordingly.

We observe that such adaptation should be controlled by an application running in the user space of the load balancer: this enforces the conclusion that network monitoring application should be resident in the user space, and controlled by the user application.

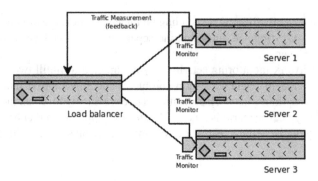

**Fig. 4** Closed loop load balancing with user level network monitoring

A consequence of the discussion above is that network monitoring may sit in a critical place concerning resource management of an application that makes use of IaaS, since it implements the feedback control, as seen in figure 4: from control theory, we know that a badly controlled feedback may make the whole system unstable.

One aspect that is not very relevant for the end user is testing liveness and reachability of virtual machines: the probability of host unreachability is drastically reduced by the service provider, which manages the underlying resources and may even relocate the virtual server in case of failure of its physical support.

## 4.2 Network monitoring on the service provider side

The service provider needs are more composite than those of the end user. We distinguish two aspects: one related to the underlying virtualization infrastructure, the other making reference to the provided service.

As mentioned in the previous section, one of the major tasks of the service provider is to guarantee that VMs are properly working and connected: virtualization infrastructures need to provide tools for such purpose.

For instance, VMware introduces the concept of *beacons* in order to verify the state of health of the virtual infrastructure.

Beacons technique is based on sending packets outside physical servers. In this way the unavailability of uplinks is detected. When coupled with Network Interface Card (NIC) teaming (a materialization of standard IEEE802.1AX [6]) we obtain a substantial increment of reliability of the networking infrastructure: *teams* of links are operated to implement a single virtual link, performing load balancing and excluding a link when diagnosed as failed.

However, pure connectivity does not exhaust the needs of a cloud computing infrastructure. The performance of the networking infrastructure is fundamental in the operation of the cloud both from the point of view of the user of the cloud infrastructure, and from the perspective of the management.

From the point of view of the user, the virtual network performance should be consistent with the agreed QoS. Here the task of network management is to enforce that such constraints are respected: this entails a selective monitoring of the connectivity services offered to a given client.

The task is addressed using end-to-end monitoring between the servers where client instances are running: packet filters are applied in order to select the traffic relevant for the specific client application, and to measure the related network performance.

We note that traffic between physical servers is probably trunked and link aggregation is also used: network monitoring may become difficult in a generic intermediate point. Therefore we conclude that network monitoring should be operated within the virtual environment (e.g., within the server) probably using passive techniques implemented, for instance, within virtual switches. Alternatives are viable, since the virtualization infrastructure may provide a promiscuous mode for switches.

These measurements might be offered as additional services to the user wanting to optimize its computation.

From the point of view of the traffic associated to the management activity, one primary concern is Virtual Machine Image (VMI) displacement: this piece of data amounts to several GBytes, and each VM instantiation entails the displacement of the corresponding VMI from a repository to the server hosting the VM. Commonly used VMIs may be disseminated throughout the Cloud infrastructure, but customized ones must not be too far from the server where the corresponding VM is instantiated. The optimization problem exhibits several degrees of freedom, and its solution is not straightforward. However VMI displacement is the kind of activity that is planned in advance, with little help from network monitoring results.

The event of the displacement of a running VM may be envisioned for fault tolerance, as well as for extreme performance reasons. This event cannot be anticipated, so its execution should be evaluated also considering instantaneous bandwidth availability. Such measurements are extremely difficult to synthesize from a link level view of the traffic: an active end-to-end measurement of residual network availability seems to be a simpler solution for this case. We note that this kind of solution may hinder or make less effective traffic engineering solutions operated on the basis of more predictable traffic.

Looking at the other aspect of network management, the compliance to the QoS agreed with user, we focus on especially demanding applications: those that require audio and video transfer.

The team working around IEEE802.1 is deeply concerned with audio/video streaming over bridged architectures: such interest materializes in a task group[6] The activity of the group covers the identification of the components of such a network, the transport of timing information [9], and end-to-end resource reservation.

---

[6] http://www.ieee802.org/1/pages/avbridges.html

Network monitoring plays a relevant role in media streaming: as a general rule, the application itself collects statistics in order to optimize buffering or for other reasons related to the real time nature of the stream. The presence of resource reservation protocols should restrict network monitoring to fault tolerance and accounting purposes.

# 5 Conclusions

Cloud computing is a concept that arises from the aggregation of new and effective techniques. Among these techniques there is a new way for network management, centered around the Virtual Local Area Network technology.

The application of this technology drastically changes the basics of network monitoring design, since tools running at level 3 in the ISO/OSI stack have a picture of the network that does not correspond to the real network, but to a synthetic abstraction.

Network level 2 implements sophisticated traffic engineering techniques:

- trunking allows a single link to support distinct virtual links, managed individually, preventing leaking with high security;
- teaming allows several links to cooperate to the implementation of a single highly reliable link;
- traffic classification allows provisioning several quality of service over the same link.

The consequence is that network phenomena at level 3 are quite different, overall exhibiting a reliable operation, with predictable performance.

The purpose of network monitoring changes accordingly. The user may want to use it primarily for accounting and secondarily to optimize, while fault detection and removal are uninteresting, since the infrastructure provides highly reliable links, and failures are beyond reach when they occur. The service provider needs data that report the dynamic evolution of the link level in order to drive mapping the VM instances requested by users to the servers, and to operate fault tolerance.

We have deliberately disregarded the utilization of network monitoring techniques to enforce security: we considered that this utilization falls outside the scope of this paper, that mostly addresses traffic control. However the potential security of VLAN based architectures must be protected against certain attacks, e.g. VLAN-hopping.

## 5.1 Looking ahead

Here we envision future directions for research on network monitoring, motivated by the above arguments:

- defining link level network monitoring features that can be embedded into virtual switches and virtual network adapters. The user may take advantage of statistics collected from within the NIC. Using virtual adapters, this feature does not need expensive specialized hardware, but the implementation of such features in the software that implements virtual adapters. Questions arise concerning how to control such features, how to implement them in a efficient way, and how to manage the data produced.
- embedding network monitoring features within developing standards. The IEEE802.1 working groups are currently active in the definition of new standards for VLANs: the inclusion of native network monitoring features within the protocol itself may reduce the overhead introduced to perform measurements;
- studying user level network monitoring infrastructures that dynamically deploy in infrastructures configured on demand. A network monitoring infrastructure may become quite complex, and its management may become a problem for itself. A network monitoring infrastructure that is automatically deployed while new VMs are instantiated may be of interest for those users that want to optimize the utilization of the virtualized infrastructure.

# References

1. Open cloud computing interface (OCCI) WG charter, March 2009.
2. Amazon Web Services LLC. *Amazon Elastic Compute Cloud - Getting Started Guide*, 2009.
3. CISCO Systems. *Overview of Routing between Virtual LANs*.
4. CISCO Systems. *Understanding VLAN Trunk Protocol (VTP)*.
5. IEEE Computer Society. *IEEE Standard for Local and metropolitan area networks - Virtual Bridged Local Area Networks*, 2005.
6. IEEE Computer Society. *IEEE Standard for Local and metropolitan area networks - Link Aggregation*, 2008.
7. Radia Perlman. An algorithm for distributed computation of a spanningtree in an extended LAN. *SIGCOMM Comput. Commun. Rev.*, 15(4):44–53, 1985.
8. Jeremy Sugerman, Ayalvadi J. Venkitachalam, Ganesh, and Beng-Hong Lim. Virtualizing I/O devices on VMware workstation's hosted virtual machine monitor. In *USENIX Annual Technical Conference*, page 14, Boston, june 2001.
9. Michael D. Johas Teener and Geoffrey M. Garner. Overview and timing performance of IEEE 802.1AS. In *International IEEE Symposium on Precision Clock Synchronization for Measurement, Control and Communication (ISPCS)*, pages 22–26, Ann Arbor (MI), September 2008.
10. VMware. *VMware Virtual Networking Concepts*.

# Acronyms

VM      Virtual Machine
VMI     Virtual Machine Image
VLAN    Virtual LAN

QoS    Quality of Service
IaaS   Infrastructure as a Service
MVRP    Multiple VLAN Registration Protocol
NIC    Network Interface Card

# Recent Advances and Research Challenges in Desktop Grid and Volunteer Computing

Gilles Fedak

**Abstract** For over a decade, Desktop Grid systems have paved the way to high throughput computing over large scale network of Desktop PCs. Nowadays, the aggregate computing power of the main Volunteer Computing projects shows performance exceeding several PetaFlops . To achieve this outstanding result, many theoretical and experimental projects and researches have investigated on how to take advantage of idle CPU's and derived the principles of Desktop Grids. After a decade of research in this prolific field of distributed computing science, time has come to survey the recent advances and results as well as understand what are the real challenge and technological issues. In this paper, we present and classify several Desktop Grid systems according to their principles and architectures. We discuss the opportunity for Data Desktop Grid and we present the future trends of this research at the age of Cloud Computing.

**Key words:** Desktop Grids, Volunteer Computing Systems

## 1 Introduction

Nowadays, Desktop Grid (DG) is a well-accepted computing platform for high throughput computing. Volunteer Computing Systems (VCS), which are a particular kind of Desktop Grids where the computing resources are provided by individuals, are among the largest distributed systems in the world. For instance, the BOINC [1] platform is used to run over 60 Internet Computing projects and scale up to 4 millions of participants. As of October 2009, the aggregated computing power provided by the participants in all projects, is over 2.7 PFlops, which is considerable computing power although it could not be compared to traditional supercomputing.

Gilles Fedak*
LIP/INRIA Rhône-Alpes, e-mail: Gilles.Fedak@inria.fr

To achieve this outstanding result, many theoretical and experimental projects and researches have investigated on how to take advantage of idle CPU's and derived the principles the of Desktop Grids. After a decade of research in this prolific field of distributed computing science, time has come to survey the recent advances and results as well as understand what are the real challenge and technological issues.

Since the late 90's, the landscape of computational distributed systems has evolved dramatically with Grid systems being deployed and run in production at large scale and the recent emergence of Cloud Computing. Because Desktop Grid systems are built around flexible and robust technologies, they remarkably well adapt to radical evolutions, as for instance, the emergence of multi-core systems or GPU processing. For instance the Folding@Home project has a significant part of its computing power contributed by PS3 gaming consoles. In this paper, we present and classify several Desktop Grid systems according to their principles and architectures. We will try to forecast and maybe envision some of the technological breakthroughs needed for Desktop grid research to sustain their growth.

The rest of the paper is organized as follows. Section 2 gives an overview of main DG systems, Section 3 discusses Data Desktop Grid, Section 4 discusses integration of DG into eScience infrastructures and we conclude in Section 5.

## 2 History and Classification of Desktop Grid Systems

In this section, we briefly present the main principles of Desktop Grid computing and examine the main research topics. We direct the reader who would like to obtain deeper information and details to this paper [2].

Origin of Desktop Grids comes from the concept of *cycle stealing* developed in the late 80's [3] : using remotely CPU's cycles when workstation are idle. Due to its high attractiveness, cycle stealing has been studied in many research projects like Condor [4], Glunix [5] or MosiX [6]. Results of these researches have been the design and development of software enabling high throughput computing over sets of idle workstation in a single administrative domain.

In the early 90's, the WWW has become increasingly popular. Beside the publication usage, the idea of using the Web as a technology to build distributed computing systems became reality by designing client/server application using http technologies. The combination of web technologies with the Master/Worker programing model has enabled the first generation of Desktop Grid systems, like SETI@Home [7], or distributed.net. The Master-Worker programming approach essentially allows the execution of bag of tasks parallel applications on loosely coupled computing resources. Because it can be combined with simple fault detection and tolerance mechanisms, it fits extremely well with the Desktop Grid platforms that are very dynamic by essence.

At the same time emerged the Java language, which was offering key benefits of virtual machine properties: high portability across heterogeneous hardware and OS, large diffusion of virtual machine in Web browsers and a strong security model associated with byte-code execution. A first approach was proposed by Web Computing projects such as Charlotte [8], Javelin [9], Bayanihan [10] , SuperWeb [11] and PopCorn [12]. At the end of the 90's these projects have proved that DG was a successful proof of concept. They have paved the way for several research works in the fields of programming model, results certification and scheduling. However, this success has been obtained at the price of simplification as they were built around a single application and only the project administrator could use the computing power provided by the whole Desktop Grids.

Lack of genericity is one of the fundamental motivations of the second generation of Global Computing systems like BOINC [1] and XtremWeb [13].

The Berkeley Open Infrastructure for Network Computing (BOINC) is a middleware dedicated to volunteer based Desktop Grid which provides several components like jobs scheduler, user forum, credits reward system, application authentication for an easy integration and deployment of VCS projects. Only the application that actually does the computation needs to be changed for each project. Results are computed by volunteers on the Internet and therefore cannot be trusted. A special component must exist which certifies that results are valid.

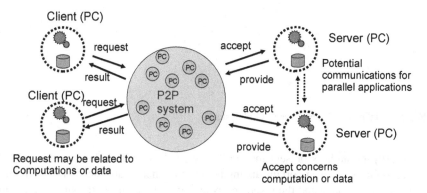

**Fig. 1** Global Desktop Grid : users can aggregate and share their computing power as well as network and storage capacity

XtremWeb [14] is an open source research project at LRI and LAL which can be classified as a Global Desktop Grid (see Figure 1) : the principle is that any participant can volunteer his computing resources, as in BOINC, but can also use other participants' computing resources or storage. In this scenario, each participant, assuming that he or she has the user rights which allow such operations, has the ability to register new applications and data and to submit new computational jobs. As a consequence, Global Desktop Grid systems need several additional components with respect to Volunteer Desktop Grids : a sandbox [15] system which protects the participant's computing resources of the users' submitted application as well as users authentication and users rights management system which defines the relationship between users/data/application/hosts.

There exists several approaches to classify Desktop Grid systems. Desktop Grids have emerged while the community was considering clustering and hierarchical designs as good performance-cost tread-offs. A first approach is to compare Desktop Grid against Clusters, Grids and P2P systems as shown in Figure 2. Several parameters distinguish Desktop Grids from clusters: scale, communication, heterogeneity and volatility. Moreover, Desktop Grids share with Grid a common objective: to extend the size and accessibility of a computing infrastructure beyond the limit of a single administration domain.

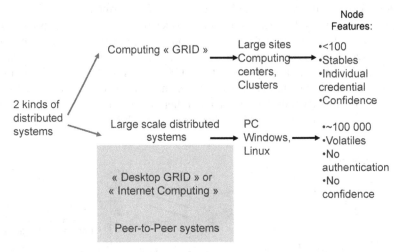

**Fig. 2** Desktop Grid Systems versus Grid System

In [16] the authors present the similarities and differences between Grids and Desktop Grids. Two important distinguishing parameters are the user community (professional or not) and the resource ownership (who own the resources and who is using them). In contrast, institutional HPC relies on few number of stable nodes and authenticated users belonging to well known institutions. Table 1 summaries the characteristics of Desktop Grid resources and the consequence over Desktop Grid systems design.

| Resources | System |
|---|---|
| High number | Requires scalable design |
| Volatility | PCs can join and leave the network at any time and appear with several identities. Requires strong fault-tolerance mechanisms. |
| Low performance | Poor communication link and unreliable storage. Requires replication mechanisms. |
| Owned by volunteer | Resources are shared between their users and the desktop grid applications and scattered across administrative domains with a wide variety of security mechanisms such as personal routers/firewalls |

**Table 1** Resources characteristics and the influence over Desktop Grid systems design.

The second approach is to classify Desktop Grid resources according to deployments and resources location. We can further subdivide Desktop Grid systems into the following categories :

*Local Desktop Grid*, also known as Enterprise Desktop Grid, consists of Desktop PC hosted within a corporation or University interconnected by LAN's. Several companies such as Entropia [17], United Devices, Platform, Mesh Technologies have specially targeted these LANs as a platform for supporting Desktop Grid applications. The Condor [4] system has shown that Enterprise Desktop Grids are an attractive platform for high throughput computing because the hosts usually have better connectivity and have relatively less volatility and heterogeneity than Desktop Grids that span the entire Internet.

*Internet Desktop Grids* aggregates resources provided by end-user Internet volunteer. At the beginning, the largest projects such as distributed.net [18] or SETI@Home [7] were running a single application. In contrast the BOINC system allows multiple application to be executed on volunteer PCs and XtremWeb allows participants to submit applications and jobs to the Desktop Grid.

Most of the Desktop Grid systems are built around three logical components : clients, servers and workers. Several instances of those components might be used at the same time. Client allows platform users to interact with the platform by submitting stand-alone jobs and retrieving results. Worker is the component running on the PC which is responsible for executing jobs. The server is a coordination service which connects clients and workers. The server receives jobs submissions from clients and distributes them to workers according to the scheduling policy. Servers also manage fault tolerance by detecting worker crash or disconnection. If needed tasks are restarted on other available workers. At the end, server retrieves and stores results before clients download them.

We can further classify Desktop Grids according to their architectural organization with respect to the three components previously mentioned.

We can see from the Figure 3 that Distributed Applications (3-a), Global Desktop Grid (3-b), and Volunteer Desktop Grid (3-c) are built around a centralized architecture where a single server and sometime client is shared by all computing resources. This design could potentially face issues with scalability and fault tolerance (single point of failure). One should expect that more computing resources also provides more network bandwidth and storage capacity. On the contrary, data distribution with BOINC for instance, relies on multiple http servers and tasks are described as a list of files locations, which can be a potential bottleneck when scheduling tasks sharing large input files.

In contrast, Collaborative Desktop Grid (3-d) and P2P Desktop Grid (3-e) are built around network of servers. The Ourgrid [19] project proposes a mechanisms for laboratories to put together their local Desktop Grids. OurGrid organizes the interconnection of Local Desktop Grid in P2P network of Peers, where each peers represent a set of Clients and Workers. A similar approach has been proposed by the Condor team under the term ock of condor [20] Several P2P Desktop Grids (P3, PowerPlant, PastryGrid [21]) have proposed which consider a flat architecture

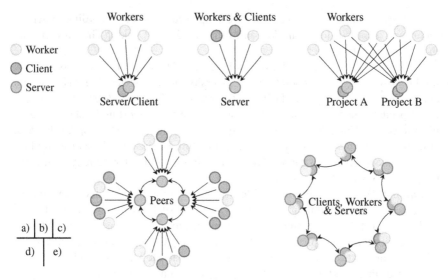

**Fig. 3** Different architectures of Desktop Grid project : a/ Distributed Application, b/ Global Desktop Grid, C/ Volunteer Computing, d/ Collaborative Desktop Grid, e/ P2P Desktop Grid

where each node provides computing resources, submits jobs and participates to the maintenance of the system.

# 3 Towards Data Desktop Grid

Data-intensive applications form an important class of applications for the e-Science community which require secure and coordinated access to large datasets, wide-area transfers and broad distribution of TeraBytes of data while keeping track of multiple data replicas. Although Desktop Grid have been very successful in the area of High Throughput Computing, data-intense computing is a promising area where some major achievements combining the huge storage potential with the processing capability are expected.

Although Data Desktop Grid tackle many research issues, we can decompose this problem in four subtopics : data distribution, data storage, data processing and handling high volume of data output. At the moment there is no single solution which solve all these issues. Instead, several significant advances have been recently achieved independently in each of this subtopics. In this section, we survey the most recent and significant ones.

There are two approaches to distribute large volume of data to large number of nodes distributed on Internet.

The first approach relies on P2P protocols where peers collaboratively participate to the distribution of the data by exchanging file chunks. In [22], authors investigate the use of the Bittorrent protocol with the XtremWeb Desktop Grid in the case of data-intense bag of tasks application. The conclusion is that Bittorrent outperforms FTP if the file is large and shared amongst a large number of nodes. In [23], authors conduct similar studies with the BOINC middleware and conclude similarly. If the P2P approach seems efficient, it assumes that volunteers would agree that their PC connects directly to another participant's machine to exchange data. Unfortunately, this could be seen as a potential security and is unlikely to be accepted widely by users. This drawbacks has so far prevented adoption of P2P protocol by major volunteer computing projects.

The second approach is to use a content delivery approach where files are distributed by a secure network of well-known and authenticated volunteers [24, 25]. This approach is followed by the ADICS project [26] (Peer-to-Peer Arhictecture for Data-Intensive Cycle Sharing), whose architecture is presented in Figure 4. Instead of retrieving files from a centralized server, workers get their input data from a network of cache peers organized in a P2P ring. This approach presents the following benefits : *i*) central servers can offload data distribution, thus reducing the server bottleneck and increasing data availability, *ii*) security criteria and replication strategies can be imposed upon data cache peers and *iii*) only workers who agree to participate to the data-sharing network have to run a P2P protocol, others use regular HTTP protocol to download files.

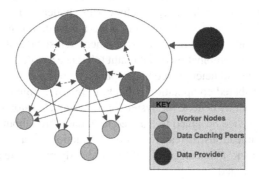

**Fig. 4** Architecture of the ADICS project (original Figure can be found in [25])

Several systems have been proposed to aggregate unused storage of desktop workstation within a LAN. Farsite [27] builds a virtual centralized file system over a set of untrusted desktop computers. It provides file reliability and availability through cryptography, replication and file caching. Freeloader [28] fulfills similar goals but unifies data storage as a unique scratch/cache space for hosting immutable datasets and exploiting data locality. Recently [29] Freeloader has been enhanced by high level features such as prefix-caching and collective file transfer in order to increase performance of applications accessing cached data. Nevertheless these projects offer a file system semantic for accessing data that is not precise enough to give users (or an agent that work on behalf of the user) control over data placement, replication and fault tolerance. However these projects target local network, an open question is how these solutions would scale to the Internet scale.

BitDew [30] is a programmable environment for automatic and transparent data management on computational Desktop Grids. BitDew relies on a specific set of meta-data to drive key data management operations, namely life cycle, distribution, placement, replication and fault-tolerance with a high level of abstraction. The Bit-dew runtime environment is a flexible distributed service architecture that integrates modular P2P components such as DHT's for a distributed data catalog and collab-orative transport protocols for data distribution. asynchronous and reliable multi-protocols transfers.

The former projects allows to persistently store data on Desktop PCs, only few initiatives associate data-intense computing with large scale distributed storage on volatile resources. In [31], authors present an architecture following the super-peer approach where the super peers serve as cache data server, handle jobs submissions and coordinate execution of parallel computations. Authors show how this frame-work is efficient when processing classical distributed data mining tasks such as solving FCIM (Frequent Closed Itemsets Mining) problem. FCIM is a widespread data mining operation which search for associations or patterns within databases.

One of the grand challenge which requires huge processing power and large vol-ume of data is to determine the DNA structure and sequences of human being and animals. Basic Local Alignment Search Tool (BLAST)[32] is one of the most im-portant and fundamental technology to achieve this challenge. BLAST computation on Desktop Grid is proposed in [33] following a data-driven master/worker. Im-plementation leverages on the BitDew environment to take benefit of multi-protocol data distribution and combination of data fault tolerance and data replication to cope with highly volatile and heterogeneous computing resources.

Massively distributed computation is likely to produce high data outputs which can be handled either by generic file system or by specialized storage. BlobSeer [34] s a data storage service designed to handled high data throughput of Desktop Grid data-intensive applications. It features blobs abstraction, data fine grain access as well as large number of concurrent clients to efficiently read/write and append huge data that are fragmented.

Another important source of output data is the checkpoint operation, which is frequent in Desktop Grid in order to cope with long running applications. StdChkpt [35] is a checkpoint storage systems which gathers local storage desktops. stdchk is specialized in many ways to for management of checkpoint images : handling of write series for high-speed I/O, support for data reliability and versionning, incre-mental checkpointing and lifetime management of checkpoint images. [36] and [37] propose to cluster nodes and use replication to improve checkpoint images reliabil-ity and performance when getting data.

Research Highlights 1 : MapReduce on Desktop Grid

MapReduce [38] is an emerging programing model for data-intense application proposed by Google, which has attracted a lot of attention recently. MapReduce borrows from functional programming : programmer defines Map task executed on data which produces intermediate output and Reduce task which combines intermediate output into a final result. Most of the current implementation, such as Hadoop[39] associates a distributed file system with a master/worker runtime which schedules Map and Reduce tasks to the nodes holding the data. MapReduce on Desktop Grid presents most of the challenges presented this section with respect to data distribution storage and processing. In addition, the reduction phase has to be considered as collective operation on files which has not been addressed yet.

# 4 Integrating Desktop Grids into Cyber-Science Infrastructures

There is a growing demand of scientific communities for large scale distributed computing infrastructures to solve their grand-challenge problems. Grid infrastructures such as EGEE [40] in Europe, NorduGrid, TeraGrid in the United States or China-Grid [41] in China, Desktop Grids and Volunteer Computing systems and the new emerging Cloud Computing such as Amazon EC2 [42] are representative of this diverse attempts to reach ever higher throughput computing. Unfortunately, these computing infrastructures are developed independently without interaction between them.

Interoperation between Service Grids (SG) and Desktop Grids (DG) has already been explored, notably by the Lattice project [43], Condor and XtremWeb [4], Superlink as well as the new the European FP7 infrastructure project: EDGeS (Enabling Desktop Grids for e-Science) [44]. EDGeS aims to build technological bridges to facilitate interoperability between the EGEE Grid and XtremWeb and BOINC Desktop Grids. EDGeS enables EGEE users to access Desktop Grid computing resources, either provided by Internet users (public DGs) or deployed within universities or enterprises (private DGs) as shown in Figure 5.

There exists two main approaches to bridge SG and DG. The superworker, proposed by the Lattice[43] project and the SZTAKI Desktop Grid[46], is the first solution. This enables the usage of several Grid or cluster resources to execute DG tasks. The superworker is a daemon between the DG server and the SG resources. From the DG server point of view, the Grid or cluster appears as one single resource with large computing capabilities. The superworker continuously fetches tasks or work units from the DG server, wraps and submits the tasks accordingly to the local Grid or cluster resources manager. When computations are finished on the SG computing nodes, the superworker sends back the results to the DG server. Thus, the

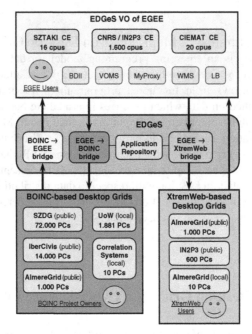

**Fig. 5** EDGeS infrastructure connects EGEE VO and XtremWeb and BOINC Desktop Grids, either public and private. (original figure can be found in [45])

superworker by itself is a scheduler which needs to continuously scan the queues of the computing resources and watch for available resources to launch jobs.

The SZTAKI 3G bridge [45] is a middleware developed within the EDGES consortium which extends this concept by providing a generic interface allowing several SG and DG technologies to work together. At the moment gLite, DC-API, BOINC and XtremWeb are supported and it is planned to support other Grid middleware such as Unicore.

Since the superworker is a centralized agent this solution has several drawbacks:

1. the superworker can become a bottleneck when the number of computing resources or the number of tasks and data increase,
2. the round trip for a work unit is increased because it has to be marshalled/unmarshalled by the superworker,
3. it introduces a single point of failure in the system, which has low fault-tolerance,
4. some allocation algorithms are needed to mediate between the different SG.

On the other hand, this centralized solution provides better security properties, concerning the integration with the Grid. First the superworker does not require modification of the infrastructure, it can be run under any user identity as long as the user has the right to submit jobs on Grid. Next, as works are wrapped by the superworker, they are run under the user identity, which conforms with the regular security usage, in contrast with the approach described in the following paragraph.

The Gliding-in approach to cluster resources spread in different Condor pool using the Global Computing system (XtremWeb) was first introduced in[47]. The main principle consists in wrapping the XtremWeb worker as regular Condor task and in submitting this task to the Condor pool. Once the worker is executed on a Condor resource, the worker pulls jobs from the DG server, executes the XtremWeb task and return the result to the XtremWeb server. As a consequence, the Condor resources communicates directly to the XtremWeb server. Similar mechanisms are now commonly employed in Grid Computing[48]. The generic approach on the Grid is called a pilot job. Instead of submitting jobs directly to the Grid gatekeeper, this system submits so-called pilot jobs. When executed, the pilot job fetches jobs from an external job scheduler.

The gliding-in or pilot job approach has several advantages. While simple, this mechanism efficiently balances the load between heterogeneous computing sites. It benefits from the fault tolerance provided by the DG server; if Grid nodes fail then jobs are rescheduled to the next available resources. Finally, as the performance study of the Falkon[49] system shows, it gives better performances because series of jobs do not have to go through the gatekeeper queues which is generally characterized by long waiting time, and communication is direct between the worker running on the computing element (CE) and the DG server without intermediate agent such as the superworker. From the security point of view, this approach breaks the Grid security rule about Pilot Jobs. This rule does not allow actual jobs owner to be different than pilot job owner. This is a well known issue of pilot jobs and new solution such as gLExec[50] are proposed to circumvent this security limitation. Furthermore, in [51], a security model is proposed which enable both authenticated an unauthenticated resources, users and application to cooperate within the same infrastructure.

Principle of Cloud computing is to provide access through web services to high-performance computing and storage infrastructure rented by companies. Recently, providing the infrastructure as a service (Iaas) has been pushed partly because the complexity of IT infrastructure is completely hidden from its users. This vision is achieved through the use of virtualization technologies where users can deploy and manage virtual images of their computing environment directly on the Cloud. These capabilities are provided at relatively low costs compared to the infrastructure and administration costs of a traditional Grid system. Amazon Web Service (AWS) [42] is set of services such as virtual cluster, storage, database and content delivery network which provides reliable and scalable cloud computing platform. AWS users relatively to the usage of the platform (CPU time, bandwidth, storage etc...). Eucalyptus[52] provides an interface which is compatible with Amazon EC2 and as such, which can be used in a LAN in place of Amazon EC2.

Virtual machine (VM) technologies are currently experiencing a resurgence in both industry and research communities. These technologies are widespread both in the server market (XEN) and the Desktop market (VMWare, Virtual Box). We think that VMs offer many desirable features such as security, ease of management,

OS customization, performance isolation, checkpointing, and migration, which can offer the technological breakthrough needed to unify the large scale distributed infrastructure.

There are several ongoing work which aims at bringing virtualization technologies to Desktop Grid. Daniel L.G et al. [53] present a method to run legacy applications on BOINC using the standard BOINC Wrapper and a special starter application to set up the environment for the application. The capability of Virtual Machines (VM) to save and resume their state image is used to provide a checkpoint/restart mechanism. LHC@Home [54] chose to use virtualization to increase the portability of the Atlas [55] physics application. Atlas requires the Athena framework which is around 8GB and it is closely tied to a specific Linux distribution. LHC@Home provides VMware images with Linux and the whole software stack needed to run Atlas plus a BOINC client executed within the virtual machine.

However, to be broadly adopted, one needs to bring new lightweight Virtual Machine technology that is generic enough to be deployed over a large range of high throughput computing infrastructures and which will feature fast deployment VM on-the-fly, VM monitoring, VM migration and VM scheduling.

### Research Highlights 2 : Cloud made of Desktop PCs

Desktop Clouds, or clouds made of Desktop PCs is disruptive new research challenge that combines virtualization and Desktop Grid technologies. This would consist in building virtual cluster such as Violin[56], WoW[57] or PVC[58] on top of volunteers PCs and which could be deeply configured on demand by DG users. The expected benefit is that a much broader range of applications could to run on Desktop Grid. Furthermore DG users would have the ability to tune OS their own VM images and deploy their prefered set of services (scheduler, file system, monitoring infrastructure) along with the application. Desktop Clouds raise many research challenges : deployment of VM images on DG resources, scheduling heuristics allowing reservation of DG resources, establishment of virtual cluster despite the network protection of firewalls and NAT, transparent checkpoint/restart of networked VM and, finally replication of communicating VM to ensure better reliability.

## 5 Conclusion

For over a decade, Desktop Grids have delivered to scientists huge computing power at a performance/price ratio unreachable otherwise. Researches around Desktop Grid Systems have been prolific in many aspects : from the system design to large scale deployment and from formal model to observation of real systems, proposing new algorithms as well as adapting existing mechanisms or systems.

At the age of Cloud Computing, Desktop Grid research faces new challenges such as data deluge caused by large experiment such as the LHC. In this paper, we have surveyed the most prominent works towards Data Desktop Grid and we have gave some perspective towards Clouds made of Desktop PCs.

# References

1. D. Anderson. BOINC: A System for Public-Resource Computing and Storage. In *Proceedings of the 5th IEEE/ACM International GRID Workshop*, Pittsburgh, USA, 2004.
2. F. Cappello, G. Fedak, D. Kondo, P. Malécot, and A. Rezmerita. *Handbook of Research on Scalable Computing Technologies*, chapter Desktop Grids: From Volunteer Distributed Computing to High Throughput Computing Production Platforms. IGI Global, 2009.
3. Matt W. Mutka and Miron Livny. Profiling workstations' available capacity for remote execution. In *Proceedings of Performance-87, The 12th IFIP W.G. 7.3 International Symposium on Computer Performance Modeling, Measurement and Evaluation*, Brussels, Belgium, 1987.
4. M. Litzkow, M. Livny, and M. Mutka. Condor - A Hunter of Idle Workstations. In *Proceedings of the 8th International Conference of Distributed Computing Systems (ICDCS)*, 1988.
5. D. Ghormley, D. Petrou, S. Rodrigues, A. Vahdat, and T. Anderson. GLUnix: a Global Layer Unix for a Network of Workstations. *Software-Practice and Experience*, 28(9), July 1998.
6. A. Barak, S. Guday, and Wheeler R. *The MOSIX Distributed Operating System, Load Balancing for UNIX*, volume 672 of *Lecture Notes in Computer Science*. Springer-Verlag, 1993.
7. W. T. Sullivan, D. Werthimer, S. Bowyer, J. Cobb, G. Gedye, and D. Anderson. A new major SETI project based on Project Serendip data and 100,000 personal computers. In *Proc. of the Fifth Intl. Conf. on Bioastronomy*, 1997.
8. A. Baratloo, M. Karaul, Z. Kedem, and P. Wyckoff. Charlotte: Metacomputing on the Web. In *Proc. of PDCS-96*, 1996.
9. P. Cappello, B. Christiansen, M. Ionescu, M. Neary, K. Schauser, and D. Wu. Javelin: Internet-Based Parallel Computing Using Java. In *Proceedings of the Sixth ACM SIGPLAN Symposium on Principles and Practice of Parallel Programming*, 1997.
10. L. Sarmenta. *Volunteer Computing*. PhD thesis, MIT, March 2001.
11. A. D. Alexandrov, M. Ibel, K. E. Schauser, and C.J. Scheiman. SuperWeb: Towards a Global Web-Based Parallel Computing Infrastructure. In *Proc. of the 11th IEEE International Parallel Processing Symposium (IPPS)*, April 1997.
12. N. Camiel, S. London, N. Nisan, and O. Regev. The PopCorn Project: Distributed Computation over the Internet in Java. In *Proc. of the 6th World Wide Web Conference*, April 1997.
13. Gilles Fedak, Cécile Germain, Vincent Néri, and Franck Cappello. XtremWeb: A Generic Global Computing Platform. In *Proceedings of 1st IEEE International Symposium on Cluster Computing and the Grid CCGRID'2001, Special Session Global Computing on Personal Devices*, pages 582–587, Brisbane, Australia, May 2001. IEEE/ACM, IEEE Press.
14. Franck Cappello, Samir Djilali, Gilles Fedak, Thomas Herault, Frédéric Magniette, Vincent Néri, and Oleg Lodygensky. Computing on Large Scale Distributed Systems: XtremWeb Architecture, Programming Models, Security, Tests and Convergence with Grid. *Future Generation Computer Systems*, 21(3):417–437, mar 2005.
15. A. C. Marosi, P. Kacsuk, and G. Fedak. Sandboxing for desktop grids using virtualization. In *To appear in PDP 2010*, Pisa, Italy, February 2010.
16. Ian T. Foster and Adriana Iamnitchi. On death, taxes, and the convergence of peer-to-peer and grid computing. 2735:118–128, 2003.
17. A. Chien, B. Calder, S. Elbert, and K. Bhatia. Entropia: Architecture and Performance of an Enterprise Desktop Grid System. *Journal of Parallel and Distributed Computing*, 2003.
18. Distributed.net. www.distributed.net.

19. Walfredo Cirne, Francisco Brasileiro, Nazareno Andrade, Lauro Costa, Alisson Andrade, Reynaldo Novaes, and Miranda Mowbray. Labs of the world, unite!!! *Journal of Grid Computing*, 4(3):225–246, September 2006.
20. J. Pruyne and M. Livny. A Worldwide Flock of Condors : Load Sharing among Workstation Clusters . *Journal on Future Generations of Computer Systems*, 12, 1996.
21. H. Abbes, C. Cérin, and M. Jemni. Pastrygrid: decentralisation of the execution of distributed applications in desktop grid. In *MGC '08: Proceedings of the 6th international workshop on Middleware for grid computing*, pages 1–6, New York, NY, USA, 2008. ACM.
22. B. Wei, G. Fedak, and F. Cappello. Towards Efficient Data Distribution on Computational Desktop Grids with BitTorrent. *Future Generation Computer Systems*, November 2007.
23. Fernando Costa, Luis Silva, Gilles Fedak, and Ian Kelley. Optimizing Data Distribution in Desktop Grid Platforms. *Parallel Processing Letters*, 18(3):391–410, September 2008.
24. C. Mastroianni, P. Cozza, D. Talia, I. Kelley, and I. Taylor. A scalable super-peer approach for public scientific computation. *Future Generation Computer Systems*, 25(3):213 – 223, 2009.
25. Ian Kelley and Ian Taylor. Bridging the data management gap between service and desktop grids. In Springer, editor, *Distributed and Parallel Systems*, Hungary, 2008.
26. Atticfs. http://www.atticfs.org.
27. Atul Adya and all. Farsite: Federated, Available, and Reliable Storage for an Incompletely Trusted Environment. *SIGOPS Oper. Syst. Rev.*, 36(SI):1–14, 2002.
28. S. Vazhkudai, V. Freeh X. Ma, J. Strickland, N. Tammineedi, and S.L. Scott. FreeLoader: Scavenging Desktop Storage Resources for Scientific Data. In *Proceedings of Supercomputing 2005 (SC'05)*, Seattle, 2005.
29. X. Ma, S. S. Vazhkudai, and Z. Zhang. Improving data availability for better access performance: A study on caching scientific data on distributed workstations. *Journal of Grid Computing–Special Issue on Volunteer Computing and Desktop Grids*, July 2009.
30. Gilles Fedak, Haiwu He, and Franck Cappello. A Data Management and Distribution Service with Multi-Protocol and Reliable File Transfer. *Journal of Network and Computer Applications*, 32(5):961–975, 2009.
31. E. Cesario, N. Caria, C. Mastroianni, and D. Talia. Distributed data mining using a public resource computing framework. In *Proc. of CoreGrid Workshop*, Delft, Nederlands, 2009.
32. Altschul, S. Gish, W. Miller, W. Myers, E.W., and D Lipman. A basic local alignment search tool. *Journal of Molecular Biology*, 215(7):403410, January 1990.
33. Haiwu He, Gilles Fedak, Bing Tran, and Franck Cappello. BLAST Application with Data-aware Desktop Grid Middleware. In *Proceedings of 9th IEEE International Symposium on Cluster Computing and the Grid CCGRID'09*, pages 284–291, Shanghai, China, May 2009.
34. Bogdan Nicolae, Gabriel Antoniu, and Luc Boug. Enabling high data throughput in desktop grids through decentralized data and metadata management: The blobseer approach. In *Proceedings of Euro-Par*, Delft, Nederlands, 2009.
35. Samer Al-Kiswany, Matei Ripeanu, Sudharshan Vazhkudai, and Abdullah Gharaibeh. stdchk: A checkpoint storage system for desktop grid computing. In *International Conference on Distributed Computing Systems (ICDCS'08)*, Beijing, China, 2008.
36. Filipe Araujo, Patricio Domingues, Derrick Kondo, , and Luis Moura Silva. Using cliques of nodes to store desktop grid checkpoints. In *Coregrid Integration Workshop*, Crete, Greece, April 2008.
37. Fatiha Bouabache, Thomas Herault, Gilles Fedak, and Franck Cappello. Hierarchical Replication Techniques to Ensure Checkpoint Storage Reliability in Grid Environments. In *Proceedings of 8th IEEE International Symposium on Cluster Computing and the Grid CCGRID'08*, pages 475–483, Lyon, France, may 2008.
38. Jeffrey Dean and Sanjay Ghemawat. Mapreduce: Simplified data processing on large clusters. pages 137–150, December 2004.
39. Dhruba Borthaku. *The hadoop distributed file system: Architecture and design*, 2007.
40. EGEE. http://www.eu-egee.org/.
41. Hai Jin. ChinaGrid: Making Grid Computing a Reality. In *Lecture Notes in Computer Science, Volume 3334*, pages 13–24, Springer-Veralag Berlin Heidelberg, 2004.

42. Amazon EC2. http://aws.amazon.com/ec2/.
43. D. S. Myers, A. L. Bazinet, and M. P. Cummings. *Expanding the reach of Grid computing: combining Globus- and BOINC-based systems*, chapter Grids for Bioinformatics and Computational Biology,. Wiley Book Series on Parallel and Distributed Computing., 2008.
44. Zoltan Balaton, Zoltan Farkas, Gabor Gombas, Peter Kacsuk, Robert Lovas, Attila Csaba Marosi, Ad Emmen, Gabor Terstyanszky, Tamas Kiss, Ian Kelley, Ian Taylor, Oleg Lodygensky, Miguel Cardenas-Montes, Gilles Fedak, and Filipe Araujo. EDGeS: the Common Boundary Between Service and Desktop Grids. *Parallel Processing Letters*, 18(3):433–453, September 2008.
45. E. Urbah, P. Kacsuk, Z. Farkas, G. Fedak, G. Kecskemeti, O. Lodygensky, A. Marosi, Z. Balaton, G. Caillat, G. Gombas, A. Kornafeld, J. Kovacs, H. He, and R. Lovas. EDGeS: Bridging EGEE to BOINC and XtremWeb. *Journal of Grid Computing*, 2009.
46. Zoltan Balaton, Gabor Gombas, Peter Kacsuk, Adam Kornafeld, Jozsef Kovacs, Attila Csaba Marosi, Gabor Vida, Norbert Podhorszki, and Tamas Kiss. Sztaki desktop grid: a modular and scalable way of building large computing grids. In *Proc. of the 21th International Parallel and Distributed Processing Symposium, 26-30 March 2007, Long Beach, California, USA*, 2007.
47. Oleg Lodygensky, Gilles Fedak, Franck Cappello, Vincent Neri, Miron Livny, and Douglas Thain. XtremWeb & Condor : Sharing Resources Between Internet Connected Condor Pools. In *Proceedings of CCGRID'2003, Third International Workshop on Global and Peer-to-Peer Computing (GP2PC'03)*, pages 382–389, Tokyo, Japan, 2003. IEEE/ACM.
48. Douglas Thain and Miron Livny. Building reliable clients and services. In *The GRID2*, pages 285–318. Morgan Kaufman, 2004.
49. Ioan Raicu, Yong Zhao, Catalin Dumitrescu, Ian Foster, and Mike Wilde. Falkon: a fast and light-weight task execution framework. In *IEEE/ACM SuperComputing*, 2007.
50. Sfiligoi1, O Koeroo2, G Venekamp2, D Yocum1, D Groep, and D Petravick. Addressing the Pilot security problem with gLExec. Technical Report FERMILAB-PUB-07-483-CD, Fermi National Laboratory, 2007.
51. Gabriel Caillat, Gilles Fedak, Haiwu He, Oleg Lodygensky, and Etienne Urbah. Towards a Security Model to Bridge Internet Desktop Grids and Service Grids. In *Proceedings of the Euro-Par 2008 Workshops (LNCS), Workshop on Secure, Trusted, Manageable and Controllable Grid Services (SGS'08)*, Las Palmas de Gran Canaria, Spain, August 2008.
52. Dan Nurmi, Rich Wolski, Chris Grzegorczyk, Graziano Obertelli, Sunil Soman, Lamia Youseff, and Dmitrii Zagorodnov. The eucalyptus open-source cloud-computing system. In *Cloud Computing and Its Applications workshop (CCA'08)*, Chicago, IL, 2008.
53. Gonzalez D.L. Gil G.G. de Vega F.F. Segal B. Centralized boinc resources manager for institutional networks. *IPDPS 2008*, pages 1–8, 2008.
54. Lhc@home. http://lhcathome.cern.ch/lhcathome.
55. Boinc and atlas. https://twiki.cern.ch/twiki/bin/view/lhcathome/boincandatlas.
56. P. Ruth, P. Mcgachey, , and Dongyan Xu. Viocluster : Virtualization for dynamic computational domains. In *IEEE International Conference on Cluster Computing*, Tsukuba, Japan, 2005.
57. Arijit Ganguly, Abhishek Agrawal, P. Oscar Boykin, and Renato J. O. Figueiredo. Wow : Self-organizing wide area overlay networks of virtual workstations. In *In HPDC15 : Proceedings of the 15th IEEE International Sympo- sium on High Performance Distributed Computing*, Paris, France, 2006.
58. Ala Rezmerita, Tangui Morlier, Vincent Neri, and Franck Cappello. Private virtual cluster : infrastructure and protocol for instant grids. In *Proc. of the Int. Euro-Par Conf. on Parallel Processing (Euro-Par 2006)*, Dresden, Germany, 2006.

# Research Challenges in Managing and Using Service Level Agreements

Omer Rana, Wolfgang Ziegler

**Abstract** A Service Level Agreement (SLA) represents an agreement between a service user and a provider in the context of a particular service provision. SLAs contain Quality of Service properties that must be maintained by a provider, and as agreed between a provider and a user/client. These are generally defined as a set of Service Level Objectives (SLOs). These properties need to be measurable and must be monitored during the provision of the service that has been agreed in the SLA. The SLA must also contain a set of penalty clauses specifying what happens when service providers fail to deliver the pre-agreed quality. Hence, an SLA may be used by both a user and a provider – from a user perspective, an SLA defines what is required – often defined using non-functional attributes of service provision. From a providers perspective, an SLA may be used to support capacity planning – especially if a provider is making it's capability available to multiple users. An SLA may be used by a client and provider to manage their behaviour over time – for instance, to optimise their long running revenue (cost) or QoS attributes (such as execution time), for instance. The lifecycle of an SLA is outlined, along with various uses of SLAs to support infrastructure management. A discussion about WS-Agreement – the emerging standard for specifying SLAs – is also provided.

## 1 Introduction

A Service Level Agreement (SLA) represents an agreement (or contract) between a service user and a provider in the context of a particular service provision. An SLA may exist between two parties, for instance, a single user and a single provider, or

Omer Rana
School of Computer Science/Welsh eScience Centre, Cardiff University, UK, e-mail: o.f.rana@ cs.cardiff.ac.uk

Wolfgang Ziegler
Fraunhofer Institute SCAI, Germany, e-mail: Wolfgang.Ziegler@scai.fraunhofer.de

between multiple parties, for example, a single user and multiple providers. SLAs contain certain Quality of Service (QoS) properties that must be maintained by a provider during service provision – generally defined as a set of Service Level Objectives (SLOs). These properties need to be measurable and must be monitored during the provision of the service that has been agreed in the SLA. The particular QoS attributes that are used must be pre-agreed between the user and provider(s), before service provision begins, as they also define the obligations of the user/client when the provider meets the quality specified in the SLA. The SLA must also contain a set of penalty clauses when service providers fail to deliver the pre-agreed quality. Although significant work exists on how SLOs may be specified and monitored, not much work has focused on actually identifying how SLOs may be impacted by the choice of specific penalty clauses. Once a violation has been detected, a number of possible actions may be undertaken, e.g. a client may initiate search for an alternative service provider, an enforcement component may initiate the process of obtaining a financial credit for the client, a service provider may release additional capacity to determine whether the agreed quality thresholds identified in the initial SLA can still be provisioned, etc.

Recent interest in Cloud computing and service aggregations or *mashups* (involving use of services such as Google maps, Amazon's EC2 and S3, etc) has increased the importance of SLAs. This is due to the aggregation of capability from multiple providers to realise a particular service – whereby each constituent of such a service is being provided by an independently managed (autonomous) entity. An SLA therefore provides some assurance to the aggregator that the combined service will be delivered according to some pre-defined criteria that has been agreed with the provider(s). Similarly, for a provider of a constituent capability within such a *mashup*, an SLA limits the liability that such a provider has towards an external user (who may be aggregating capability from multiple providers). Such multi-tier SLAs also become significant with the emerging interest in virtualised infrastructures, where a resource provider (for instance, managing storage or computational capacity) needs to identify how many virtual machine instances to support – i.e. decide how to divide its total capacity across the multiple users requesting access.

Given this context, it is necessary to better understand: (i) what could be contained within an SLA; (ii) how an SLA is used once it has been defined; (iii) how an SLA is monitored during service provisioning; and (iv) what actions need to be undertaken if a violation is detected. To better understand these issues, it is necessary to identify the various stages within an SLA lifecycle. Assuming that an SLA is initiated by a client application, these stages include:

- Identifying the provider: this could either be "hard wired" (i.e. pre-determined) or obtained through the use of a discovery (registry) service. Provider selection is an activity often considered outside the scope of SLA lifecycle, but nevertheless an important requirement to be fulfilled.
- Defining the SLA: this stage involves identifying the particular terms that should be included in the SLA. These terms may relate to QoS attributes that must subsequently be monitored, and also form the basis for penalty clauses. The definition also includes the period over which the SLA is valid. This is an important

parameter, as this determines the time period over which the provider has an obligation towards a particular user. Once this time interval expires, the provider can re-allocate capacity to other users.

- Agreeing on the terms of the SLA: this stage involves identifying the constraints that must be met by a provider during service provisioning. A negotiation process may be used to converge on such constraints. This stage would also involve identifying penalty clauses.
- Provisioning: this stage involves using the previously agreed SLA, and actually provisioning the required service. This stage involves the interaction with execution management services to setup resources and services accordingly.
- Execution and Monitoring: this stage involves executing the service and monitoring the agreed terms and ensuring that these are not being violated. Who does the monitoring and how often is an aspect that needs to be considered at this stage.
- Destroying SLAs: once a service provision has completed, the SLA must be destroyed.
- Penalties for SLA violation: once a service provision has completed, the monitoring data may be used to determine if any penalties need to be imposed on the service provider. Conversely, if an SLA has not been violated, the client has an obligation to carry out the action agreed upon in the SLA (this generally involves paying the provider for the service carried out). Payment mechanisms can also differ, such as providing a payment before, during or after use of a service.

More details about each of these stages can be found in [9].

## 2 SLA Research Landscape

Figure 1 relates work in SLA research to various other areas, indicating issues that are necessary when considering the description of SLAs, and areas of work that are impacted by the choice of SLAs. An SLA generally contains a number of Quality of Service (QoS) terms that have been agreed between two parties, identifying that a capability from a provider must be provisioned subject to these QoS constraints to a client – generally in return for some monetary payment to be made by the client to the provider. Terms used in the SLA are only useful if they can be subsequently monitored, to ensure that the pre-agreed QoS attributes are not being violated. What constitutes as a violation can also differ, as outlined in [10], and it is therefore necessary for a client and a provider to also agree on what constitutes a violation of the original SLA. Once a violation has been detected, it is subsequently necessary to identify the appropriate penalty clause that must be invoked. A penalty, generally, can contain a refund being made to a client in the event of the provider being unable to deliver on the pre-agreed SLA.

Once an SLA has been defined, it may be used to support capacity planning – whereby a resource provider can determine how many additional client requests it can handle over a given time frame. Based on SLAs that a provider has already

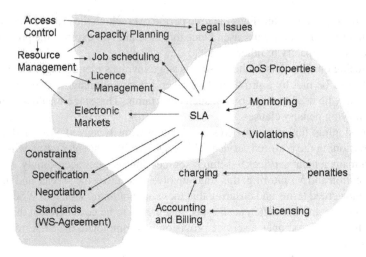

**Fig. 1** SLA Landscape

agreed to support, a provider can decided whether new SLAs can be accepted, and more importantly, how such SLAs will interfere with existing ones. Such capacity planning becomes particularly relevant in the context of virtualised infrastructures, where new virtual machine instances can be dynamically generated with small overhead. Identifying how many such instances to create (even though creation of each instance may not incur significant cost) becomes an important decision for the provider. An SLA may also form the basis for a legal agreement between a client and a provider – although this is often hard to realise in practice. Even when the legal directives (based on eCommerce law, for instance) are in use, it does not mean that this agreement will be upheld in a legal dispute. One of the primarily limitations relate to the issue of *jurisdiction* when a service provider resides in a geographically different location to the user – thereby making it difficult to decide which legal directive (i.e. of which area) applies. Another concern relates to the legal position held by the provider or user in the context of a particular service provision – i.e. whether the service is being provided as part of the *main work activity* associated with a provider, or whether the service capability is being offered on a voluntary basis. Some work has been undertaken in associating economic and legal issues with SLAs [7]. There is often a paper contract (counterpart) for a dynamic electronic SLA, which outlines legal obligations on the parties involved in the SLA. An SLA may also form the basis for job scheduling, as a single SLA may be associated with either each job or a batch. This provides an alternative to job scheduling using a queuing policy, as each job would contain it's own SLA, and would need to be handled differently by the resource owner. As an SLA can include monetary attributes (such as cost, penalty, etc), it is possible to use an SLA as a basis for establishing an electronic market, where resource providers attempt to maximise their revenue while clients attempt to minimise their cost. Such a market place can use an auction mechanism to enable providers and consumer to alter their bids and offers, respectively, based on changes in demand. Section 3 provides a discussion of the use of SLAs witihn electronic markets, and section 4 provides a discussion about the relationship between SLAs and licence management.

# 3 Electronic Markets

An architecture of a SLA management framework to support electronic markets is shown in figure 2, and based on work undertaken within the SORMA project [6]. The focus of the SORMA project was to develop a platform to support dynamic trading of computational and data resources "on-demand". Such a platform is intended to support both resource trading and providing the necessary interfaces to the resource management capabilities supported on these purchased resources. The internal resource management therefore becomes transparent for the users, who can leave their job execution constraints to the SORMA system – which is then responsible for matching requirements of user jobs with capabilities being made available by resource providers. The architecture consists of the following components: a Consumer, Trading Management, Contract Management, SLA Enforcement, Resource Management, and a Provider. The Trading Management component is the access point for the consumers to a marketplace where they can find the offered services and place their bids. The role of the Trading Management component is to perform matchmaking between bids from consumers and offers from providers, and orchestrate the bidding process in an auction scenario. Once the auction is cleared, the details of the winning bid and offer are submitted to the Contract Management component. Based on the matched bid/offer couplet, a SLA is generated between the consumer and the provider – which is then submitted to SLA Enforcement to enable subsequent monitoring of terms contained within the agreement. The SLA prediction component parses the SLA to extract the monitorable attributes and ascertain the most suitable monitoring frequency to attach to these attributes. Alternatively (and in most cases), the monitoring frequency is a parameter that is defined by an administrator. SLA Enforcement then issues a call to the Resource Management component to retrieve real time monitored data about a provider. The Resource Management component acts as a management interface for a provider, to enable performing operations such as resource monitoring, resource scheduling and offer injection. The SLA Enforcement service analyzes the monitored data received from the Resource Management component to predict if a possible SLA violation has either: (i) already occurred; (ii) is likely to occur at some time in the future. SLA Enforcement service also interacts with the Resource Management component to perform reactive measures on the detection of any SLA violations. The SLA Enforcement Service is made of two primary components: (1) SLA prediction, and (2) SLA reaction. The SLA prediction and reactive components provide consumers with a certain degree of "assurance" on the likely completion of one or more SLAs that they may hold with a provider. If the prediction indicates the occurrence of a possible violation, the reactive component interacts with the Resource Management component to identify if suitable corrective actions can be undertaken to enable the SLA to complete as originally intended. The reaction component may interact with the Trading Management component to re-initiate the matchmaking and bidding process to either add an additional resource provider or replace the provider.

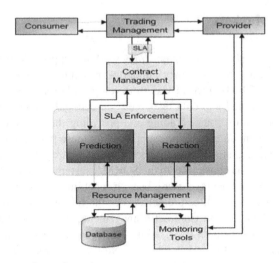

**Fig. 2** SLA to support electronic markets

The SLAs in the SORMA project are created using WS-Agreement specifications for generating an SLA template, and the Job Submission Description Language (JSDL) specification is used as the language for defining the job to be carried out. It is therefore necessary that any user defined terms are also encoded in JSDL. In order to capture the necessary economic data, JSDL is enveloped by an extended term language developed by the consortium: EJSDL [11]. This economic data is also captured in the SLA. The SLA mainly consists of a set of monitorable resource attributes (e.g. number of processors allocated, size of memory allocated, etc), which were specified by the resource consumer in their bid for resources. This can loosely be modelled as their basic requirements for service provisioning. Both the consumer and SLA Enforcement expect the resource provider to fulfil these requirements during the service provision.

# 4 Smart Licencing

IT infrastructure paradigms in recent years have changed to require greater support for flexibility and reduced costs at the same time. Similarly, computer-based simulations tend to become more complex and demanding with respect to the computational requirements. Several approaches to address these issues evolved, driven by academia and industry. Grid computing aims at providing infrastructure for sharing or pooling resources in a collaborative manner. Similarly, recent interest in Cloud computing has focused on resource provisioning, e.g. for peak demand or when customer owned infrastructure is overloaded or its use is not appropriate for any reason. However, extending a company's business or a research institution's information processing beyond the borders of the respective administrative domain raises a number of issues, one of them is the use of license-protected software. Software protection and licensing are important topics for both the independent software vendors and software users. In Grid and Cloud environments, the use of license-protected applications is almost impossible and becomes a challenging task. The reasons are twofold: (i) there are – with a few exceptions for the Amazon EC2 environment that have been introduced recently – no business models of the independent software vendors for Grids or Clouds and (ii) there is no licensing technology suitable for Grid environments. The European SmartLM [3] project took these shortcomings as a starting point for the development of a generic and flexible technology for virtualisation of software licensing. SmartLM makes use of external resources for running a license protected application, and provides support for additional business models across organizational boundaries.

Key aspects of the SmartLM developments are the token-based license mechanism, which renders licenses as mobile objects and the expression of licenses as SLAs: successful license requests from a user result in an SLA covering all terms of the license to be used, the time frame and the (maximum) price for the license usage. For creating the SLAs, WS-Agreement is used based on the WS-Agreement for Java (WSAG4J) framework [5]. SmartLM supports two ways for creating agreements (i) single-step negotiation (basic WS-Agreement functionality) and (ii) multi-round negotiation (an extension of WS-Agreement). The multi-round negotiation is a compatible extension with additional messages for negotiation and the corresponding data structures.

The rationale for implementing negotiation in SmartLM is that licenses are scarce resources. Avoiding blocking of licenses by jobs waiting for execution, and allocating the license when jobs are queued at the scheduler, allows the license to be used by other users before the application actually needs it. Thus, negotiation encompasses the availability of a license over time leading to advance reservation of a license settled by a SLA. This guarantees the application the availability of the license at runtime without blocking the license in the meantime. Naturally, these SLAs can be created by an orchestrator when co-allocating computing resources and licenses. On the other hand, re-negotiation of an existing SLA will provide the means for both provider and consumer to extend or limit license usage at run-time in terms of both license features and time.

Goals of WS-Agreement Negotiation implemented in SmartLM have been keeping modifications of WS-Agreement to a minimum, while providing the basic mechanism to allow negotiation *on top of* WS-Agreement, including the later extensibility for re-negotiation of agreements. In contrast, it was not intended for the implementation to provide general strategies to support negotiation. However, the current WS-Agreement Negotiation provides the basic multi-round negotiation mechanisms necessary to create sophisticated strategies, such as auctions or strategies developed in the agents community.

# 5 WS-Agreement

A number of schemes exist for representing SLAs – the Contract Net Protocol [12] is one of the first protocols for negotiating electronic service contracts. This specification has been widely used in the multi-agent systems community, and has also been used in service-oriented applications. Additional languages for specifying SLAs include: WSLA [8], SLAng [13], WS-Agreement [1] and RBSLA [14]. In this section we present a brief overview of the current specification of WS-Agreement: purpose, state-machine, protocol and structure. We focus on WS-Agreement as it is the most widely used specification within Grid projects. The Web Services Agreement Specification Version 1.0 [1] developed at the Open Grid Forum describes a protocol for establishing an agreement on the use of services between a service provider and a consumer. It defines a language and a protocol to represent the services of providers, create agreements based on offers and monitor agreement compliance at runtime. An agreement defines a relationship between two parties that is dynamically established and dynamically managed. The objective of this relationship is to deliver a service by one of the parties. In the agreement each party agrees on the respective roles, rights and obligations.

A provider in an agreement offers a service according to conditions described in the agreement. A consumer enters into an agreement with the intent of obtaining guarantees on the availability of one or more services from the provider. Agreements can also be negotiated by entities acting on behalf the provider and / or the consumer. An agreement creation process usually consists of three steps: the initiator (often the service or resource consumer) retrieves a template from the responder (often the service or resource provider), which advertises the types of offers the responder is willing to accept. The initiator then makes an offer, which is either accepted or rejected by the responder.

The underlying protocol as specified in WS-Agreement version 1.0 does not contain elements to allow further negotiation based on an initial offer. Especially, the responder has no possibility to reply with a counter offer, which could express more precisely the SLOs a provider is able to fulfil at that time. Thus, once the initial offer is rejected by the responder, the initiator can only *guess* which part of the offer can not be fulfilled, modifying the offer accordingly and sending the offer to the responder again. Obviously, a tedious process with limited chances to reach an agreement, especially if the agreement contains variable terms that have to be agreed upon, e.g. the time when a certain service is required, or if there are multiple QoS objectives to be reached. The agreement states as proposed in the WS-Agreement protocol version 1.0 are depicted in figure 3. An agreement consists of the agreement name, its context and the agreement terms as shown in figure 4.

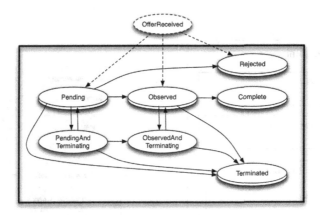

**Fig. 3** WS-Agreement Version 1.0 state machine

The context contains information about the involved parties and metadata such as the duration of the agreement. Agreement terms define the content of an agreement: Service Description Terms (SDTs) define the functionality that is delivered under an agreement. A SDT includes a domain-specific description of the offered or required functionality (the service itself). Guarantee Terms define assurance on service quality of the service described by the SDTs – defining the associated Service Level Objectives (SLOs). The Web Services Agreement Specification allows the usage of any domain specific or standard condition expression language to define SLOs. The specification of domain-specific term languages is explicitly left open. For example, in the structure of agreements depicted in Figure 5 a term language to express properties of software licenses is used to express the SDTs, where as in the SORMA project (described in section 3) the JSDL specification is used.

As mentioned before the built-in negotiation capabilities of WS-Agreement as specified in version 1.0 are limited to a simple offer accept/reject procedure. Thus, either party can send an offer and the respective other party may accept this offer or reject it. To overcome this limitation, a multi-round negotiation process was defined by the GRAAP working group of the Open Grid Forum that allows negotiation on top of WS-Agreement without requiring incompatible changes of WS-Agreement. The resulting protocol extensions are described in the following sections. Figure 6 presents an overview of the negotiation process.

## 5.1 Initialisation of the negotiation process

The negotiation initiator first initializes the process by querying a set of SLA templates from agreement providers, sending a standard WS-Agreement message (the getResourceProperty request) to agreement providers. Within the SmartLM environment, any resource scheduler or any client who wants to reserve a license will be

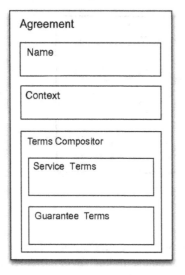

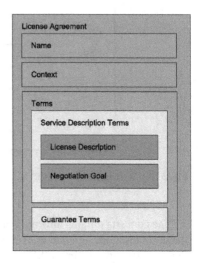

**Fig. 4** Structure of an agreement following the WS-Agreement specification

**Fig. 5** Structure of an agreement for software licenses

the negotiation initiator and any SmartLM server can act as an agreement provider. In general, the agreement provider uses site-specific mechanisms to advertise the available templates and to provide access to them. The initiator, in SmartLM the user, chooses the most suitable template as a starting point for the negotiation process. This template defines the context of the subsequent iterations. All subsequent offers must refer to this agreement template. This is required in order to enable an agreement provider to validate the creation constraints of the original template during the negotiation process, and therefore the validity of an offer.

## 5.2 Negotiation of the template

After the negotiation initiator has chosen an agreement template, it will create a new negotiation quote based on the chosen template. This quote must contain a reference to the originating template within its context. Furthermore, the agreement initiator may adjust the content of the quote, i.e. service description terms, the service property terms and the guarantee terms. These changes must be performed according to the creation constraints defined in the original template.

After the initiator created the negotiation quote according to its requirements, it is sent to responders via a negotiate message. The agreement provider checks

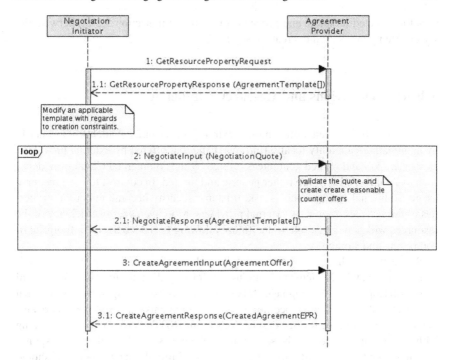

**Fig. 6** Overview of the negotiation process.

whether the service defined in the request could be provided or not. If the service can be provided, it just returns an agreement template to the client, indicating that an offer based on that template will potentially be accepted. Otherwise, the provider employs some strategy to create reasonable counter offers.

The relationship between dynamically created templates and original ones must be reflected by updating the context of the new templates accordingly. After creating the counter offers the provider sends them back to the negotiation initiator (negotiate response).

## 5.3 Post-processing of the templates

After the negotiation initiator receives the counter offers (templates) from the negotiation responder, it checks whether one or more meets its requirements. Sending multiple counter offers allow to speed up the negotiation process but it is not mandatory for the negotiation responder to send more than one counter offer. If there is no such template, the initiator can either stop the negotiation process, or start again (as outlined in section 5.1). If there is an applicable template, the initiator validates whether there is need for an additional negotiation step or not. If yes, the initiator uses the selected template and proceeds (as outlined in section 5.2), otherwise the selected template is used to create a new SLA.

# 6 Future Directions and Research Challenges

Cloud computing systems offer more flexibility in resource availability, primarily by aggregating capability locally (in-house) and that offered by external providers. However, QoS and related guarantees offered by the commercial Cloud providers - such as Amazon's EC2 - are rather generic and limited. In contrast to local resource usage, additional aspects such as risk, trust and security become important properties of the services offered by external providers. Moreover, energy efficiency of the resources will play a key role in the future allowing to reduce the $CO_2$ footprint of computing and storage.

While the mechanisms for negotiating and creating SLAs, e.g. through WS-Agreement, may be implemented one-to-one for Cloud environments there are still gaps with respect to term languages for creating SLAs expressing the non-functional properties risk, trust, Cloud-specific security requirements, and aspects of energy efficiency. Here, suitable service descriptions terms (SDTs) have to be defined along with appropriate metrics for the service level objectives (SLOs) and the corresponding guarantee terms. In order to achieve interoperability these developments should be captured in micro-specifications of the OGF.

A key limitations with Cloud computing environments that aggregate multiple systems is the difficultly of translating an SLA across systems. Hence, there is not just a need to agree on a common term language and metrics, but also on ensuring that provisioning policies across multiple systems are congruent, and facilitate the dynamic provisioning capability often associated with Clouds. The ability to define policies that can then be aggregated to support the scale up (or "Cloud burst") capability in an efficient manner remains another challenge.

## *6.1 Conclusions and Research Directions*

Two research projects, and the WS-Agreement specification have been used to highlight existing work on SLAs and their use. To generalize, we identify the following future research directions for SLAs:

- Research Challenge 1: What should be part of an SLA? How should this be encoded (rules, constraints, keywords)? This challenge relates to identifying suitable term languages and metrics (i.e. monitorable parameters) that could be used within an SLA. When aggregating capacity across multiple systems, in Cloud computing for instance, development of such a term language becomes significant.

- Research Challenge 2: What can we do with an SLA once it has been defined? – e.g. capacity planning, pricing services, etc. This issue becomes especially relevant in the context of emerging infrastructure – such as Cloud computing – where virtualised resources are being made available to external users. It is also useful to note that an SLA may be used at different levels – between an application and the resource management system, and between the resource manager and various underlying infrastructure. Relating SLAs that occur at these different levels is also a significant challenge.
- Research Challenge 3: What types of SLAs are most beneficial to an end user community in computational science (e-Science)? Can we encourage their use to facilitate greater resource sharing – especially the concurrent use of distributed resources? This challenge primarily relates to evaluating user requirements for SLAs from an applications perspective, and the types of application characteristics that could differentiate them in their use of nationally (e.g. TeraGrid) or regionally (e.g. EGEE) funded infrastructure. [16] reports that very few (existing) scientific applications utilize distributed resources within the TeraGrid, primarily due to the way they are written, but also due to the lack of suitable programming abstractions. The development of SLAs could provide the necessary incentive mechanisms to enable resource providers to make available suitable programming libraries to enable greater use of distributed infrastructures.
- Research Challenge 4: How can business or institutional policy be mapped into operational SLAs? This challenge primarily relates to mapping business policies (relating to issues such as revenue) to operational policies (relating to issues such as number of servers to allocate to a given user application, etc). This is important to ensure that metrics used within an SLA can eventually be traced back to some overall business or institutional objective. Identifying suitable policy languages that enable this type of tracking is therefore an important challenge in gaining more wide-spread adoption of SLAs. A useful discussion is provided in [4]
- Research Challenge 5: What are the infrastructure capabilities associated with different stages of SLA lifecycle (monitoring, (re-)negotiation, etc)? This challenge relates to the need for tools and APIs that enable interoperable use of SLAs across multiple types of infrastructures, at different stages of the SLA lifecycle.

**Acknowledgements:** We are grateful to work undertaken by Simon Caton and Vikas Deora (at Cardiff University) for work on SLAs in electronic markets – as part of the EU FP6 SORMA project under grant number 034286. Additionally, some of the work reported here has been funded by the European Commission's ICT programme in the FP7 project SmartLM under grant number 216759.

# References

1. A. Andrieux, K. Czajkowski, A. Dan, K. Keahey, H. Ludwig, T. Nakata, J. Pruyne, J. Rofrano, S. Tuecke, and M. Xu. Web Services Agreement Specification (WS-Agreement). *GRAAP Working Group at the Open Grid Forum*, May 2007. available at: http://www.ogf.org/documents/GFD.107.pdf.
2. *GRAAP Working Group at the Open Grid Forum*. available at: http://www.ogf.org/gf/group_info/view.php?group=graap-wg.
3. *SmartLM project web site*. available at: http://www.smartlm.eu.
4. Y. Chen, S. Iyer, X. Liu, D. Milojicic, and A. Sahai. SLA Decomposition: Translating Service Level Objectives to System Level Thresholds. *HPL-2007-17*, 2007.
5. Fraunhofer Institute, "WS-Agreement for Java". See Web site at: http://packcs-e0.scai.fraunhofer.de/wsag4j/. Last accessed: November 2009.
6. Self-Organising ICT Resource Management (SORMA) project, 2009. Web site at: http://sorma-project.org/. Last accessed: November 2009.
7. Davide M. Parrilli, "The Determination of Jurisdiction in Grid and Cloud Service Level Agreements", Grid Economics and Business Models workshop, Proceedings of GECON 2009 workshop (Eds: Altmann, Buyya and Rana), August 2009, LNCS 5745, Springer Verlag.
8. A. Keller and H. Ludwig, "The WSLA Framework: Specifying and Monitoring Service Level Agreements for Web Services", *Journal of Network and Systems Management*, 11(1):57–81, 2003.
9. Jordi Guitart, Mario Macas, Omer Rana, Philipp Wieder, Ramin Yahyapour and Wolfgang Ziegler, "SLA-based Resource Management and Allocation", Chapter 12 in book "Market Oriented Grid and Utility Computing", Eds: Rajkumar Buyya and Kris Bubendorfer, John Wiley, 2009.
10. Omer F. Rana, Martijn Warnier, Thomas B. Quillinan and Frances M. T. Brazier, "Monitoring and Reputation Mechanisms for Service Level Agreements", Proceedings of GECON 2008, LNCS 5206, Springer Verlag.
11. Nikolay Borissov, Simon Caton, Omer F. Rana, Aharon Levine, "Message Protocols for Provisioning and Usage of Computing Services". Proceedings of GECON workshop (Eds: Altmann, Buyya and Rana), August 2009, LNCS 5745, Springer Verlag.
12. R. G. Smith, "The Contract Net Protocol: High-Level Communication and Control in a Distributed Problem Solver", IEEE Transactions on Computers, Vol. C-29, No. 12, December 1980.
13. D. Davide Lamanna, James Skene, Wolfgang Emmerich: SLAng: A Language for Defining Service Level Agreements. Proceedings of FTDCS 2003.
14. Adrian Paschke, "RBSLA A declarative Rule-based Service Level Agreement Language based on RuleML", Proceedings of CIMCA/IAWTIC 2005.
15. E. Wustenhoff, "Service Level Agreement in the Data Center", *Sun Microsystems Professional Series*, April 2002.
16. Shantenu Jha, Daniel S. Katz, Manish Parashar, Omer Rana, and Jon Weissman, "Critical Perspectives on Large-Scale Distributed Applications and Production Grids", IEEE Grid 2009 Conference, Banff, Canada, October 2009. IEEE Computer Society Press.